Henry Home Kames

Sketches of the history of man

Volume III

Henry Home Kames

Sketches of the history of man
Volume III

ISBN/EAN: 9783743401174

Manufactured in Europe, USA, Canada, Australia, Japa

Cover: Foto ©ninafisch / pixelio.de

Manufactured and distributed by brebook publishing software (www.brebook.com)

Henry Home Kames

Sketches of the history of man

SKETCHES

OF THE

HISTORY

OF

MAN.

CONSIDERABLY IMPROVED IN

A SECOND EDITION.

IN FOUR VOLUMES.

VOLUME III.

EDINBURGH:

Printed for W. STRAHAN, and T. CADELL, *London;*
and for W. CREECH, *Edinburgh.*

MDCCLXXVIII.

SKETCHES

OF THE

HISTORY OF MAN.

BOOK II.

Progress of MEN IN SOCIETY.

SKETCH IX.

Military Branch of Government.

DURING the infancy of a nation, every member depends on his own industry for procuring the necessaries of life : he is his own mason, his own tailor, his own physician; and on himself he chiefly relies for offence as well as defence. Every savage can say, what few beggars among us can say, *Omnia mea mecum porto;* and hence the apti-

　　　tude

tude of a favage for war, which makes little alteration in his manner of living. In early times accordingly, the men were all warriors, and every known art was exercifed by women; which continues to be the cafe of American favages. And even after arts were fo much improved as to be exercifed by men, none who could bear arms were exempted from war. In feudal governments, the military fpirit was carried to a great height: all gentlemen were foldiers by profeffion; and every other art was defpifed, as low, if not contemptible.

Even in the unnatural ftate of the feudal fyftem, arts made fome progrefs, not excepting thofe for amufement; and many conveniencies, formerly unknown, became neceffary to comfortable living. A man accuftomed to manifold conveniencies, cannot bear with patience to be deprived of them: he hates war, and clings to the fweets of peace. Hence the neceffity of a military eftablifhment, hardening men by ftrict difcipline to endure the fatigues of war. By a ftanding army, war is carried on more regularly and fcientifically than in a feudal government; but as it is carried on with infinitely greater expence, na-

tions

tions are more referved in declaring war
than formerly. Long experience has at
the fame time made it evident, that a nation feldom gains by war ; and that agriculture, manufactures, and commerce,
are the only folid foundations of power
and grandeur. Thefe arts accordingly
have become the chief objects of European
governments, and the only rational caufes
of war. Among the warlike nations of
Greece and Italy, how would it have
founded, that their effeminate defcendents
would employ foldiers by profeffion to
fight their battles! And yet this is unavoidable in every country where arts and
manufactures flourifh ; which, requiring
little exercife, tend to enervate the body,
and of courfe the mind. Gain, at the
fame time, being the fole object of induftry, advances felfifhnefs to be the ruling paffion, and brings on a timid anxiety
about property and felf-prefervation. Cyrus, tho' enflamed with refentment againft
the Lydians for revolting, liftened to the
following advice, offered by Crœfus, their
former King. " O Cyrus, deftroy not
" Sardis, an ancient city, famous for arts
" and arms ; but, pardoning what is paft,
A 2   " demand

" demand all their arms, encourage lu-
" xury, and exhort them to inftruct their
" children in every art. of gainful com-
" merce. You will foon fee, O King, that
" inftead of men, they will be women."
The Arabians, a brave and generous people,
conquered Spain; and drove into the in-
acceffible mountains of Bifcay and Afturia,
the few natives who ftood out. When no
longer an enemy appeared, they turned
their fwords into ploughfhares, and became a rich and flourifhing nation. The
inhabitants of the mountains, hardened
by poverty and fituation, ventured, after
a long interval, to peep out from their
ftrong holds, and to lie in wait for ftrag-
gling parties. Finding themfelves now a
match for a people, whom opulence had
betrayed to luxury and the arts of peace to
cowardice; they took courage to difplay
their banners in the open field; and after
many military atchievements, fucceeded
in reconquering Spain. The Scots, inhabiting the mountainous parts of Cale-
donia, were an overmatch for the Picts,
who occupied the fertile plains, and at laft
fubdued them *.

* See the note on the following page.

Benjamin de Tudele, a Spaniſh Jew, who wrote in the twelfth century, obſerves, that by luxury and effeminacy the Greeks had contracted a degree of ſoftneſs, more proper for women than for men; and that the Greek Emperor was reduced to the neceſſity of employing mercenary troops, to defend his country againſt the Turks. In the year 1453, the city of Conſtantinople, defended by a garriſon not exceeding 6000 men, was beſieged by the Turks, and reduced to extremity; yet

A note referred to in the preceding page.

* Before the time that all Scotland was brought under one king, the highlanders, divided into tribes or clans, made war upon each other; and continued the ſame practice irregularly many ages after they ſubmitted to the king of Scotland. Open war was repreſſed, but it went on privately by depredations and repriſals. The clan-ſpirit was much depreſſed by their bad ſucceſs in the rebellion 1715; and totally cruſhed by the like bad ſucceſs in the rebellion 1745. The mildneſs with which the highlanders have been treated of late, and the pains that have been taken to introduce induſtry among them, have totally extirpated depredations and repriſals, and have rendered them the moſt peaceable people in Scotland; but have at the ſame time reduced their military ſpirit to a low ebb. To train them for war, military diſcipline has now become no leſs neceſſary than to others.

not

not a fingle inhabitant had courage to take arms, all waiting with torpid defpondence the hour of utter extirpation. Venice, Genoa, and other fmall Italian ftates, became fo effeminate by long and fuccefsful commerce, that not a citizen ever thought of ferving in the army; which obliged them to employ mercenaries, officers as well as private men. Thefe mercenaries at firft, fought confcientioufly for their pay; but reflecting, that the victors were no better paid than the vanquifhed, they learned to play booty. In a battle particularly between the Pifans and Florentines, which lafted from fun-rifing to fun-fetting, there was but a fingle man loft, who, having accidentally fallen from his horfe, was trodden under foot. Men at that time fought on horfeback, covered with iron from head to heel. Machiavel mentions a battle between the Florentines and Venetians which lafted half a day, neither party giving ground; fome horfes wounded, not a man flain. He obferves, that fuch cowardice and diforder was in the armies of thofe times, that the turning of a fingle horfe either to charge or retreat, would have decided a battle.

Charles

Charles VIII. of France, when he invaded Italy *anno* 1498, underftood not fuch mock battles ; and his men were held to be devils incarnate, who feemed to take delight in fhedding human blood. The Dutch, who for many years have been reduced to mercenary troops, are more indebted to the mutual jealoufy of their neighbours for their independence, than to their own army. In the year 1672, Lewis of France invaded Holland, and in forty days took forty walled towns. That country was faved, not by its army, but by being laid under water. Froft, which is ufual at that feafon, would have put an end to the feven United Provinces.

The fmall principality of Palmyra is the only inftance known in hiftory, where the military fpirit was not enervated by opulence. Pliny defcribes that country as extremely pleafant, and bleffed with plenty of fprings, tho' furrounded with dry and fandy deferts. The commerce of the Indies was at that time carried on by land ; and the city of Palmyra was the centre of that commerce between the Eaft and the Weft. Its territory being very fmall, little more than fufficient for villas and plea-

fure-

fure-grounds, the inhabitants, like thofe of Hamburgh, had no way to employ their riches for profit but in trade. At the fame time, being fituated between the two mighty empires of Rome and Parthia; it required great addrefs and the moft affiduous military difcipline, to guard it from being fwallowed up by the one or the other. This ticklifh fituation preferved the inhabitants from luxury and effeminacy, the ufual concomitants of riches. Their fuperfluous wealth was laid out on magnificient buildings, and on embellifhing their country-feats. The fine arts were among them carried to a high degree of perfection. The famous Zenobia, their Queen, being led captive to Rome after being deprived of her dominions, was admired and celebrated for fpirit, for learning, and for an exquifite tafte in the fine arts.

Thus, by accumulating wealth, a manufacturing and commercial people become a tempting object for conqueft; and by effeminacy become an eafy conqueft. The military fpirit feems to be at a low ebb in Britain: will no phantom appear, even in a dream, to difturb our downy reft?

I

reft? Formerly, plenty of corn in the temperate regions of Europe and Afia, proved a tempting bait to northern favages who wanted bread: have we no caufe to dread a fimilar fate from fome warlike neighbour, impelled by hunger, or by ambition, to extend his dominions? The difficulty of providing for defence, confiftent with induftry, has produced a general opinion among political writers, that a nation, to preferve its military fpirit, muft give up induftry; and to preferve induftry, muft give up a military fpirit. In the former cafe, we are fecure againft any invader: in the latter, we lie open to every invader. A military plan that would fecure us againft enemies, without hurting our induftry and manufactures, would be a rich prefent to Britain. That fuch a plan is poffible, will appear from what follows; tho' I am far from hoping that it will meet with univerfal approbation. To prepare the reader, I fhall premife an account of the different military eftablifhments that exift, and have exifted, in Europe, with the advantages and difadvantages of each. In examining thefe, who

knows whether fome hint may not occur
of a plan more perfect than any of them.

The moft illuftrious military eftablifhment of antiquity is that of the Romans,
by which they fubdued almoft all the
known world. The citizens of Rome were
all of them foldiers: they lived upon their
pay when in the field; but if they happened not to be fuccefsful in plundering,
they ftarved at home. An annual diftribution of corn among them, became neceffary; which in effect correfponded to
the halfpay of our officers. It is believed,
that fuch a conftitution would not be adopted by any modern ftate. It was a
forc'd conftitution; contrary to nature,
which gives different difpofitions to men,
in order to fupply hands for every neceffary art. It was a hazardous conftitution,
having no medium between univerfal conqueft and wretched flavery. Had the
Gauls who conquered Rome, entertained
any view but of plunder, Rome would never have been heard of. It was on the
brink of ruin in the war with Hannibal.
What would have happened had Hannibal been victorious? It is eafy to judge,
by comparing it with Carthage. Carthage

thage was a commercial ftate, the people
all employ'd in arts, manufactures, and
navigation.   The Carthaginians were fubdued ; but they could not be reduced to
extremity, while they had accefs to the
fea.   In fact, they profpered fo much by
commerce, even after they were fubdued,
as to raife jealoufy in their mafters ; who
thought themfelves not fecure while a
houfe remained in Carthage.   On the o-
ther hand, what refource for the inhabitants of Rome, had they been fubdued ?
They muft have perifhed by hunger ; for
they could not work.   In a word, ancient
Rome refembles a gamefter who ventures
all upon one decifive throw : if he lofe, he
is undone.

I take it for granted, that our feudal
fyftem will not have a fingle vote.   It was
a fyftem that led to confufion and anar-
chy, as little fitted for war as for peace.
And as for mercenary troops, it is unneceffary to bring them again into the field,
after what is faid of them above.

The only remaining forms that merit
attention, are a ftanding army, and a militia ; which I fhall examine in their order, with the objections that lie againft

B 2   each.

each. The firft ftanding army in modern
times was eftablifhed by Charles VII. of
France, on a very imperfect plan. He
began with a body of cavalry termed *com-
panies of ordonnance*. And as for infantry,
he, *anno* 1448, appointed each parifh to
furnifh an archer: thefe were termed
franc-archers, becaufe they were exempted
from all taxes. This little army was intended for reftoring peace and order at
home, not for difturbing neighbouring
ftates. The King had been forc'd into
many perilous wars, fome of them for re-
ftraining the turbulent fpirit of his vaffals,
and moft of them for defending his crown
againft an ambitious adverfary, Henry V.
of England. As thefe wars were carried
on in the feudal mode, the foldiers, who
had no pay, could not be reftrained from
plundering; and inveterate practice rendered them equally licentious in peace and
in war. Charles, to leave no pretext for
free quarters, laid upon his fubjects a
fmall tax, no more than fufficient for regular pay to his little army *.

Firft

---

* This was the firft tax impofed in France without confent of the three eftates : and, however un-
conftitutional,

First attempts are commonly crude and defective. The franc-archers, difperfed one by one in different villages, and never collected but in time of action, could not eafily be brought under regular difcipline: in the field, they difplay'd nothing but vicious habits, a fpirit of lazinefs, of diforder, and of pilfering. Neither in peace were they of any ufe: their character of foldier made them defpife agriculture, without being qualified for war: in the army they were no better than peafants: at the plough, no better than idle foldiers. But in the hands of a monarch, a ftanding army is an inftrument of power, too valuable ever to be abandoned: if one fove-

conftitutional, it occafioned not the flighteft murmur, becaufe its vifible good tendency reconciled all the world to it. Charles, befide, was a favourite of his people; and juftly, as he fhewed by every act his affection for them. Had our firft Charles been fuch a favourite, who knows whether the taxes he impofed without confent of parliament, would have met with any oppofition? Such taxes would have become cuftomary, as in France; and a limited monarchy would, as in France, have become abfolute. Governments, like men, are liable to many revolutions: we remain, it is true, a free people; but for that bleffing we are perhaps more indebted to fortune, than to patriotic vigilance.

reign

reign entertain fuch an army, others in
felf-defence muft follow. Standing armies are now eftablifhed in every European ftate, and are brought to a competent degree of perfection.

This new inftrument of government,
has produced a furprifing change in manners. We now rely on a ftanding army,
for defence as well as offence : none but
thofe who are trained to war, ever think
of handling arms, or even of defending
themfelves againft an enemy : our people
have become altogether effeminate, terrified at the very fight of a hoftile weapon.
It is true, they are not the lefs qualified
for the arts of peace ; and if manufacturers be protected from being obliged to
ferve in the army, I difcover not any in-
compatibility between a ftanding army
and the higheft induftry. Hufbandmen
at the fame time make the beft foldiers : a
military fpirit in the lower claffes arifes
from bodily ftrength, and from affection
to their natal foil. Both are eminent in
the hufbandman : conftant exercife in the
open air renders him hardy and robuft ;
and fondnefs for the place where he finds
comfort and plenty, attaches him to his
country

country in general *. An artiſt or manufacturer, on the contrary, is attached to
no country but where he finds the beſt
bread; and a ſedentary life, enervating
his body, renders him puſillanimous. For
theſe reaſons, among many, agriculture
ought to be honoured and cheriſhed a-
bove all other arts. It is not only a fine
preparation

* Numquam credo potuiſſe dubitari, aptiorem
armis ruſticam plebem, quæ ſub divo et in labore
nutritur; ſolis patiens; umbræ negligens; balnea-
rum neſcia; deliciarum ignara; ſimplicis animi;
parvo contenta; duratis ad omnem laborum tole-
rantiam membris: cui geſtare ferrum, foſſam du-
cere, onus ferre, conſuetudo de rure eſt. Nec in-
ficiandum eſt, poſt urbem conditam, Romanos ex
civitate profectos ſemper ad bellum :. ſed tunc nullis
voluptatibus, nullis deliciis frangebantur. Sudorem
curſu et campeſtri exercitio collectum nando juven-
tus abluebat in Tybere. Idem bellator, idem agri-
cola, genera tantum mutabat armorum. *Vegetius,
De re militari, l. 1. cap. 3.* — [*In Engliſh thus :* " I
" believe it was never doubted, that the country-
" labourers were, of all others, the beſt ſoldiers.
" Inured to the open air, and habitual toil, ſub-
" jected to the extremes of heat and cold, ignorant
" of the uſe of the bath, or any of the luxuries of
" life, contented with bare neceſſaries, there was
" no ſeverity in any change they could make : their
" limbs, accuſtomed to the uſe of the ſpade and
" plough, and habituated to burden, were capable
" of

preparation for war, by breeding men who love their country, and whom labour and sobriety qualify for being soldiers; but is also the best foundation for commerce, by furnishing both food and materials to the industrious.

But several objections occur against a standing army, that call aloud for a better model than has hitherto been established, at least in Britain. The subject is interesting, and I hope for attention from every man who loves his country. During the vigour of the feudal system which made every land-proprietor a soldier, every inch of ground was tenaciously disputed with an invader: and while a sovereign retained any part of his dominions, he never lost hopes of recovering the whole. At present, we rely entirely on a standing

" of the utmost extremity of toil. Indeed, in the
" earliest ages of the commonwealth, while the city
" was in her infancy, the citizens marched out from
" the town to the field: but at that time they were
" not enfeebled by pleasures, nor by luxury: The
" military youth, returning from their exercise and
" martial sports, plunged into the Tyber to wash
" off the sweat and dust of the field. The warrior
" and the husbandman were the same, they chan-
" ged only the nature of their arms."]

army,

army, for defence as well as offence;
which has reduced every nation in Europe
to a precarious ſtate.   If the army of a
nation happen to be defeated, even at the
moſt diſtant frontier, there is little reſource
againſt a total conqueſt.   Compare the
hiſtory of Charles VII. with that of Lewis
XIV. Kings of France.   The former, tho'
driven into a corner by Henry V. of England, was however far from yielding : on
the contrary, relying on the military ſpirit
of his people, and indefatigably intent on
ſtratagem and ſurpriſe, he recovered all
he had loſt.   When Lewis XIV. ſucceeded
to the crown, the military ſpirit of the
people was contracted within the narrow
ſpan of a ſtanding army.   Behold the conſequence.   That ambitious monarch, having provoked his neighbours into an al-
liance againſt him, had no reſource againſt
a more numerous army, but to purchaſe
peace by an abandon of all his conqueſts,
upon which he had laviſhed much blood
and treaſure (*a*).   France at that period
contained ſeveral millions capable of bearing arms ; and yet was not in a condition

(*a*) Treaty of St Gertrudenberg.

to make head againſt a diſciplined army of
70,000 men. Poland, which continues
upon the ancient military eſtabliſhment,
wearied out Charles XII. of Sweden; and
had done the ſame to ſeveral of his prede-
ceſſors. But Saxony, defended only by a
ſtanding army, could not hold out a ſingle
day againſt the prince now mentioned, at
the head of a greater army. Mercenary
troops are a defence ſtill more feeble, a-
gainſt troops that fight for glory, or for
their country. Unhappy was the invention of a ſtanding army; which, without
being any ſtrong bulwark againſt enemies,
is a grievous burden on the people; and
turns daily more and more ſo. Liſten to
a firſt-rate author on that point. " Sitôt
" qu' un état augmente ce qu'il appelle
" ſes troupes, les autres augmentent les
" leurs; de façon qu'on ne gagne rien
" par-là que la ruine commune. Chaque
" monarque tient ſur pied toutes les ar-
" mées qu'il pourroit avoir ſi ſes peuples
" étoient en danger d' être exterminées;
" et on nomme paix cet état d'effort de ·
" tous contre tous. Nous ſommes pau-
" vres avec les richeſſes et le commerce de
" tout l'univers; et bientôt à force d'avoir
            " des

" des foldats, nous n'aurons plus que des
" foldats, et nous ferons comme de Tar-
" tares * (*a*)."

But with refpect to Britain, and every
free nation, there is an objection ftill more
formidable ; which is, that a ftanding army is dangerous to liberty. It avails very
little to be fecure againft foreign enemies,
fuppofing a ftanding army to afford fecurity, if we have no fecurity againft an e-
nemy at home. If a warlike king, head-
ing his own troops, be ambitious to render himfelf abfolute, there are no means
to evade the impending blow ; for what
avail the greateft number of effeminate

---

* " As foon as one ftate augments the number of
" its troops, the neighbouring ftates of courfe do
" the fame ; fo that nothing is gained, and the ef-
" fect is, the general ruin. Every prince keeps as
" many armies in pay, as if he dreaded the exter-
" mination of his people from a foreign invafion ;
" and this perpetual ftruggle, maintained by all a-
" gainft all, is termed *peace*. With the riches and
" commerce of the whole univerfe, we are in a ftate
" of poverty ; and by thus continually augmenting
" our troops, we fhall foon have none elfe but fol-
" diers, and be reduced to the fame fituation as the
" Tartars."

(*a*) L'efprit des loix. liv. 13 chap. 17.

cowards

cowards againſt a diſciplined army, devoted to their prince, and ready implicitly
to execute his commands ? In a word, by
relying entirely on a ſtanding army, and
by truſting the ſword in the hands of men
who abhor the reſtraints of civil law, a ſolid foundation is laid for military government. Thus a ſtanding army is dangerous to liberty, and yet no ſufficient bulwark againſt powerful neighbours.

Deeply ſenſible of the foregoing objections,
Harrington propoſes a militia as a remedy.
Every male between eighteen and thirty, is
to be trained to military exerciſes, by frequent meetings, where the youth are ex-
cited by premiums to contend in running,
wreſtling, ſhooting at a mark, &c. &c.
But Harrington did not advert, that ſuch
meetings, enflaming the military ſpirit,
muſt create an averſion in the people to
dull and fatiguing labour. His plan evidently is inconſiſtent with induſtry and
manufactures : it would be ſo at leaſt in
Britain. An unexceptionable plan it would
be, were defence our ſole object ; and not
the leſs ſo by reducing Britain to ſuch poverty as ſcarce to be a tempting conqueſt.
Our late war with France is a conſpicuous
                                    inſtance

inftance of the power of a commercial ftate, entire in its credit ; a power that a-maz'd all the world, and ourfelves no lefs than others. Politicians begin to confider Britain, and not France, to be the formi-dable power that threatens univerfal mo-narchy. Had Harrington's plan been a-dopted, Britain muft have been reduced to a level with Sweden or Denmark, ha-ving no ambition but to draw fubfidies from its more potent neighbours.

In Switzerland, it is true, boys are, from the age of twelve, exercifed in run-ning, wreftling, and fhooting. Every male who can bear arms is regimented, and fubjeced to military difcipline. Here is a militia in perfection upon Harring-ton's plan, a militia neither forc'd nor mercenary ; invincible when fighting for their country. And as the Swifs are not an idle people, we learn from this inftance, that the martial fpirit is not an invincible obftruction to induftry. But the original barrennefs of Switzerland, compelled the inhabitants to be fober and induftrious : and induftry hath among them become a fecond nature; there fcarcely being a child above fix years of age but who is employ'd,

not

not excepting children of opulent families. England differs widely in the nature of its foil, and of its people. But there is little occafion to infift upon that difference; as Switzerland affords no clear evidence, that a fpirit of induftry is perfectly compatible with a militia: the Swifs, it is true, may be termed induftrious; but their induftry is confined to neceffaries and conveniencies: they are lefs ambitious of wealth than of military glory; and they have few arts or manufactures, either to fupport foreign commerce, or to excite luxury.

Fletcher of Salton's plan of a militia, differs little from that of Harrington. Three camps are to be conftantly kept up in England, and a fourth in Scotland; into one or other of which, every man muft enter upon completing his one and twentieth year. In thefe camps, the art of war is to be acquired and practifed: thofe who can maintain themfelves muft continue there two years, others but a fingle year. Secondly, Thofe who have been thus educated, fhall for ever after have fifty yearly meetings, and fhall exercife four hours every meeting. It is not faid,

faid, by what means young men are compelled to refort to the camp; nor is any
exception mentioned of perfons deftin'd
for the church, for liberal fciences, or for
the fine arts. The weak and the fickly
muft be exempted; and yet no regulation
is propofed againft thofe who abfent themfelves on a falfe pretext. But waving thefe,
the capital objection againft Harrington's
plan ftrikes equally againft Fletcher's, That
by roufing a military fpirit, it would ali-
enate the minds of our people from arts
and manufactures, and from conftant and
uniform occupation. The author himfelf
remarks, that the ufe and exercife of arms,
would make the youth place their honour
upon that art, and would enflame them
with love of military glory; not advert-
ing, that love of military glory, diffufed
through the whole mafs of the people,
would unqualify Britain for being a manufacturing and commercial country, rendering it of little weight or confideration
in Europe.

The military branch is effential to every
fpecies of government: the Quakers are
the only people who ever doubted of it.
Is it not then mortifying, that a capital
branch

branch of government, fhould to this day remain in a ftate fo imperfect? One would fufpect fome inherent vice in the nature of government, that counteracts every effort of genius to produce a more perfect mode. I am not difpofed to admit any fuch defect, efpecially in an article effential to the well-being of fociety; and rather than yield to the charge, I venture to propofe the following plan, even at the hazard of being thought an idle projector. And what animates me greatly to make the attempt, is a firm conviction that a military and an induftrious fpirit are of equal importance to Britain; and that if either of them be loft, we are undone. To reconcile thefe feeming antagonifts, is my chief view in the following plan; to which I fhall proceed, after paving the way by fome preliminary confiderations.

The firft is, that as military force is effential to every ftate, no man is exempted from bearing arms for his country: all are bound; becaufe no perfon has right to be exempted more than another. Were any difference to be made, perfons of figure and fortune ought firft to be called to that fervice, as being the moft interefted in the

I   welfare

welfare of their country. Liften to a good
foldier delivering his opinion on that fubject. " Les levées qui fe font par fuper-
" cherie font tout auffi odieufes ; on met
" de l'argent dans la pochette d'un hom-
" me, et on lui dit qu'il eft foldat. Celles
" qui fe font par force, le font encore
" plus ; c'eft une defolation publique,
" dont le bourgeois et l'habitant ne fe fau-
" vent qu'à force d'argent, et dont le fond
" eft toujours un moyen odieux. Ne vou-
. " droit-il pas mieux établer, par une loi,
" que tout homme, de quelque condition ·
" qu'il fût, feroit obligé de fervir fon
" prince et fa patrie pendant cinq ans ?
" Cette loi ne fçauroit être defapprouvée,
" parce qu'il eft naturel et jufte que les
" citoyens s'emploient pour la défenfe de
" l'état. Cette methode de lever des trou-
" pes feroit un fond inépuifable de belles
" et bonnes recrues, qui ne feroient pas
" fujetes a déferter. L'on fe feroit même,
" par la fuite, un honneur et un devoir
" de ferver fa tâche. Mais, pour y par-
" venir, il faudroit n'en excepter aucune
" condition, être févére fur ce point, et
" s'attacher a faire exécuter cette loi de
" préférence aux nobles et aux riches.

VOL. III.   D   " Perfonne

" Perfonne n'en murmureroit. Alors
" ceux qui auroient fervi leur temps, ver-
" roient avec mépris ceux qui repugneroi-
" ent à cette loi, et infenfiblement on fe
" feroit un honneur de fervir : le pauvre
" bourgeois feroit confolé . par l'example
" du riche ; et celui-ci n'oferoit fe plain-
" dre, voyant fervir le noble (a) *."

Take

(a) Les reveries du Comte de Saxe.

* " The method of inlifting men, by putting a
" trick upon them, is fully as odious. They flip a
" piece of money into a man's pocket, and then tell
" him he is a foldier. Inlifting by force is ftill more
" odious. It is a public calamity, from which the
" citizen has no means of faving himfelf but by
" money ; and it is confequently the worft of all
" the refources of government. Would it not be
" more expedient to enact a law, obliging every
" man, whatever be his rank, to ferve his King and
" country for five years ? This law could not be
" difapproved of, becaufe it is confiftent both with
" nature and juftice, that every citizen fhould be
" employed in the defence of the ftate. Here would
" be an inexhauftible fund of good and able fol-
" diers, who would not be apt to defert, as every
" man would reckon it both his honour and his
" duty to have ferved his time. But to effect this,
" it muft be a fixed principle, That there fhall be
" no exception of ranks. This point muft be ri-
" goroufly attended to, and the law muft be en-
" forced, by way of preference, firft among the
" nobility

Take another preliminary confideration. While there were any remains among us of a martial fpirit, the difficulty was not great of recruiting the army. But that tafk hath of late years become trouble-fome; and more difagreeable ftill than troublefome, by the neceffity of ufing de-ceitful arts for trepanning the unwary youth. Nor are fuch arts always fuccefs-ful: in our late war with France, we were neceffitated to give up even the appearance of voluntary fervice, and to recruit the army on the folid principle, that every man fhould fight for his country; the ju-ftices of peace being empowered to force into the fervice fuch as could be beft fpa-red from civil occupation. If a fingle claufe had been added, limiting the fer-vice to five or feven years, the meafure

" nobility and the men of wealth. There would
" not be a fingle man who would complain of it. A
" perfon who had ferved his time, would treat with
" contempt another who fhould fhow reluctance to
" comply with the law; and thus, by degrees, it
" would become a tafk of honour. The poor citi-
" zen would be comforted and infpirited by the ex-
" ample of his rich neighbour; and he again would
" have nothing to complain of, when he faw that
" the nobleman was not exempted from fervice."

would

would have been unexceptionable, even in
a land of liberty. To relieve officers of
the army from the neceſſity of practiſing
deceitful arts, by ſubſtituting a fair and
conſtitutional mode of recruiting the army,
was a valuable improvement. It was of
importance with reſpect to its direct intendment; but of much greater, with reſpect to its conſequences. One of the few
diſadvantages of a free ſtate, is licentiouf-
neſs in the common people, who may
wallow in diſorder and profligacy without
control, if they but refrain from groſs
crimes, puniſhable by law. Now, as it appears to me, there never was deviſed a
plan more efficacious for reſtoring induſtry and ſobriety, than that under conſi-
deration. Its ſalutary effects were conſpicuous, even during the ſhort time it ſub-
ſiſted. The dread of being forc'd into the
ſervice, rendered the populace peaceable
and orderly: it did more; it rendered
them induſtrious in order to conciliate favour. The moſt beneficial diſcoveries have
been accidental: without having any view
but for recruiting the army, our legiſlature ſtumbled upon an excellent plan, for
reclaiming the idle and the profligate; a

matter,

matter, in the prefent depravity of manners, of greater importance than any o-
ther that concerns the police of Britain.
A perpetual law of that kind, by promoting induftry, would prove a fovereign remedy againft mobs and riots, difeafes of
a free ftate, full of people and of manufactures *. Why were the foregoing fta-
tutes, for there were two of them, limited
to a temporary exiftence? There is not
on record another ftatute better intitled to
immortality.

And now to the project, which after all
my efforts I produce with trepidation; not
from any doubt of its folidity, but as ill
fuited to the prefent manners of this i-
fland. To hope that it will be put in
practice, would indeed be highly ridiculous : this can never happen, till patriotifm flourifh more in Britain than it has

---

* Several late mobs in the fouth of England, all
of them on pretext of fcarcity, greatly alarmed the
adminiftration. A fact was difcovered by a private
perfon (*Six-weeks tour through the fouth of England*) which our minifters ought to have difcovered, that thefe mobs conftantly happened where wages were high and provifions low ; confequently
that they were occafioned, not by want, but by wan-
tonnefs.

done

done for some time past. Suppoſing now an army of 60,000 men to be ſufficient for Britain, a rational method for raiſing ſuch an army, were there no ſtanding forces, would be, that land-proprietors, in proportion to their valued rents, ſhould furniſh men to ſerve ſeven years, and no longer *. But as it would be no leſs unjuſt than imprudent, to diſband at once our preſent army, we begin with moulding gradually the old army into the new, by filling up vacancies with men bound to ſerve ſeven years and no longer. And for raiſing proper men, a matter of much delicacy, it is propoſed, that in every ſhire a ſpecial commiſſion be given to certain landholders of rank and figure, to raiſe recruits out of the lower claſſes, ſelecting always thoſe who are the leaſt uſeful at home.

Second. Thoſe who claim to be diſmiſſed after ſerving the appointed time, ſhall never again be called to the ſervice, ex-

* In Denmark, every land-proprietor of a certain rent, is obliged to furniſh a militia-man, whom he can withdraw at pleaſure upon ſubſtituting another; an excellent method for taming the peaſants, and for rendering them induſtrious.

cept

cept in cafe of an actual invafion. They
fhall be intitled each of them to a premium of eight or ten pounds, for enabling them to follow a trade or calling,
without being fubjected to corporation-
laws. The private men in France are inlifted but for fix years; and that mode
has never been attended with any incon-
venience *.

Third. With refpect to the private men,
idlenefs muft be totally and for ever banifhed. Suppofing three months yearly
to be fufficient for military difcipline; the
men, during the reft of the year, ought
to be employ'd upon public works, forming roads, erecting bridges, making rivers
navigable, clearing harbours, &c. &c.
Why not alfo furnifh men for half-pay to
private undertakers of ufeful works ? And
fuppofing the daily pay of a foldier to be

* Had the plan of difcharging foldiers after a
fervice of five or feven years been early adopted by
the Emperors of Rome, the Pretorian bands would
never have become mafters of the ftate. It was a
grofs error to keep thefe troops always on foot
without change of members; which gave them a
confidence in one another, to unite in one folid
body, and to be actuated as it were by one mind.

ten

ten pence, it would greatly encourage extenſive improvements, to have at command a number of ſtout fellows under ſtrict diſcipline, at the low wages of five pence a-day. An army of 60,000 men thus employ'd, would not be ſo expenſive to the public, as 20,000 men upon the preſent eſtabliſhment: for beſide the money contributed by private undertakers, public works carried on by ſoldiers would be miſerably ill contrived, if not cheaply purchaſed with their pay *.

The moſt important branch of the project, is what regards the officers. The neceſſity of reviving in our people of rank ſome military ſpirit, will be acknowledged by every perſon of reflection; and in that view, the following articles are propoſed. Firſt, That there be two claſſes of officers, one ſerving for pay, one without pay. In filling up every vacant office of cornet or enſign, the latter are to be preferred; but in progreſſive advancement,

* Taking this for granted, I bring only into the computation the pay of the three months ſpent in military diſcipline; and the calculation is very ſimple, the pay of 20,000 for twelve months amounting to a greater ſum than the pay of 60,000 for three months.

no diftinction is to be made between the claffes. An officer who has ferved feven years without pay, may retire with ho-nour.

Second. No man fhall be privileged to reprefent a county in parliament, who has not ferved feven years without pay ; and, excepting an actual burgefs, none but thofe who have performed that fervice, fhall be privileged to reprefent a borough. The fame qualification fhall be neceffary to every one who afpires to ferve the public or the King in an office of dignity ; excepting only churchmen and lawyers with regard to offices in their refpective profeffions. In old Rome, none were ad-mitted candidates for any civil employ-ment, till they had ferved ten years in the army.

Third. Officers of this clafs are to be exempted from the taxes impofed on land, coaches, windows, and plate ; not for fa-ving a trifling fum, but as a mark of di-ftinction.

The military fpirit muft in Britain be miferably low, if fuch regulations prove not effectual to decorate the army with of-ficers of figure and fortune. Nor need we to apprehend any bad confequence from a number of raw officers who ferve without pay : among men of birth, emulation will have a more commanding influence than pay or profit ; and at any rate, there will always be a fufficiency of old and experienc'd officers receiving pay, ready to take the lead in every difficult enterprife.

To improve this army in military difcipline, it is propofed, that when occafion offers, 5 or 6000 of them be maintained by Great Britain, as auxiliaries to fome ally at war. And if that body be changed from time to time, knowledge and practice in war will be diffufed thro' the whole army.

Officers who ferve for pay, will be greatly benefited by this plan : frequent removes of thofe who ferve without pay, make way for them ; and the very nature of the plan excludes buying and felling.

I proceed to the alterations neceffary for accommodating this plan to our prefent military eftablifhment. As a total revolution at one inftant would breed confufion, the firft ftep ought to be a fpecimen only, fuch as the levying two or three regiments

on

on the new model; the expence of which ought not to be grudged, as the forces prefently in pay, are not fufficient, even in peace, to anfwer the ordinary demands of government. And as the profpect of civil employments, will excite more men of rank to offer their fervice than can be taken in, the choice muft be in the crown, not only with refpect to the new regiments, but with refpect to the vacant offices of cornet and enfign in the old army. But as thefe regulations will not inftantly produce men qualified to be fecretaries of ftate or commiffioners of treafury, fo numerous as to afford his Majefty a fatisfactory choice; that branch of the plan may be fufpended, till thofe who have ferved feven years without pay, amount to one hundred at leaft. The article that concerns members of parliament muft be ftill longer fufpended: it may however, after the firft feven years, receive execution in part, by privileging thofe who have ferved without pay to reprefent a borough, refufing that privilege to others, except to actual burgeffes. We may proceed one ftep farther, That if in a county there be five gentlemen who have the qualification under confideration, over and above the ordinary legal qualifications ; one of the five muft be chofen, leaving the electors free as to their other reprefentative.

With refpect to the private men of the old army, a thoufand of fuch as have ferved the longeft may be difbanded annually, if fo many be willing to retire ; and in their ftead an equal number may be inlifted to ferve but feven years. Upon fuch a plan, it will not be difficult to find recruits.

The advantage of this plan, in one particular, is eminent. It will infallibly fill the army with gallant officers : Other advantages concerning the officers themfelves, fhall be mentioned 'afterward. An appetite for military glory, cannot fail to be roufed in officers who ferve without pay, when their fervice is the only paffport to employments of truft and honour. And may we not hope, that officers who ferve for pay, will, by force of imitation, be infpired with the fame appetite ? Nothing ought to be more feduloufly inculcated into every officer, than to defpife riches, as a mercantile object below the dignity of a foldier. Often has the courage of victo-

rious

rjous troops been blunted by the pillage of an opulent city ; and may not rich captures at sea have the same effect ? Some sea-commanders have been suspected, of bestowing their fire more willingly upon a merchantman, than upon a ship of war. A triumph, an ovation, a civic crown, or some such mark of honour, were in old Rome the only rewards for military atchievements *. Money, it is true, was sometimes distributed among the private men, as an addition to their pay, after a fatiguing campaign ; but not as a recompence for their good behaviour, because all shared alike. It did not escape the penetrating Romans, that wealth, the parent of luxury and selfishness, fails not to era-

---

* A Roman triumph was finely contrived to excite heroism ; and a sort of triumph no less splendid, was usual among the Fatemite Califs of Egypt. After returning from a successful expedition, the Calif pitched his camp in a spacious plain near his capital, where he was attended by all his grandees, in their finest equipages. Three days were commonly spent in all manner of rejoicings, feasting, music, fireworks, &c. He marched into the city with this great cavalcade, through roads covered with rich carpets, strewed with flowers, gums, and odoriferous plants, and lined on both sides with crouds of congratulating subjects.

dicate

dicate the military fpirit. The foldier who
to recover his baggage performed a bold
action, gave an inftructive leffon to all
princes. Being invited by his general to
try his fortune a fecond time; " Invite
" (fays the foldier) one who has loft his
" baggage." Many a bold adventurer
goes to the Indies, who, returning with a
fortune, is afraid of every breeze. Britain, I fufpect, is too much infected with
the fpirit of gain. Will it be thought ridiculous in any man of figure, to prefer
reputation and refpect before riches ; provided only he can afford a frugal meal,
and a warm garment ? Let us compare an
old officer, who never deferted his friend
nor his country, and a wealthy merchant,
who never indulged a thought but of gain :
the wealth is tempting ; — and yet does
there exift a man of fpirit, who would not
be the officer rather than the merchant,
even with his millions ? Sultan Mechmet
granted to the Janifaries a privilege of im-
porting foreign commodities free of duty :
was it his intention to metamorphofe foldiers into merchants, loving peace, and
hating war ?

In the war 1672 carried on by Lewis
XIV.

XIV. againft the Dutch, Dupas was made governor of Naerden, recommended by the Duke of Luxembourg ; who wrote to M. de Louvois, that he wifhed nothing more ardently, than that the Prince of O-, range would befiege Naerden, being certain of a defence fo fkilful and vigorous, as to furnifh an opportunity for another victory over the Prince. Dupas had ferved long in honourable poverty ; but in this rich town he made a fhift to amafs a confiderable fum. Terrified to be reduced to his former poverty, he furrendered the town on the firft fummons. He was degraded in a court-martial, and condemned to perpetual prifon and poverty. Having obtained his liberty at the folicitation of the Vifcount de Turenne, he recovered his former valour, and ventured his life freely on all occafions.

But tho' I declare againft large appointments beforehand, which, inftead of promoting fervice, excite luxury and effeminacy ; yet to an officer of character, who has fpent his younger years in ferving his king and country, a government or other fuitable employment that enables him to, pafs the remainder of his life in cafe and affluence,

affluence, is a proper reward for merit, reflecting equal honour on the prince who
beſtows, and on the ſubject who receives;
beſide affording an enlivening proſpect to
others, who have it at heart to do well.

With reſpect to the private men, the
rotation propoſed, aims at improvements
far more important than that of making
military ſervice fall light upon individuals.
It tends to unite the ſpirit of induſtry with
that of war; and to form the ſame man to
be an induſtrious labourer, and a good
ſoldier. The continual exerciſe recommended, cannot fail to produce a ſpirit of
induſtry; which will occaſion a demand
for the private men after their ſeven years
ſervice, as valuable above all other labourers, not only for regularity, but for activity. And with reſpect to ſervice in war,
conſtant exerciſe is the life of an army,
in the literal as well as metaphorical ſenſe.
Boldneſs is inſpired by ſtrength and agi-
lity, to which conſtant motion mainly
contributes. The Roman citizens, trained
to arms from their infancy and never allowed to reſt, were invincible. To mention no other works, ſpacious and durable
roads carried to the very extremities of that

I   vaſt

vaft empire, fhow clearly how the foldiers were employ'd during peace; which hardened them for war, and made them orderly and fubmiffive (*a*). So effential was labour held by the Romans for training an army, that they never ventured to face an enemy with troops debilitated with idlenefs. The Roman army in Spain, having ·been worfted in feveral engagements and confined within their entrenchments, were funk in idlenefs and luxury. Scipio Nafica, having demolifhed Carthage, took the command of that army; but durft not oppofe it to the enemy, till he had accuftomed the foldiers to temperance and hard labour. He exercifed them without relaxation, in marching and countermarching, in fortifying camps and demolifhing them, in digging trenches and filling them up, in building high walls and· pulling them down; he himfelf, from morning till e-·vening, going about, and directing every operation. Marius, before engaging· the Cimbri, exercifed his army in turning the courfe of a river. Appian relates, that Antiochus, during his winter-quarters at

(*a*) Bergiere hiftoire des grands chemins, vol. 2. p. 152.

Calchis, having married a beautiful virgin
with whom he was greatly enamoured,
fpent the whole winter in pleafure, aban-
doning his army to vice and idlenefs ; and
that when the time of action returned with
the fpring, he found his foldiers unfit for
fervice. It is reported of Hannibal, that
to preferve his troops from the infection
of idlenefs, he employ'd them in making
large plantations of olive trees. The Emperor Probus exercifed his legions in covering with vineyards the hills of Gaul
and Pannonia. The idlenefs of our foldiers in time of peace, promoting debauchery and licentioufnefs, is no lefs deftructive to health than to difcipline. Unable for the fatigues of a firft campaign,
our private men die in thoufands, as if
fmitten with a peftilence *. We never
read

* The idlenefs of Britifh foldiers appears from a
tranfaction of the commiffioners of the annexed e-
ftates in Scotland. After the late war with France,
they judged, that part of the King's rents could not
be better applied, than in giving bread to the difbanded foldiers. Houfes were built for them, portions of land given them to cultivate at a very low
rent, and maintenance afforded them till they could
reap a crop. Thefe men could not wifh to be better
accommodated :

read of any mortality in the Roman legions, tho' frequently engaged in climates
very different from their own. Let us
liften to a judicious writer, to whom every
one liftens with delight: " Nous remar-
" quons aujourd'hui, que nos armées pé-
" riffent beaucoup par le travail immo-
" déré des foldats ; et cependant c'étoit
" par un travail immenfe que les Romains
" fe confervoient. La raifon en eft, je
" croix, que leurs fatigues étoient conti-
" nuelles ; au lieu que nos foldats paffent
" fans ceffe d'un travail extreme à une ex-
" treme oifivété, ce qui eft la chofe du
" monde la plus propre à les faire perir.
" Il faut que je rapporte ici ce que les au-
" teurs nous difent de l'education de fol-
" dats Romains. On les accoutumoit à
" aller le pas militaire, c'eft-a-dire, à faire
" en cinq heures vingt milles, et quelque-
" fois vingt-quatre. Pendant ces mar-
" ches, on leur faifoit porter de poids de

accommodated : but fo accuftomed they had been
to idlenefs and change of place, as to be incapable
of any fort of work : they deferted their farms one
after another, and commenced thieves and beggars.
Such as had been made ferjeants muft be excepted :
thefe were fenfible fellows, and profpered in their
little farms.

F 2 " foixante

" foixante livres. On les entretenoit dans
" l'habitude de courir et de fauter tout
" armés ; ils prénoient dans leurs exerci-
" ces des epées, de javelots, de flêches,
" d'une péfanteur double des armes ordi-
" naires ; et ces exercices étoient conti-
" nuels. Des hommes fi endurcis étoient
" ordinairement fains ; on ne remarque
" pas dans les auteurs que les armées Ro-
" maines, qui faifoient la guerre en tant
" de climats, periffoient beaucoup par les
" maladies ; au lieu qu'il arrive prefque
" continuellement aujourd'hui, que des
" armèes, fans avoir combattu, fe fon-
" dent, pour ainfi dire, dans une cam-
" pagne * (a)." Our author muft be here
underftood

(a) Montefquieu, Grandeur de Romains, chap. 2.

* " We obferve now-a-days, that our armies
" are confumed by the fatigues and fevere labour of
" the foldiers ; and yet it was alone by labour and
" toil that the Romans preferved themfelves from
" deftruction. I believe the reafon is, that their
" fatigue was continual and unremitting, while the
" life of our foldiers is a perpetual tranfition from
" fevere labour to extreme indolence, a life the
" moft ruinous of all others. I muft here recite the
" account which the Roman authors give of the e-
" ducation of their foldiers. They were continu-
" ally habituated to the military pace, which was,
" to

underſtood of the early times of the Roman ſtate. Military diſcipline was much
ſunk in the fourth century when Vegetius
wrote (Lib. 3. cap. 14. 15.). The ſword
and Pilum, theſe formidable weapons of
their forefathers, were totally laid aſide
for ſlings and bows, the weapons of effeminate people. About this time it was,
that the Romans left off fortifying their
camps, a work too laborious for their
weakly conſtitutions. Mareſchal Saxe, a
ſoldier, not a phyſician, aſcribes to the
uſe of vinegar the healthineſs of the Roman legions: were vinegar ſo ſalutary, it
would of all liquors be the moſt in requeſt.
Exerciſe without intermiſſion, during

" to march in five hours twenty, and ſometimes
" twenty-four miles. In theſe marches each ſoldier
" carried ſixty pounds weight. They were accu-
" ſtomed to run and leap in arms ; and in their mi-
" litary exerciſes, their ſwords, javelins, and ar-
" rows, were of twice the ordinary weight. Theſe
" exerciſes were continual, which ſo ſtrengthened
" the conſtitution of the men, that they were al-
" ways in health. We ſee no remarks in the Ro-
" man authors, that their armies, in the variety of
" climates where they made war, ever periſhed by
" diſeaſe ; whilſt now-a-days it is not unuſual, that
" an army, without ever coming to an engagement,
" dwindles away by diſeaſe in one campaign."

peace

peace as well as during war, produced
that salutary effect; which every prince
will find, who is difpofed to copy the Roman difcipline *. The Marefchal guefles
better with refpect to a horfe. Difcour-
fing of cavalry, he obferves, that a horfe
becomes hardy and healthful by conftant
exercife, and that a young horfe is unable
to bear fatigue; for which reafon he declares againft young horfes for the fervice
of an army.

- That the military branch of the Britifh
government is fufceptible of improvements, all the world will admit. To improve it, I have contributed my mite;

* Rei militaris periti, plus quotidiana armorum
exercitia ad fanitatem militum putaverunt prodeffe,
quam medicos. Ex quo intelligitur quanto ftudio-
fius armorum artem docendus fit femper exercitus,
cum ei laboris confuetudo et in caftris fanitatem, et
in conflictu poffit præftare victoriam. *Vegetius, De
re militari, lib.* 3. *cap.* 2.—[*In Englifh thus :* " Our
" mafters of the art-military were of opinion,
" that daily exercife in arms contributed more to
" the health of the troops, than the fkill of the
" phyfician : from which we may judge, what care
" fhould be taken, to habituate the foldiers to the
" exercife of arms, to which they owe both their
" health in the camp, and their victory in the
" field."]

which

which is humbly fubmitted to the public, a judge from which there lies no appeal. It is fubmitted in three views. The firft is, Whether an army, modelled as above, would not fecure us againft the boldeft invader; the next, Whether fuch an army be as dangerous to liberty, as an army in its prefent form; and the laft, Whether it would not be a fchool of induftry and moderation to our people.

With refpect to the firft, we fhould, after a few years, have not only an army of fixty thoufand well-difciplined troops, but the command of another army, equally numerous and equally well difciplined. It is true, that troops inured to war have an advantage over troops that have not the fame experience: but with affurance it may be pronounced impracticable, to land at once in Britain an army that can ftand againft 100,000 Britifh foldiers well difciplined, fighting, even the firft time, for their country, and for their wives and children.

A war with France raifes a panic on every flight threatening of an invafion. The fecurity afforded by the propofed plan, would enable us to act offenfively

at

at fea, inftead of being reduced to keep our fhips at home for guarding our coafts. Would Britain any longer be obliged to fupport her continental connections? No fooner does an European prince augment his army or improve military difcipline, than his neighbours, taking fright, muft do the fame. May not one hope, that by the plan propofed, or by fome fuch, Britain would be relieved from jealoufy and folicitude about its neighbours?

With refpect to the fecond view, having long enjoy'd the fweets of a free government under a fucceffion of mild princes, we begin to forget that our liberties ever were in danger. But droufy fecurity is of all conditions the moft dangerous; becaufe the ftate may be overwhelmed before we even dream of danger. Suppofe only, that a Britifh King, accomplifhed in the art of war and beloved by his foldiers, heads his own troops in a war with France; and after more than one fuccefsful campaign, gives peace to his enemy, on terms advantageous to his people: what fecurity have we for our liberties, when he returns with a victorious army,

2   devoted

devoted to his will? I am talking of a ftanding army in its prefent form. Troops modelled as above would not be fo obfequious: a number of the prime nobility and · gentry ferving without pay, who could be under no temptation to enflave themfelves and their country, would prove a firm barrier againft the ambitious views of fuch a prince. And even fuppofing that army to be totally corrupted, the prince could have little hope of fuccefs a-gainft the nation, fupported by a veteran army, that might be relied on as champions for their country.

And as to the laft view mentioned, the plan propofed would promote induftry and virtue, not only among the foldiers, but among the working people in general. To avoid hard labour and fevere difcipline in the army, men would be fober and induftrious at home; and fuch untraclable fpirits as cannot be reached by the mild laws of a free government, would be effectually tamed by military law. At the fame time, as fobriety and innocence are conftant attendants upon induftry, the manners of our people would be much purified; a circumftance of infinite importance to Britain. The falutary influence of the plan, would reach perfons in a higher fphere. A young gentleman, whipt at fchool, or falling behind at college, contracts an a-verfion to ftudy; and flies to the army, where he is kept in countenance by num-bers, idle and ignorant like himfelf. How many young men are thus daily ruined, who, but for the temptation of idlenefs and gaiety in the army, would have be-come ufeful fubjects! In the plan under confideration, the officers who ferve for pay would be fo few in number, and their profpect of advancement fo clear, that it would require much intereft to be admit-ted into the army. None would be ad-mitted but thofe who have been regular-ly educated in every branch of military knowledge; and idle boys would be re-mitted to their ftudies.

Here is difplay'd an agreeable fcene with relation to induftry. Suppofing the whole threefcore thoufand men to be ab-folutely idle; yet, by doubling the indu-ftry of thofe who remain, I affirm, that the fum of induftry would be much greater than before. And the fcene becomes en-chanting, when we confider, that thefe
threefcore

threefcore thoufand men, would not only
be of all the moft induftrious, but be pat-
terns of induftry to others.

Upon conclufion of a foreign war, we
fuffer grievoufly by difbanded foldiers,
who muft plunder or ftarve. The prefent
plan is an effectual remedy : men accuftomed to hard labour under ftrict difcipline, can never be in want of bread :
they will be fought for every where, even
at higher than ordinary wages ; and they
will prove excellent mafters for training
the peafants to hard labour.

' A man indulges emulation more freely
in behalf of his friend or his country,
than of himfelf: emulation in the latter
cafe is felfifh ; in the former, is focial.
Doth not that give us reafon to hope, that
the feparating military officers into different claffes will excite a laudable emulation,
prompting individuals to exert themfelves
on every occafion for the honour of their
clafs ? Nor will fuch emulation, a virtuous
paffion, be any obftruction to private
friendlhip between members of different
claffes. May it not be expected, that
young officers of birth and fortune, zea-
lous to qualify themfelves at their own

expence

expence for ferving their country, will cling for inftruction to officers of experience, who have no inheritance but perfonal merit? Both find their account in that connection: men of rank become adepts in military affairs, a valuable branch of education for them; and officers who ferve for pay, acquire friends at court, who will embrace every opportunity of teftifying their gratitude.

The advantages mentioned are great and extenfive; and yet are not the only advantages. Will it be thought extravagant to hope, that the propofed plan would form a better fyftem of education for young men of fortune, than hitherto has been known in Britain? Before pronouncing fentence againft me, let the following confiderations be weigh'd. Our youth go abroad to *fee* the world in the literal fenfe; for to pierce deeper than eyefight, cannot be expected of boys. They refort to gay courts, where nothing is found for imitation but pomp, luxury, diffembled virtues, and real vices: fuch fcenes make an impreffion too deep on young men of a warm imagination. Our plan would be an antidote to fuch poifonous education. Suppofing eighteen to be

the

the earlieft time for the army ; here is an
object held up to our youth of fortune,
for roufing their ambition : they will endeavour to make a figure, and emulation
·will animate them to excel : fuppofing a
young man to have no ambition, fhame
however will pufh him on. To acquire
the military art, to difcipline their men,
to direct the execution of public works,
and to conduct other military operations,
would occupy their whole time, and banifh idlenefs. A young gentleman, thus
guarded againft the enticing vices and
fauntering follies of youth, muft be fadly
deficient in genius, if, during his feven
years fervice, reading and meditation have
been totally neglected.   Hoping better
things from our youth of fortune, I take
for granted, that during their fervice they
have made fome progrefs, not only in military knowledge, but in morals, and in
the fine arts, fo as at the age of twenty-
five to be qualified for profiting, inftead
of being undone, by *feeing* the world *.

Further,

* Whether hereditary nobility may not be neceffary in a monarchical government to fupport the
King againft the multitude, I take not on me to
pronounce :

Further, young men of birth and fortune, acquire indeed the fmoothnefs and fupplenefs of a court, with refpect to their fuperiors ; but the reftraint of fuch manners, makes their temper break out againft inferiors, where there is no reftraint. Infolence of rank, is not fo vifible in Britain as in countries of lefs freedom ; but it is fufficiently vifible to require correction. To that end, no method promifes more fuccefs than military fervice ; as command and obedience alternately, are the beft difcipline for acquiring temper and moderation. Can pride and infolence be more effectually ftemmed, than to be under command of an inferior ?

Still upon the important article of education. Where pleafure is the ruling paffion in youth, intereft will be the ruling paffion in age : the felfifh principle is the foundation of both ; the object only is

pronounce : but this I pronounce with affurance, that fuch a conftitution is unhappy with refpect to education ; and appears to admit no remedy, if it be not that above mentioned, or fome fuch. In fact, few of thofe who received their education while they were the eldeft fons of Peers, have been duly qualified to manage public affairs.

varied.

varied. This obfervation is fadly verified
in Britain: our young men of rank, loath-
ing an irkfome and fatiguing courfe of e-
ducation, abandon themfelves to pleafure.
Trace thefe very men through the more
fettled part of life, and they will be found
grafping at power and profit, by means of
court-favour; with no regard to their
country, and with very little to their
friends. The education propofed, holding
up a tempting prize to virtuous ambition,
is an excellent fence againft a life of indolent pleafure. A youth of fortune, engaged with many rivals in a train of public
fervice, acquires a habit of bufinefs; and
as he is conftantly employ'd for the public, patriotifm becomes his ruling paffion *.

The

---

* The following portrait is fketched by a good
hand, (Madame Pompadour); and if it have any
refemblance, it fets our plan in a confpicuous light.
The French noblefle, fays that lady, fpending their
lives in diflipation and idlenefs, know as little of politics as of economy. A gentleman hunts all his
life in the country, or perhaps comes to Paris to
ruin himfelf with an opera-girl. Thofe who are
ambitious to be of the miniftry, have feldom any
merit, if it be not in caballing and intrigue. The
French noblefle have courage, but without any ge-

nius

The advantages of a military education, fuch as that propofed, are not yet exhauft-ed. Under regular government promo-ting the arts of peace, focial intercourfe refines, and fondnefs for company in-creafes in proportion. And hence it is, that the capital is crouded with every per-fon who can afford to live there. A man of fortune, who has no tafte but for a city life, happens to be forc'd into the country by bufinefs : finding bufinefs and the country equally infipid, he turns impa-tient, and flies to town, with a difguft at every rural amufement. In France, the country has been long deferted : in Bri-tain the fame fondnefs for a town-life is gaining ground. A ftranger confidering the immenfe fums expended in England upon country-feats, would conclude, in appearance with great certainty, that the Englifh fpend moft of their time in the country. But how would it furprife him

---

nius for war, the fatigue of a foldier's life being to them unfupportable. The King has been reduced to the neceffity of employing two ftrangers for the fafety of his crown : had it not been for the Counts Saxe and Louendahl, the enemies of France might have laid fiege to Paris.

to be told, not only that people of fashion in England pass little of their time there, but that the immenfe fums laid out upon gardening and pleafure-grounds, are the effect of vanity more than of tafte! In fact, fuch embellifhments are beginning to wear out of fafhion; appetite for fociety leaving neither time nor inclination for rural pleafures. If the progrefs of that difeafe can be ftay'd, the only means is military education. In youth lafting impreffions are made; and men of fortune who take to the army, being confined moftly to the country in prime of life, contract a liking for country occupations and amufements: which withdraw them from the capital, and contribute to the health of the mind, no lefs than of the body.

A military life is the only cure for a difeafe much more dangerous. Moft men of rank are ambitious of fhining in public. They may affume the patriot at the beginning; but it is a falfe appearance, for their patriotifm is only a difguife to favour their ambition. A court life becomes habitual and engroffes their whole foul: the minifter's nod is a law to them: they dare not difobey; for to be reduced to a

private ſtation, would to them be a cruel
misfortune. This impotence of mind is
in France ſo exceſſive, that to baniſh a
courtier to his country ſeat, is held an a-
dequate puniſhment for the higheſt miſde-
meanor. This ſort of ſlavery is gaining
ground in Britain; and it ought to be
dreaded, for ſcarce another circumſtance
will more readily pave the way to abſolute
power, if adverſe fate ſhall afflict us with
an ambitious King. There is no effectual
remedy to the ſervility of a court life, but
the military education here recommended.

A military education would contribute
equally to moderation in ſocial enjoyments. The pomp, ceremony, and expence, neceſſary to thoſe who adhere to a
court and live always in public, are not a
little fatiguing and oppreſſive. Man is naturally moderate in his deſire of enjoyment; and it requires much practice to
make him bear exceſs without ſatiety and
diſguſt. The pain of exceſs, prompts men
of opulence to paſs ſome part of their time
in a ſnug retirement, where they live at
eaſe, free from pomp and ceremony.
Here is a retirement, which can be reached without any painful circuit; a port of
ſafety

fafety and of peace, to which we are pi-
loted by military education, avoiding e-
very dangerous rock, and every fatiguing
agitation.

Reflecting on the advantages of military
education above difplay'd, is it foolifh to
think, that our plan might produce a total
alteration of manners in our youth of birth
and fortune? The idler, the gamefter, the
profligate, compared with our military
men, would make a defpicable figure:
fhame, not to talk of pride, would compel
them to reform.

How conducive to good government
might the propofed plan be, in the hands
of a virtuous king, fupported by a public-
fpirited miniftry! In the prefent courfe of
advancement, a youth of quality who a-
fpires to ferve his country in a civil employment, has nothing to rely on but par-
liamentary intereft. The military education propofed, would afford him opportunity to improve his talents, and to convince the world of his merit. Honour
and applaufe thus acquired, would intitle
him to demand preferment; and he ought
to be employ'd, not only as deferving, but
as an encouragement to others. Frequent

inftances of neglecting men who are pa-
tronized by the public, might perhaps
prove dangerous to a Britifh minifter.

If I have not all this while been dreaming, here are difplay'd illuftrious advantages of the military education propofed.
Fondnefs for the fubject excites me to pro-
long the entertainment; and I add the
following reflection on the education of
fuch men as are difpofed to ferve in a public ftation. The fciences are mutually connected: a man cannot be perfect in any one,
without being in fome degree acquainted
with every one. The fcience of politics in
particular, being not a little intricate, cannot be acquired in perfection by any one
whofe ftudies have been confined to a fingle
branch, whether relative to peace or to war.
The Duke of Marlborough made an eminent figure in the cabinet, as well as in
the field; and fo did equally the illuftrious
Sully, who may ferve as a model to all
minifters. The great aim in modern politics is, to fplit government into the
greateft number poffible of departments,
trufting nothing to genius. China affords
fuch a government in perfection. National affairs are there fo fimplified by divifion,

vifion, as to require fcarce any capacity in
the mandarines. Thefe officers, having
little occafion for activity either of mind
or of body, fink down into floth and fen-
fuality : motives of ambition or of fame
make no impreffion : they have not even
the delicacy to blufh when they err : and
as no punifhment is regarded but what
touches the perfon or the purfe, it is not
unufual to fee a mandarine beaten with
many ftripes, fometimes for a very flight
tranfgreffion. Let arts be fubdivided into
many parts : the more fubdivifions the
better. But I venture to pronounce, that
no man ever did, nor ever will, make a
capital figure in the government of a ftate,
whether as a judge, a general, or a minifter, whofe education is rigidly confined
to one fcience *.

Senfible I am that the foregoing plan is
in feveral refpects imperfect ; but if it be
found at bottom, polifh and improvement
are eafy operations. My capital aim has

---

* Phocion is praifed by ancient writers, for ftrug-
gling againft an abufe that had crept into his country of Attica, that of making war and politics different profeffions. In imitation of Ariftides and of
Pericles, he ftudied both equally.

been,

been, to obviate the objections that press hard against every military plan, hitherto embraced or proposed. A standing army, in its present form, is dangerous to liberty; and but a feeble bulwark against superior force.   On the other hand, a nation in which every subject is a soldier, must not indulge any hopes of becoming powerful by manufactures and commerce: it is indeed vigorously defended, but is scarce worthy of being defended.   The golden mean of rotation and constant labour in a standing army, would discipline multitudes for peace as well as for war. And a nation so defended would be invincible.

SKETCH

SKETCH X.

Public Police with respect to the Poor.

AMong the industrious nations of Europe, regulations for the poor, make a considerable branch of public police. These regulations are so multipled and so anxiously framed, as to move one to think, that there cannot remain a single person under a necessity to beg. It is however a sad truth, that the disease of poverty, instead of being eradicated, has become more and more inveterate. England in particular overflows with beggars, tho' in no other country are the indigent so amply provided for. Some radical defect there must be in these regulations, when, after endless attempts to perfect them, they prove abortive. Every writer, dissatisfied with former plans, fails not to produce one of his own ; which, in its turn, meets with as little approbation as any of the foregoing.

The first regulation of the states of Holland

land concerning the poor, was in the year 1614, prohibiting all begging. The next was in the year 1649. " It is enacted, " That every town, village, or parish, " shall maintain its poor out of the in- " come of its charitable foundations and " collections. And in cafe thefe means " fall short, the magistrates shall maintain " them at the general expence of the in- " habitants, as can most conveniently be " done : Provided always, that the poor " be obliged to work either to merchants, " farmers, or others, for reasonable wages, " in order that they may, as far as pof- " fible, be fupported that way ; provided " also, that they be indulged in no idle- " nefs nor infolence." The advice or in- struction here given to magistrates, is fen- fible; but falls short of what may be termed a *law*, the execution of which can be enforc'd in a court of justice.

In France, the precarious charity of monasteries proving ineffectual, a hofpital was erected in the city of Paris *anno* 1656, having different apartments ; one for the innocent poor, one for putting vagabonds to hard labour, one for foundlings, and one for the fick and maimed ; with cer-

tain

tain funds for defraying the expence of each, which produce annually much about the fame fum. In imitation of Paris, hofpitals of the fame kind were erected in every great town of the kingdom.

The Englifh began more early to think of their poor; and in a country without induftry, the neceffity probably arofe more early. The firft Englifh ftatute bears date in the year 1496, directing, " That every " beggar unable to work, fhall refort to " the hundred where he laft dwelt or was " born; and there fhall remain, upon " pain of being fet in the ftocks three days " and three nights, with only bread and " water, and then fhall be put out of " town." This was a law againft vagrants, for the fake of order. There was little occafion, at that period, to provide for the innocent poor; their maintenance being a burden upon monafteries. But monafteries being put down by Henry VIII. a ftatute, 22d year of his reign, cap. 12. impowered the . juftices of every county, to licenfe poor aged and impotent perfons to beg within a certain diftrict; thofe who beg without it, to be whipt, or fet in the ftocks. In the firſt year of Edward VI. cap. 3. a ſtatute was made in favour of impotent, maimed, and aged perſons, that they ſhall have convenient houſes provided for them, in the cities or towns where they were born, or where they reſided for three years, to be relieved by the *willing and charitable diſpoſition* of the pariſhioners. By 2d and 3d Philip and Mary, cap. 5. the former ſtatutes of Henry VIII. and Edward VI. were confirmed, of gathering weekly relief for the poor by charitable collections. " A " man licenſed to beg, ſhall wear a badge " on his breaſt and back openly."

The firſt compulſory ſtatute was 5° Eliſab. cap. 3. empowering juſtices of peace to raiſe a weekly ſum for the poor, by taxing ſuch perſons as obſtinately refuſe to contribute, after repeated admonitions from the pulpit. In the next ſtatute, 14° Eliſab. cap. 5. a bolder ſtep was made, empowering juſtices to tax the inhabitants of every pariſh, in a weekly ſum for their poor. And taxations for the poor being now in ſome degree familiar, the remarkable ſtatutes, 39° Eliſab. cap. 3. and 43° Eliſab. cap. 2. were enacted, which are the ground-work of all the ſubſequent ſtatutes

ſtatutes concerning the poor. By theſe ſtatutes, certain houſeholders, named by the juſtices, are, in conjunction with the church-wardens, appointed overſeers for the poor ; and theſe overſeers, with conſent of two juſtices, are empowered to tax the pariſh in what ſums they think proper, for maintaining the poor.

Among a people ſo tenacious of liberty as the Engliſh are, and ſo impatient of oppreſſion, is it not ſurpriſing, to find a law, that without ceremony ſubjects individuals to be taxed at the arbitrary will of men, who ſeldom either by birth or education deſerve that important truſt ; and without even providing any effectual check againſt embezzlement ? At preſent, a Britiſh parliament would reject with ſcorn ſuch an abſurd plan ; and yet, being familiarized to it, they never ſeriouſly have attempted a repeal. We have been always on the watch to prevent the ſovereign's encroachments, eſpecially with regard to taxes : but as pariſh-officers are low perſons who inſpire no dread, we ſubmit to have our pockets pick'd by them, almoſt without repining. There is provided, it is true, an appeal to the general ſeſſions

for redreſſing inequalities in taxing the pariſhioners. But it is no effectual remedy:
artful overſeers will not over-rate any man
ſo groſsly as to make it his intereſt to
complain, conſidering that theſe overſeers
have the poor's money to defend themſelves with. Nor will the general ſeſſions
readily liſten to a complaint, that cannot
be verified but with much time and
trouble. If the appeal have any effect, it
makes a ſtill greater inequality, by relieving men of figure at the expence of their
inferiors ; who muſt ſubmit, having little
intereſt to obtain redreſs.

The Engliſh plan, beſide being oppreſ-
five, is groſsly unjuſt. If it ſhould be reported of ſome diſtant nation, that the
burden of maintaining the idle and profligate, is laid upon the frugal and induſtrious, who work hard for a maintenance to
themſelves ; what would one think of ſuch
a nation ? Yet this is literally the caſe of
England. I ſay more : the plan is not
only oppreſſive and unjuſt, but miſerably
defective in the checking of maladmini-
ſtration. In fact, great ſums are levied
beyond what the poor receive : it requires
briguing to be named a church-warden :
the

the nomination, in London efpecially, gives him credit at once; and however meagre at the commencement of his office, he is round and plump before it ends. To wax fat and rich by robbing the poor! Let us turn our eyes from a fcene fo horrid *.

Inequality in taxing, and embezzlement of the money levied, which are notorious, poifon the minds of the people; and imprefs them with a notion, that all taxes raifed by public authority are ill managed.

Thefe evils are great, and yet are but flight compared with what follow. As the

---

* In the parifh of St George, Hanover Square, a great reform was made fome years ago. Inhabitants of figure, not excepting men of the higheft rank, take it in turn to be church-wardens; which has reduced the poor-rates in that parifh to a trifle. But people, after acquiring a name, foon tire of drudging for others. The drudgery will be left to low people as formerly, and the tax will again rife as high in that parifh as in others. The poor-rates, in Dr Davenant's time, were about L. 700,000 yearly. In the year 1764, they amounted to L. 2,200,000. In the year 1773, they amounted to L. 3,000,000, equal to fix fhillings in the pound land-tax.

number

number of poor in England, as well as the expence of maintenance, are increafing daily; proprietors of land, in order to be relieved of a burden fo grievous, drive the poor out of the parifh, and prevent all perfons from fettling in it who are likely to become a burden: cottages are demolifhed, and marriage obftructed. . Influenced by the prefent evil, they look not forward to depopulation, nor to the downfall of hufbandry and manufactures by fcarcity of hands. Every parifh is in a ftate of war with every other parifh, concerning *pauper* fettlements and removals.

The price of labour is generally the fame in the different fhires of Scotland, and in the different parifhes. A few exceptions are occafioned by the neighbourhood of a great town, or by fome extenfive manufacture that requires many hands. In Scotland, the price of labour refembles water, which always levels itfelf: if high in any one corner, an influx of hands brings it down. The price of labour varies in every parifh of England: a labourer who has gain'd a fettlement in a parifh, on which he depends for bread when he inclines to be idle, dares not remove to
another

another parifh where wages are higher, fearing to be cut out of a fettlement altogether. England is in the fame condition with refpect to labour, that France lately was with refpect to corn; which, however plentiful in one province, could not be exported to fupply the wants of another. The pernicious effect of the latter with refpect to food, are not more obvious, than of the former with refpect to manufactures.

Englifh manufactures labour under a ftill greater hardfhip than inequality of wages. In a country where there is no fund for the poor but what nature provides, the labourer muft be fatisfied with fuch wages as are cuftomary: he has no refource; for pity is not moved by idlenefs. In England, the labourers command the market: if not fatisfied with cuftomary wages, they have a tempting refource; which is, to abandon work altogether, and to put themfelves on the parifh. Labour is much cheaper in France than in England: feveral plaufible reafons have been affigned; but in my judgement, the difference arifes from the poor-laws. In England, every man is entitled to be idle;

becaufe

becaufe every idler is entitled to a maintenance. In France, the funds allotted for
the poor, yield the fame fum annually:
that fum is always preoccupied; and
France, with refpect to all but thofe on
the lift, is a nation that has no fund provided by law for the poor.

Depopulation, inequality in the price of
labour, and extravagant wages, are deplorable evils. But the Englifh poor-laws
are productive of evils ftill more deplorable: they are fubverfive both of morality and induftry. This is a heavy charge,
but no lefs true than heavy. Fear of want
is the only effectual motive to induftry
with the labouring poor: remove that
fear, and they ceafe to be induftrious.
The ruling paffion of thofe who live by
bodily labour, is to fave a pittance for
their children, and for fupporting themfelves in old age: ftimulated by defire of
accomplifhing thefe ends, they are frugal
and induftrious; and the profpect of fuccefs is to them a continual feaft. Now,
what worfe can malice invent againft fuch
a man, under colour of friendfhip, than
to fecure bread to him and his children
whenever he takes a diflike to work; which

effectually

effectually deadens his fole ambition, and
with it his honeft induftry? Relying on
the certainty of a provifion againft want,
he relaxes gradually till he finks into idlenefs : idlenefs leads to profligacy : profligacy begets difeafes : and the wretch becomes an object of public charity before
he has run half his courfe. Such are the
genuine effects of the Englifh tax for the
poor, under a miftaken notion of charity.
There never was known in any country,
a fcheme for the poor more contradictory
to found policy. Might it not have been
forefeen, that to a groveling creature, who
has no fenfe of honour and fcarce any of
fhame, the certainty of maintenance would
prove an irrefiftible temptation to idlenefs
and debauchery? The poor-houfe at Lyons contained originally but forty beds,
of which twenty only were occupied. The
eight hundred beds it contains at prefent,
are not fufficient for thofe who demand
admittance. A premium is not more fuccefsful in any cafe, than where given to
promote idlenefs *. A houfe for the poor

was

* A London alderman named *Harper*, who was
cotemporary with James I. or his fon Charles, be-

was erected in a French village, the revenue of which by economy became confi-

queathed ten or twelve acres of meadow ground in
the parish of St Andrew's Holborn, London, for
the benefit of the poor in the town of Bedford.
This ground has been long covered with houses,
which yield from L. 4000 to L. 5000 yearly. That
sum is laid out upon charity-schools, upon defraying the expence of apprenticeships, and upon a
stock to young persons when they marry; an encouragement that attracts to the town of Bedford
great numbers of the lower classes. So far well:
but mark the consequence. That encouragement
relaxes the industry of many, and adds greatly to
the number of the poor. Hence it is, that in few
places of England does the poor's rate amount so
high as in the town of Bedford. An extensive common in the parish of Charley, Suffex, is the chief
cause of an extravagant affessment for the poor, no
less than nine shillings in the pound of rack rent.
Give a poor man access to a common for feeding
two or three cows, you make him idle by a dependence upon what he does not labour for. The town
of Largo in Fife has a small hospital, erected many
years ago by a gentleman of the name of Wood;
and confined by him to the poor of his own name.
That name being rare in the neighbourhood, access to the hospital is easy. One man in particular
is entertained there, whose father, grandfather, and
great-grandfather, enjoy'd succeffively the same benefit; every one of whom probably would have
been useful members of society, but for that temptation to idleness.

derable,

derable. Upon a reprefentation by the curate of the parifh that more beds were neceffary, the proprietor undertook the management. He fold the houfe, with the furniture.; and to every proper object of charity, he ordered a moderate proportion of bread and beef. The poor and fick were more comfortably lodged at home, than formerly in the poor-houfe. And by that management, the parifh-poor decreafed, inftead of increafing as at Lyons. How few Englifh manufacturers labour the whole week, if the work of four or five days afford them maintenance? Is not this a demonftration, that the malady of idlenefs is widely fpread? In Briftol, the parifh-poor twenty years ago did not exceed four thoufand : at prefent, they amount to more than ten thoufand. But as a malady, when left to itfelf, commonly effectuates its own cure ; fo it will be in this cafe : when, by prevailing idlenefs, every one without fhame claims parifh-charity, the burden will become intolerable, and the poor will be left to their fhifts.

The immoral effects of public charity are not confined to thofe who depend on

K 2　　　　　　　　　it,

it, but extend to their children. The constant anxiety of a labouring man to provide for his issue, endears them to him. Being relieved of that anxiety by the tax for the poor, his affection cools gradually, and he turns at last indifferent about them. Their independence, on the other hand, weans them from their duty to him. And thus, affection between parent and child, which is the corner-stone of society, is in a great measure obliterated among the labouring poor. In a plan published by the Earl of Hilsborough, an article is proposed to oblige parents to maintain their indigent children, and children to maintain their indigent parents. Natural affection must be at a low ebb, where such a regulation is necessary: but it is necessary, at least in London, where it is common to see men in good business neglecting their aged and diseased parents, for no better reason than that the parish is bound to find them bread : *Proh tempora, proh mores !*

The immoral effects of public charity spread still wider. It fails not to extinguish the virtue of charity among the rich ; who never think of giving charity,

when

when the public undertakes for all. In a scheme publifhed by Mr Hay, one article is, to raife a ftock for the poor by voluntary contributions, and to make up the deficiency by a parifh-tax. Will individuals ever contribute, when it is not to relieve the poor, but to relieve the parifh? Every hofpital has a poor-box, which feldom produces any thing *. The great comfort of fociety is affiftance in time of need; and its firmeft cement is, the beftowing and receiving kindly offices, efpecially in diftrefs. Now to unhinge or fufpend the exercife of charity by rendering it unneceffary, relaxes every focial virtue by fupplanting the chief of them. The confequence is difmal: exercife of benevolence to the diftreffed is our firmeft guard againft the encroachments of felfifhnefs: if that guard be withdrawn, felfifhnefs will prevail, and become the ruling paffion. In fact, the tax for the poor has contributed greatly to the growth of

---

* One exception I am fond to mention. The poor-box of the Edinburgh infirmary was neglected two or three years, little being expected from it. When opened, L. 74 and a fraction was found in it; contributed probably by the lower fort, who were afhamed to give their mite publicly.

that

that groveling paſſion, ſo conſpicuous at
preſent in England.

English authors who turn their thoughts
to the poor, make heavy complaints of de-
caying charity, and increaſing poverty:
never once dreaming, that theſe are the
genuine effects of a legal proviſion for the
poor; which on the one hand eradicates
the virtue of charity, and on the other is
a violent temptation to idleneſs. Wonderfully ill contrived muſt the Engliſh cha-
rity-laws be, when their conſequences are
to ſap the foundation of voluntary charity; to deprive the labouring poor of
their chief comfort, that of providing for
themſelves and children; to relax mutual
affection between parent and child; and
to reward, inſtead of puniſhing, idleneſs
and vice. Conſider whether a legal proviſion for the poor, be ſufficient to atone
for ſo many evils.

No man had better opportunity than
Fielding to be acquainted with the ſtate of
the poor: let us liſten to him. " That
" the poor are a very great burden, and
" even a nuiſance to the kingdom; that
" the laws for relieving their diſtreſſes and
" reſtraining their vices, have not anſwer-
                                    " ed;

" ed ; and that they are at prefent very
" ill provided for and much worfe go-
" verned, are truths which every one will
" acknowledge. Every perfon who hath
" property, muft feel the weight of the
" tax that is levied for the poor ; and e-
" very perfon of underftanding, muft fee
" how abfurdly it is applied. So ufelefs
" indeed is this heavy tax and fo wretched
" its difpofition, that it is a queftion,
" whether the poor or rich are actually
" more diffatisfied ; fince the plunder of
" the one ferves fo little to the real advan-
" tage of the other ; for while a million
" yearly is raifed among the rich, many
" of the poor are ftarved ; many more
" languifh in want and mifery ; of the
" reft, numbers are found begging or pil-
" fering in the ftreets to-day, and to-
" morrow are locked up in gaols and
" Bridewells. If we were to make a pro-
" grefs through the outfkirts of the me-
" tropolis and look into the habitations of
" the poor, we fhould there behold fuch
" pictures of human mifery, as muft
" move the compaffion of every heart
" that deferves the name of human.
" What indeed muft be his compofition,
                                    " who

" who could fee whole families in want of
" every neceffary of life, oppreffed with
" hunger, cold, nakednefs, and filth ; and
" with difeafes, the certain confequence
" of all thefe ! The fufferings indeed of
" the poor are lefs known than their mif-
" deeds ; and therefore we are lefs apt to
" pity them. They ftarve, and freeze,
" and rot, among themfelves ; but they
" beg, and fteal, and rob, among their
" betters. There is not a parifh in the li-
" berty of Weftminfter, which doth not
" raife thoufands annually for the poor ;
" and there is not a ftreet in that liberty,
" which doth not fwarm all day with beg-
" gars, and all night with thieves."

There is not a fingle beggar to be feen
in Penfylvania. Luxury and idlenefs have
got no footing in that happy country ;
and thofe who fuffer by misfortune, have
maintenance out of the public treafury.
But luxury and idlenefs cannot for ever
be excluded ; and when they prevail, this
regulation will be as pernicious in Penfylvania, as the poor-rates are in Britain.

Of the many propofals that have been
publifhed for reforming the poor-laws, not
one has pierced to the root of the evil.

2

None

None of the authors entertain the flighteft
doubt of a legal provifion being neceffary,
tho' all our diftreffes arife evidently from
that very caufe. Travellers complain, of
being infefted with an endlefs number of
beggars in every Englifh town; a very
different fcene from what they meet with
in Holland or Switzerland. How would
it furprife them to be told, that this proceeds from an overflow of charity in the
good people of England!

Few inftitutions are more ticklifh than
thofe of charity. In London, common
proftitutes are treated with fingular humanity : a hofpital for them when pregnant,
difburdens them of their load, and nurfes
them till they be again fit for bufinefs :
another hofpital cures them of the venereal
difeafe : and a third receives them with o-
pen arms, when, inftead of defire, they
become objects of averfion. Would not
one imagine, that thefe hofpitals have been
erected for encouraging proftitution? They
undoubtedly have that effect, tho' far from
being intended. Mr Stirling, fuperintend-
ant of the Edinburgh poor-houfe, deferves
a ftatue for a fcheme he contrived to reform common proftitutes. A number of

them were confined in a houfe of correction, on a daily allowance of three pence;
and even part of that fmall pittance was
embezzled by the fervants of the houfe.
Pinching hunger did not reform their
manners; for being abfolutely idle, they
encouraged each other in vice, waiting
impatiently for the hour of deliverance.
Mr Stirling, with confent of the magiftrates, removed them to a clean houfe;
and inftead of money, which is apt to be
fquandered, appointed for each a pound of
oat-meal daily, with falt, water, and fire
for cooking. Relieved now from diftrefs,
they longed for comfort: what would they
not give for milk or ale? Work, fays he,
will procure you plenty. To fome who
offered to fpin, he gave flax and wheels,
engaging to pay them half the price of
their yarn, retaining the other half for the
materials furnifhed. The fpinners earned
about nine pence weekly, a comfortable
addition to what they had before. The
reft undertook to fpin, one after another;
and before the end of the firft quarter,
they were all of them intent upon work.
It was a branch of his plan, to fet free
fuch as merited that favour; and fome of
them

them appeared fo thoroughly reformed, as to be in no danger of a relapfe.

The ingenious author of *The Police of France*, who wrote in the year 1753, ob-ferves, that notwithftanding the plentiful provifion for the poor in that kingdom, mentioned above, there was a general complaint of the increafe of beggars and vagrants ; and adds, that the French po-litical writers, diffatisfied with their own plan, had prefented feveral memorials to the miniftry, propofing to adopt the Eng-lifh parochial affeffments, as greatly pre-ferable. This is a curious fact ; for at that very time, people in London, no lefs diffatisfied with thefe affeffments, were writing pamphlets in praife of the French hofpitals. One thing is certain, that no plan hitherto invented, has given fatisfac-tion. Whether an unexceptionable plan is at all poffible, feems extremely doubt-ful.

In every plan for the poor that I have feen, workhoufes make one article ; to provide work for thofe who are willing, and to make thofe work who are unwilling. With refpect to the former, men need ne-ver be idle in England for want of em-

L 2   ployment;

ployment; and they always fucceed the
beft at the employment they chufe for
themfelves. With refpeć to the latter,
punifhment will not compel a man to labour: he may affume the appearance, but
will make no progrefs ; and the pretext of
ficknefs or weaknefs is ever at hand for an
excufe. The only compulfion to make a
man work ferioufly, is fear of want.

A hofpital for the fick, for the wounded, and for the maimed, is a right eftablifhment ; being produćive of good,
without doing any harm. Such a hofpital fhould depend partly on voluntary charity ; to procure which, a convićion of
its being well managed, is neceffary. Hofpitals that have a fufficient fund of their
own, and that have no dependence on the
good will of others, are commonly ill managed.

Lies there any objećion againft a workhoufe, for training to labour, deftitute orphans, and begging children ? It is an article in Mr Hay's plan, that the workhoufe
fhould relieve poor families of all their
children above three. This has an enticing appearance, but is unfound at bottom. Children require the tendernefs of

a

a mother, during the period of infantine difeafes; and are far from being fafe in the hands of mercenaries, who ftudy nothing but their own eafe and intereft. Would it not be better, to diftribute fmall fums from time to time among poor families overburdened with children, fo as to relieve them from famine, not from labour? And with refpect to orphans and begging children, I incline to think, that it would be a more falutary meafure, to encourage mechanicks, manufacturers, and farmers above all, to educate fuch children. A premium for each, the half in hand, and the other half when they can work for themfelves, would be a proper encouragement. The beft-regulated orphan-hofpital I am acquainted with, is that of Edinburgh. Orphans are taken in from every corner, provided only they be not under the age of feven, nor above that of twelve: under feven, they are too tender for a hofpital; above twelve their relations can find employment for them. Befide the being taught to read and write, they are carefully inftructed in fome art, that may afford them comfortable fubfiftence.

No

No man ever called in queftion the utility of the marine fociety; which will re-
flect honour on the members as long as we
have a navy to protect us: they deferve a
rank above that of gartered knights. That
inftitution is the moft judicious exertion of
charity and patriotifm, that ever exifted in
any country.

A fort of hofpital for fervants who for
twenty years have faithfully adhered to
the fame mafter, would be much to my
tafte; with a few adjoining acres for a kit-
chen-garden. The fund for purchafing,
building, and maintenance, muft be raifed by contribution; and none but the
contributors fhould be entitled to offer fervants to the houfe. By fuch encouragement, a malady would be remedied, that
of wandering from mafter to mafter for
better wages, or eafier fervice; which feldom fail to corrupt fervants. They ought
to be comfortably provided for, adding to
the allowance of the houfe what pot-herbs
are raifed by their own labour. A number of virtuous men thus affociated, would
end their days in comfort; and the profpect of attaining a fettlement fo agreeable,
would form excellent fervants. How advantageous

vantageous would fuch a hofpital prove to
hufbandry in particular! But I confine
this hofpital to fervants who are fingle.
Men who have a family will be better
provided feparately.

Of all the mifchiefs that have been en-
gendered by over-anxiety about the poor,
none have proved more fatal than a founds
ling-hofpital. They tend to cool affection
for children, ftill more effectually than the
Englifh parifh-charity. At every occa-
fional pinch for food, away goes a child
to the hofpital; and parental affection a-
mong the lower fort turns fo languid, that
many who are in no pinch, relieve themfelves of trouble by the fame means. It is
affirmed, that of the children born annually in Paris, about a third part are
fent to the foundling-hofpital. The Paris
almanack for the year 1768, mentions,
that there were baptifed 18,576 infants, of
whom the foundling-hofpital received
6025. The fame almanack for the year
1773 bears, that of 18513 children born
and baptifed, 5989 were fent to the foundling-hofpital. The proportion originally
was much lefs; but vice advances with a
fwift pace. How enormous muft be the
degeneracy

degeneracy of the Parisian populace, and
their want of parental affection!

Let us next turn to infants shut up in
this hospital. Of all animals, infants of
the human race are the weakest : they require a mother's affection to guard them
against numberless diseases and accidents ;
a wise appointment of Providence to connect parents and children in the strictest
union. In a foundling-hospital, there is
no fond mother to watch over her tender
babe ; and the hireling nurse has no fond-
ness but for her own little profit. Need
we any other cause for the destruction of
infants in a foundling - hospital, much
greater in proportion than of those under
the care of a mother? And yet there is another cause equally potent, which is corrupted air. What Mr Hanway observes
upon parish-workhouses, is equally applicable to a foundling-hospital. " To at-
" tempt," says he, " to nourish an infant
" in a workhouse, where a number of
" nurses are congregated into one room,
" and consequently the air become putrid,
" I will pronounce, from intimate know-
" ledge of the subject, to be but a small
" remove from slaughter ; *for the child*

I   " *must*

" *muſt die.*" It is computed, that of the
children in the London foundling-hoſpital,
the half do not live a year. It appears by
an account given in to parliament, that the
money beſtow'd on that hoſpital from its
commencement till December 1757 a-
mounted to L.166,000; and yet during that
period, 105 perſons only were put out to
do for themſelves. Down then with
foundling-hoſpitals, more noxious than
peſtilence or famine. An infant expoſed
at the door of a dwelling-houſe, muſt be
taken up : but in that caſe, which ſeldom
happens, the infant has a better chance
for life with a hired nurſe than in a hoſpital ; and a chance perhaps little worſe,
bad as it is, than with an unnatural mother. I approve not indeed of a quarterly
payment to ſuch a nurſe : would it not do
better to furniſh her bare maintenance for
three years ; and if the child be alive at
the end of that time, to give her a hand-
ſome addition ?

A houſe of correction is neceſſary for
good order ; but belongs not to the preſent eſſay, which concerns maintenance of
the poor, not puniſhment of vagrants. I
ſhall only by the way borrow a thought

from Fielding, that fafting is the proper
punifhment of profligacy, not any punifhment that is attended with fhame. Punifhment, he obferves, that deprives a man
of all fenfe of honour, never will contribute to make him virtuous.

Charity-fchools may have been proper,
when few could read, and fewer write;
but thefe arts are now fo common, that
in moft families children may be taught
to read at home, and to write in a private
fchool at little expence. Charity-fchools
at prefent are more hurtful than beneficial: young perfons who continue there
fo long as to read and write fluently, become too delicate for hard labour, and too
proud for ordinary labour. Knowledge
is a dangerous acquifition to the labouring poor: the more of it that is poffeffed
by a fhepherd, a ploughman, or any
drudge, the lefs fatisfaction he will have
in labour. The only plaufible argument
for a charity-fchool, is, " That children
" of the labouring poor are taught there
" the principles of religion and of mora-
" lity, which they cannot acquire at
" home." The argument would be invincible, if without regular education we
            could

could have no knowledge of thefe principles. But Providence has not left man in
a ftate fo imperfect: religion and morality are ftamped on his heart; and none
can be ignorant of them, who attend to
their own perceptions. Education is indeed of ufe to ripen fuch perceptions; and
it is of fingular ufe to thofe who have time
for reading and thinking: but education
in a charity-fchool is fo flight, as to render it doubtful, whether it be not more
hurtful by foftering lazinefs, than advantageous by conveying inftruction. The
natural impreffions of religion and morality, if not obfcured by vitious habits, are
fufficient for good conduct: preferve a
man from vice by conftant labour, and
he will not be deficient in his duty either
to God or to man. Hefiod, an ancient
and refpectable poet, fays, that God hath
placed labour as a guard to virtue. More
integrity accordingly will be found among
a number of induftrious poor, taken at
random, than among the fame number in
any other clafs.

I heartily approve every regulation that
tends to prevent idlenefs. Chief Juftice
Hale fays, " That prevention of poverty

" and

" and idlenefs would do more good than
" all the gibbets, whipping-pofts, and
" gaols in the kingdom." In that view,
gaming-houfes ought to be heavily taxed,
as well as horfe-racing, cock-fighting, and
all meetings that encourage idlenefs. The
admitting low people to vote for members
of parliament, is a fource of idlenefs, corruption, and poverty. The fame privilege
is ruinous to every fmall parliament-bo-
rough. Nor have I any difficulty to pronounce, that the admitting the populace
to vote in the election of a parifh-minifter,
a frequent practice in Scotland, is productive of the fame pernicious effects.

What then is to be the refult of the
foregoing enquiry? Is it from defect of
invention that a good legal eftablifhment
for the poor is not yet difcovered? or is it
impracticable to make any legal eftablifhment that is not fraught with corruption?
I incline to the latter, for the following
reafon, no lefs obvious than folid, That
in a legal eftablifhment for the poor, no
diftinction can be made between virtue
and vice; and confequently that every
fuch eftablifhment muft be a premium for
idlenefs. And where is the neceffity, after

ter all, of any public eftablifhment? By
what unhappy prejudice have people been
led to think, that the Author of our nature, fo beneficent to his favourite man in
every other refpect, has abandoned the indigent to famine and death, if municipal
law interpofe not? We need but infpect
the human heart to be convinced, that
perfons in diftrefs are his peculiar care.
Not only has he made it our duty to afford them relief, but has fuperadded the
paffion of pity to enforce the performance
of that duty. This branch of our nature
fulfils in perfection all the falutary purpofes of charity, without admitting any
one of the evils that a legal provifion is
fraught with. The contrivance, at the
fame time, is extremely fimple: it leaves
to every man the objects as well as meafure of his charity. No man efteems it a
duty to relieve wretches reduced to poverty by idlenefs and profligacy: they
move not our pity; nor do they expect
any good from us. Wifely therefore is it
ordered by Providence, that charity fhould
in every refpect be voluntary, to prevent
the idle and profligate from depending on
it for fupport.

This

This plan is in many refpects excellent. The exercife of charity, when free from compulfion, is highly pleafant. There is indeed little pleafure where charity is rendered unneceffary by municipal law; but were that law láid afide, the gratification of pity would become one of our fweeteft enjoyments. Charity, like other affections, is envigorated by exercife, and no lefs enfeebled by difufe. Providence withal hath fcattered benevolence among the fons of men with a liberal hand : and notwithftanding the obftruction of municipal law, feldom is there found one fo obdurate, as to refift the impulfe of compaffion, when a proper object is prefented. In a well regulated government, promoting induftry and virtue, the perfons who need charity are not many; and fuch perfons may with affurance depend on the charity of their neighbours *.

It may at the fame time be boldly affirmed, that thofe who need charity, would be more comfortably provided for by the

* The Italians are not more remarkable for a charitable difpofition, than their neighbours. No fewer however than feventy thoufand mendicant friars live there upon voluntary charity ; and I have not heard that any one of them ever died of want.

plan

plan of Providence, than by any legal e-
ftablifhment. Creatures loathfome by difeafe or naftinefs, affect the air in a poor-
houfe; and have little chance for life,
without more care and kindlinefs than can
be expected from fervants, rendered cal-
lous by continual fcenes of mifery. Confider, on the other hand, the confequences
of voluntary charity, equally agreeable to
the giver and receiver. The kindly connection it forms between them, grows
ftronger and ftronger by reiteration; and
fquallid poverty, far from being an obftruction, excites a degree of pity, proportioned to the diftrefs. It may happen for
a wonder, that an indigent perfon is overlooked; but for one who will fuffer by
fuch neglect, multitudes fuffer by compelled charity.

But what I infift on with peculiar fatif-
faction is, that natural charity is an illuftrious fupport to virtue. Indigent virtue
can never fail of relief, becaufe it never
fails to enflame compaffion. Indigent vice,
on the contrary, raifes indignation more
than pity (*a*); and therefore can have little
profpect of relief. What a glorious en-

(*a*) Elements of Criticifm, ch. 2. part 7.

citement

citement to induſtry and virtue, and how
diſcouraging to idleneſs and vice! Will
it be thought chimerical to obſerve further, that to leave the indigent on Providence, will tend to improve manners as
well as virtue among the lower claſſes?
No 'man can think himſelf ſecure againſt
being reduced to depend on his neighbours
for bread. The influence of that thought,
will make every one ſolicitous to acquire
the good will of others. Lamentable it is,
that ſo beautiful a ſtructure ſhould be ra-
zed to the foundation by municipal law,
which, in providing for the poor, makes
no diſtinction between virtue and vice.
The execution of the poor-laws would be
impracticable, were ſuch a diſtinction attempted by enquiring into the conduct
and character of every *pauper*. Where are
judges to be found who will patiently follow out ſuch a dark and intricate expiſca-
tion? To accompliſh the taſk, a man
muſt abandon every other concern.

In the firſt Engliſh ſtatutes mentioned
above, the legiſlature appear carefully to
have avoided compulſory charity: every
meaſure for promoting voluntary charity
was firſt try'd, before the fatal blow was

ſtruck,

ftruck, empowering parifh-officers to im-
pofe a tax for the poor. The legiflature
certainly did not forefee the baneful confequences : but how came they not to fee
that they were diftrufting Providence, declaring in effect, that the plan eftablifhed
by our Maker for the poor, is infufficient?
Many are the municipal laws that enforce
the laws of nature, by additional rewards
and punifhments ; but it was fingularly
bold to abolifh the natural law of charity,
by eftablifhing a legal tax in its ftead.
Men will always be mending : what a confufed jumble do they make, when they attempt to mend the laws of Nature ! Leave
Nature to her own operations : fhe under-
ftands them the beft.

Few regulations are more plaufible than
what are political ; and yet few are more
deceitful. A writer, blind with partiality
for his country, makes the following obfervations upon the 43° Elifab. eftablifhing a maintenance for the poor. " Laws
" have been enacted in many other coun-
" tries, which have punifhed the idle beg-
" gar, and exhorted the rich to extend
" their charity to the poor : but it is pe-
" culiar to the humanity of England, to

Vol. III.   N   " have

" have made their support a matter of
" obligation and neceffity on the more
" wealthy. The Englifh feem to be the
" firft nation in Europe in fcience, arts,
" and arms: they likewife are poffeffed
" of the freeft and moft perfect of confti-
" tutions, and the bleffings confequential
" to that freedom. If virtues in an indi-
" vidual are fometimes fuppofed to be re-
" warded in this world, I do not think it
" too prefumptuous to fuppofe, that na-
" tional virtues may likewife meet with
" their reward. England hath, to its pe-
" culiar honour, not only made their poor
" free, but hath provided a certain and
" folid eftablifhment to prevent their ne-
" ceffities and indigence, when they a-
" rife from what the law calls *the act of*
" *God:* and are not thefe beneficent and
" humane attentions to the miferies of our
" fellow-creatures, the firft of thofe poor
" pleas which we are capable of offering,
" in behalf of our imperfections, to an all-
" wife and merciful Creator!" To this
writer I oppofe another, whofe reflections
are more found. " In England, there is
" an act of the legiflature, obliging every
" parifh to maintain its own poor. Scarce
             " any

" any man living, who has not feen the
" effects of this law, but muft approve of
" it ; and yet fuch are its effects, that the
" ftreets of London are filled with objects
" of mifery beyond what is feen in any
" other city. The labouring poor, de-
" pending on this law to be provided in
" ficknefs and old age, are little folicitous
" to fave, and become habitually profufe.
" The principle of charity is eftablifhed
" by Providence in the human heart, for
" relieving thofe who are difabled to work
" for themfelves. And if the labouring
" poor had no dependence but on the
" principle of charity, they would be
" more religious ; and if they were influ-
" enced by religion, they would be lefs a-
" bandoned in their behaviour. Thus
" this feeming-good act turns to a na-
" tional evil : there is more diftrefs a-
" mong the poor in London than any
" where in Europe ; and more drunken-
" nefs both in males and females (*a*)."

I am aware, that during the reign of E-
lifabeth, fome compulfion might be neceffary to preferve the poor from ftarving.

(*a*) Author of Angeloni's letters.

N 2   Her

Her father Henry had fequeftered all the hofpitals, a hundred and ten in number, and fquandered their revenues; he had alfo demolifhed all the abbeys. By thefe means, the poor were reduced to a miferable condition; efpecially as private charity, for want of exercife, was at a low ebb. That critical juncture required indeed help from the legiflature: and a temporary provifion for the poor would have been a proper meafure; fo contrived as not to fuperfede voluntary charity, but rather to promote it. Unlucky it is for England, that fuch a meafure was overlooked; but Queen Elifabeth and her parliaments had not the talent of forefeeing confequences without the aid of experience. A perpetual tax for the poor was impofed, the moft pernicious tax that ever was impofed in any country.

With refpect to the prefent times, the reafon now given pleads againft abolifhing at once a legal provifion for the poor. It may be taken for granted, that charity is in England not more vigorous at prefent, than it was in the days of Elifabeth. Would our miniftry but lead the way, by fhowing fome zeal for a reformation, expedients

pedients would probably be invented for
fupporting the poor, without unhinging
voluntary charity. The following expedient is propofed, merely as a fpecimen.
Let a tax be impofed by parliament on e-
very parifh for their poor, variable in proportion to the number; but not to exceed
the half of what is neceffary: directing
the landholders to make up quarterly, a
lift of the names and condition of fuch
perfons as in their opinion deferve charity;
with an eftimate of what each ought to
have weekly. The public tax makes the
half, and the other half is to be raifed by
voluntary contribution. To prevent col-
lufion, the roll of the poor, and their
weekly appointment, with a fubfcription
of gentlemen for their part of the fum,
fhall be examined by the juftices of peace
at a quarterly meeting; who, on receiving
fatisfaction, muft order the fum arifing
from the public tax to be diftributed a-
mong the poor contained in the roll, according to the eftimate of the landholders.
As the public fund lies dead till the fubfcription be completed, it is not to be imagined that any gentleman will ftand out
it would be a public imputation on his
                                    character.

character. Far from apprehending any
deficiency, confident I am, that every
gentleman would confider it as honourable to contribute largely. This agreeable
work muft be blended with fome degree
of feverity, that of excluding from the roll
every profligate, male or female. If that
rule be ftrictly followed out, the innocent
poor will diminifh daily ; fo as in time to
be fafely left upon voluntary charity, without neceffity of any tax.

But muft miferable wretches reduced to
poverty by idlenefs or intemperance, be,
in a Chriftian country, abandoned to difeafes and famine. This is the argument, fhallow as it is, that has corrupted the induftry of England, and reduced multitudes to
difeafes and famine. Thofe who are able to
work, may be locked up in a houfe of correction, to be fed with bread and water ;
but with liberty of working for themfelves.
And as for the remainder, their cafe is not
defperate, when they have accefs to fuch
tender-hearted perfons as are more eminent for pity than for principle. If by neglect or overfight any happen to die of
want, the example will tend more to reformation,

formation, than the moſt pathetic diſcourſe from the pulpit.

Even at the hazard of loſing a few lives
by neglect or overſight, common begging
ought abſolutely to be prohibited. The
moſt profligate, are the moſt impudent
and the moſt expert at feigning diſtreſs. If
begging be indulged to any, all will ruſh
into the public: idlers are fond of that
wandering and indolent ſort of life; and
there is no temptation to idleneſs more
ſucceſsful, than liberty to beg. In order to
be relieved from common beggars, it has
been propoſed, to fine thoſe who give them
alms. Little penetration muſt they have,
to whom the inſufficiency of ſuch a remedy is not palpable. It is eaſy to give
alms without being ſeen; and compaſſion
will extort alms, even at the hazard of
ſuffering for it; not to mention, that every
one in ſuch a caſe would avoid the odious
character of an informer. The following
remedy is ſuggeſted, as what probably may
anſwer. An officer muſt be appointed in
every pariſh, with a competent ſalary, for
apprehending and carrying to the work-
houſe every ſtrolling beggar; under the
penalty of loſing his office, with what ſalary

lary is due to him, if any beggar be found ftrolling four and twenty hours after the fact comes to his knowledge. In the workhoufe fuch beggars fhall be fed with bread and water for a year, but with liberty of working for themfelves.

I declare refolutely againft a perpetual tax for the poor. But if there muft be fuch a tax, I know of none lefs fubverfive of induftry and morals than that eftablifhed in Scotland, obliging the landholders in every parifh to meet at ftated times, in order to provide a fund for the poor; but leaving the objects of their charity, and the meafure, to their own humanity and difcretion. In this plan, there is no encroachment on the natural duty of charity, but only that the minority muft fubmit to the opinion of the majority.

In large towns, where the character and circumftances of the poor are not fo well known as in country-parifhes, the following variation is propofed. Inftead of landholders, who are proper in country-parifhes; let there be in each town-parifh a ftanding committee chofen by the proprietors of houfes, the third part to be changed annually. This committee with the

I   minifter,

minifter, make up a lift of fuch as deferve charity, adding an eftimate of what, with their own labour, may be fufficient for each of them. The minifter, with one or two of the committee, carry about this lift to every family that can afford charity, fuggefting what may be proper for each to contribute. This lift, with an addition of the fum contributed or promifed by each houfeholder, muft be affixed on the principal door of the parifh-church, to honour the contributors, and to inform the poor of the provifion made for them. Some fuch mode may probably be effectual, without tranfgreffing the bounds of voluntary charity. But if any one obftinately refufe to contribute after feveral applications, the committee at their difcretion may tax him. If it be the poffeffor who declines contributing, the tax muft be laid upon him, referving relief againft his landlord.

In great towns, the poor, who ought to be prohibited from begging, are lefs known than in country-parifhes : and among a croud of inhabitants, it is eafier for an individual to efcape the public eye when he with-holds charity, than in country-pa-

rifhes. Both defects would be remedied
by the plan above propofed : it will bring
to light, in great cities, the poor who deferve charity ; and it will bring to light e-
very perfon who with-holds charity.

In every regulation for the poor, Englifh
and Scotch, it is taken for granted, that
the poor are to be maintained in their own
houfes. Parochial poor-houfes are creep-
ing into fafhion : a few are already erected both in England and Scotland ; and
there is depending in parliament a plan for
eftablifhing poor-houfes in every part of
England. Yet whether they ought to be
preferred to the accuftomed mode, deferves
ferious confideration. The erection and
management of a poor-houfe are expenfive
articles ; and if they do not upon the
whole appear clearly beneficial, it is better
to ftop fhort in time.

Economy is the great motive that inclines people to this new mode of providing for the poor. It is imagined, that
numbers collected at a common table, can
be maintained at lefs expence than in feparate houfes ; and foot-foldiers are given
for an example, who could not live on
their pay if they did not mefs together.
But

But the cafes are not parallel. Soldiers, having the management of their pay, can club for a bit of meat. But as the inhabitants of a poor-houfe are maintained by the public, the fame quantity of provifions muft be allotted to each ; as there can be no good rule for feparating thofe who eat much from thofe who eat little. The confequence is what may be expected : the bulk of them referve part of their victuals for purchafing ale or fpirits. It is vain to expect work from them : poor wretches void of fhame will never work ferioufly, where the profit accrues to the public, not to themfelves. Hunger is the only effectual means for compelling fuch perfons to work.

Where the poor are fupported in their own houfes, the firft thing that is done, or ought to be done, is to eftimate what each can earn by their own labour ; and as far only as that falls fhort of maintenance, is there place for charity. They will be as induftrious as poffible, becaufe they work for themfelves ; and a weekly fum of charity under their own management, will turn to better account, than in a poor-houfe, under the direction of mer-

O 2   cenaries.

cenaries. The quantity of food for health depends greatly on cuftom. Bufbequius obferves, that the Turks eat very little flefh-meat; and that the Janizaries in particular, at that time a moft formidable infantry, were maintained at an expence far below that of a German. Wafers, cakes, boiled rice, with fmall bits of mutton or pullet, were their higheft entertainment, fermented liquors being abfolutely prohibited. The famous Montecuculi fays, that the Janizaries eat but once a-day, about fun-fet; and that cuftom makes it eafy. Negroes are maintain'd in the Weft Indies at a very fmall expence. A bit of ground is allotted to them for raifing vegetables, which they cultivate on Sunday, being employ'd all the reft of the week in labouring for their mafters. They receive a weekly allowance of dry'd fifh, about a pound and a half; and their only drink is water. Yet by vegetables and water with à morfel of dry'd fifh, thefe people are fufficiently nourifhed to perform the hardeft labour in a moft enervating climate. I would not have the poor to be pampered, which might prove a bad example to the induftrious: if they be fupported

ported in the moft frugal manner, the duty of charity is fulfilled. And in no other manner can they be fupported fo frugally, as to leave to their own difpofal what they receive in charity. Not a penny will be laid out on fermented liquors, unlefs perhaps as a medicine in ficknefs. Nor does their low fare call for pity. Ale makes no part of the maintenance of thofe in Scotland who live by the fweat of their brows. Water is their only drink; and yet they live comfortably, without ever thinking of pitying themfelves. Many gentlemen drink nothing but water; who feel no decay either in health or vigour. The perfon however who fhould propofe to banifh ale from a poor-houfe, would be exclaimed againft as hard-hearted and void of charity. The difference indeed is great between what is done voluntarily, and what is done by compulfion. It is provoking to hear of the petulance and even luxury of the Englifh poor. Not a perfon in London who lives by the parifh-charity will deign to eat brown bread; and in feveral parts of England, many who receive large fums from thar fund, are in the conftant cuftom of drinking tea

twice

twice a-day. Will one incline to labour where idlenefs and beggary are fo much encouraged ?

But what objection, it will be urged, lies againft adopting in a poor-houfe the plan mentioned, giving to no perfon in money more than what his work, juftly eftimated, falls fhort of maintenance? It is eafy to forefee, that this plan can never anfwer in a poor-houfe. The materials for work muft be provided by mercenary officers; who muft alfo be trufted with the difpofal of the made work, for behoof of the poor people. Thefe operations may go on fweetly a year or two, under the influence of novelty and zeal for improvement; but it would be chimerical to expect for ever ftrict fidelity in mercenary officers, whofe management cannot eafily be checked. Computing the expence of this operofe management, and giving allowance for endlefs frauds in purchafing and felling, I boldly affirm, that the plan would turn to no account. Confider next the weekly fum given in charity : people confined in a poor-houfe have no means for purchafing neceffaries but at a futlery, where

where they will certainly be impofed on, and their money go no length.

We are now ripe for a comparifon with refpect to economy. Many a houfeholder in Edinburgh makes a fhift to maintain a family with their gain of four fhillings *per* week, amounting to ten pounds eight fhillings yearly. Seldom are there fewer than four or five perfons in fuch a family ; the hufband, the wife, and two or three children. Thus four or five perfons can be maintain'd under eleven pounds yearly. But are they maintain'd fo cheap in the Edinburgh poor-houfe ? Not a fingle perfon there but at an average cofts the public at leaft four pounds yearly. Nor is this all. A great fum remains to be taken into the computation, the intereft of the fum for building, yearly reparations, expence of management, wages to fervants, male and female. A proportion of this great fum muft be laid upon each perfon, which fwells the expence of their maintenance. And when every particular is taken into the account, I have no hefitation to pronounce, that laying afide labour altogether, a man can make a fhift to maintain him-

felf

self privately at half of the expence that is neceſſary in a poor-houſe.

So far we have travelled on ſolid ground; and what follows is equally ſolid. Among the induſtrious, not many are reduced ſo low, but that they can make ſome ſhift for themſelves. The quantity of labour that can be performed by thoſe who require aid, cannot be brought under any accurate eſtimation. To pave the way to a conjecture, thoſe who are reduced to poverty by diſſoluteneſs or ſheer idleneſs, ought abſolutely to be rejected as unworthy of public charity. If ſuch wretches can prevail on the tender-hearted to relieve them privately, ſo far well: they ought not to be indulged with any other hope. Now laying theſe aſide, the quantity of labour may be fairly computed as half maintenance. Here then is another great article ſaved to the public. If a man can be maintained privately at half of what is neceſſary in a poor-houſe, his work, reckoning it half of his maintenance, brings down the ſum to the fourth part of what is neceſſary in a poor-houſe.

Undiſtinguiſhed charity to the deſerving and undeſerving, has multiply'd the poor;

2   and

and will multiply them more and more
without end.   Let it be publicly known
that the diffolute and idle have no chance
to be put on a charity-roll; the poor, inftead of increafing, will gradually diminifh, till none be left but proper objects of
charity, fuch as have been reduced to indigence by old age or innocent misfortune.
And if that rule be ftrictly adhered to, the
maintenance of the poor will not be a
heavy burden.   After all, a houfe for the
poor may poffibly be a frugal fcheme in
England where the parifh-rates are high,
in the town of Bedford for example.   In
Scotland, it is undoubtedly a very unfru-
gal fcheme.

Hitherto of a poor-houfe with refpect
to economy.   There is another point of
ftill greater moment; which is to confider
the influence it has on the manners of the
inhabitants.   A number of perfons, ftrangers to each other, and differing in temper
and manners, can never live comfortably
together: will ever the fober and innocent
make a tolerable fociety with the idle and
profligate? In our poor-houfes accordingly, quarrels and complaints are endlefs.
The family fociety and that of a nation un-

VOL. III.   P   der

der government, are prompted by the common nature of man; and none other. In monafteries and nunneries, envy, detraction, and heart-burning, never ceafe. Sorry I am to obferve, that in feminaries of learning concord and good-will do not always prevail, even among the profeffors. What adds greatly to the difeafe in a poorhoufe, is that the people fhut up there, being fecure of maintenance, are reduced to a ftate of abfolute idlenefs, for it is in vain to think of making them work: they have no care, nothing to keep the blood in motion. Attend to a ftate fo different from what is natural to us. Thofe who are innocent and harmlefs, will languifh, turn difpirited, and tire of life. Thofe of a buftling and reftlefs temper, will turn four and peevifh for want of occupation: they will murmur againft their fuperiors, pick quarrels with their neighbours, and fow difcord every where. The worft of all is, that a poor-houfe never fails to corrupt the morals of the inhabitants: nothing tends fo much to promote vice and immorality, as idlenefs among a number of low people collected in one place. Among no fet of people does profligacy more abound,

bound, than among the feamen in Greenwich hofpital.

A poor-houfe tends to corrupt the body no lefs than the mind. It is a nurfery of difeafes, foftered by dirtinefs and crouding.

To this fcene let us oppofe the condition of thofe who are fupported in their own houfes. They are laid under the neceffity of working with as much affiduity as ever; and as the fum given them in charity is at their own difpofal, they are careful to lay it out in the moft frugal manner. If by parfimony they can fave any fmall part, it is their own; and the hope of encreafing this little ftock, fupports their fpirits and redoubles their induftry. They live innocently and comfortably, becaufe they live induftrioufly; and induftry, as every one knows, is the chief pleafure of life to thofe who have acquired the habit of being conftantly employ'd.

P 2   S K E T C H

A Great City considered in Physical, Moral, and Political Views.

IN all ages an opinion has been prevalent, that a great city is a great evil; and that a capital may be too great for the state, as a head may be for the body. Considering however the very shallow reasons that have been given for this opinion, it should seem to be but slightly founded. There are several ordinances limiting the extent of Paris, and prohibiting new buildings beyond the prescribed bounds; the first of which is by Henry II. *ann.* 1549. These ordinances have been renewed from time to time, down to the 1672, in which year there is an edict of Louis XIV. to the same purpose. The reasons assigned are, " First, That by enlarging the city, the " air would be rendered unwholesome. " Second, That cleaning the streets would " prove a great additional labour. Third, " That adding to the number of inhabi- " tants would raise the price of provi-

" sions,

" fions, of labour, and of manufactures.
" Fourth, That ground would be covered
" with buildings inftead of corn, which
" might hazard a fcarcity. Fifth, That
" the country would be depopulated by
" the defire that people have to refort to
" the capital. And, laftly, That the dif-
" ficulty of governing fuch numbers,
" would be an encouragement to robbery
" and murder."

In thefe reafons, the limiting the extent
of the city and the limiting the number of
inhabitants are jumbled together, as if
they were the fame. The only reafons
that regard the former, are the fecond and
fourth ; and thefe, at beft, are trifling.
The firft reafon urged againft enlarging
the city, is a folid reafon for enlarging
it, fuppofing the numbers to be limited ;
for crouding is an infallible means to render the air unwholefome. Paris, with the
fame number of inhabitants that were in
the days of the fourth Henry, occupies
thrice the fpace, much to the health as
well as comfort of the inhabitants. Had
the ordinances mentioned been made effectual, the houfes in Paris muft all have
been built ftory above ftory, afcending to
the

the fky like the tower of Babel. Before
the great fire *anno* 1666, the plague was
frequent in London; but by widening the
ftreets and enlarging the houfes, there has
not fince been known in that great city,
any contagious diftemper that deferves
the name of a plague. The third, fifth,
and laft reafons, conclude againft permitting any addition to the number of inhabitants; but conclude nothing againft enlarging the town. In a word, the meafure adopted in thefe ordinances has little
or no tendency to correct the evils com-
plained of; and infallibly would enflame
the chief of them. The meafure that
ought to have been adopted, is to limit
the number of inhabitants, not the extent
of the town.

Queen Elifabeth of England, copying
the French ordinances, iffued a proclamation *anno* 1602, prohibiting any new
buildings within three miles of London.
The preamble is in the following words:
" That forefeeing the great and manifold
" inconveniencies and mifchiefs which
" daily grow, and are likely to increafe,
" in the city and fuburbs of London, by
" confluence of people to inhabit the
                                    " fame;

" fame; not only by reafon that fuch
" multitudes can hardly be governed, to
" ferve God and obey her Majefty, with-
" out conftituting an addition of new of-
" ficers, and enlarging their authority;
" but alfo can hardly be provided of food
" and other neceffaries at a reafonable
" price; and finally, that as fuch multi-
" tudes of people, many of them poor
" who muft live by begging or worfe
" means, are heaped up together, and in
" a fort fmothered with many children
" and fervants in one houfe or fmall te-
" nement; it muft needs follow, if any
" plague or other univerfal ficknefs come
" amongft them, that it would prefently
" fpread through the whole city and con-
" fines, and alfo into all parts of the realm."

There appears as little accuracy in this
proclamation, as in the French ordinances.
The fame error is obfervable in both,
which is the limiting the extent of the
city, inftead of limiting the number of
inhabitants. True it is indeed, that the
regulation would have a better effect in
London than in Paris. As ftone is in
plenty about Paris, houfes there may be
carried to a very great height; and are

actually

actually fo carried in the old town : but there being no ftone about London, the houfes formerly were built of timber, now of brick ; materials too frail for a lofty e-difice.

Proceeding to particulars, the firft ob-jection, which is the expence of governing a great multitude, concludes againft the number of inhabitants, not againft the ex-tent of the city. At the fame time, the objection is at beft doubtful in point of fact. Tho' vices abound in a great city, requiring the ftricteft attention of the ma-giftrate ; yet with a well-regulated police, it appears lefs expenfive to govern 600,000 in one city, than the fame number in ten different cities. The fecond objection, viz. the high price of provifions, ftrikes only againft numbers, not extent. Befide, whatever might have been the cafe in the days of Elifabeth, when agriculture and internal commerce were in their infancy ; there are at prefent not many towns in England, where a temperate man may live cheaper than in London. The hazard of contagious diftempers, which is the third objection, is an invincible argument againft limiting the extent of a great town.

I   It

It is mentioned above, that from the year 1666, when the ftreets were widened and the houfes enlarged, London has never been once vifited by the plague. If the proclamation had taken effect, the houfes muft have been fo crouded upon each o-ther, and the ftreets fo contracted, as to have occafioned plagues ftill more fre-quently than before the year 1666.

The Queen's immediate fucceffors were not more clear-fighted than fhe had been. In the year 1624, King James iffued a pro-clamation againft building in London up-on new foundations. Charles I. iffued two proclamations to the fame purpofe; one in the year 1625, and one in the year 1630.

The progrefs of political knowledge has unfolded many bad effects of a great city, more weighty than any urged in thefe proclamations. The firft I fhall mention, is, that people born and bred in a great city are commonly weak and effe-minate. Vegetius (*a*) obferving, that men bred to hufbandry make the beft foldiers, adds what follows. " Interdum tamen

(*a*) De re militari, lib. 1: cap. 3.

" neceſſitas exigit, etiam urbanos ad ar-
" ma compelli : qui ubi nomen dedere
" militiæ, primum laborare, decurrere,
" portare pondus, et ſolem pulveremque
" ferre, condiſcant ; parco victu utantur
" et ruſtico ; interdum ſub divo, inter-
" dum ſub papilionibus, commorentur.
" Tunc demum ad uſum erudiantur ar-
" morum : et ſi longior expeditio emergit,
" in angariis plurimum detinendi ſunt,
" proculque habendi a civitatis illecebris :
" ut eo modo, et corporibus eorum robur
" accedat, et animis *." The luxury of
a great city deſcends from the higheſt to

* " But ſometimes there is a neceſſity for arming
" the townſpeople, and calling them out to ſervice.
" When this is the caſe, it ought to be the firſt
" ca.e, to enure them to labour, to march them
" up and down the country, to make them carry
" heavy burdens, and to harden them againſt the
" weather. Their food ſhould be coarſe and ſcanty,
" and they ſhould be habituated to ſleep alternately
" in their tents, and in the open air. Then is the
" time to inſtruct them in the exerciſe of their arms.
" If the expedition is a diſtant one, they ſhould be
" ch.fly employ'd in the ſtations of poſts or ex-
" preſſes, and removed as much as poſſible from
" the dangerous allurements that abound in large
" cities ; that thus they may be envigorated both
" in mind and body."

the

the loweft, infecting all ranks of men; and there is little opportunity in it for fuch exercife as to render the body vigorous and robuft.

The foregoing is a phyfical objection againft a great city: the next regards morality. Virtue is exerted chiefly in reftraint: vice, in giving freedom to defire. Moderation and felf-command form a character the moft fufceptible of virtue: fuperfluity of animal fpirits, and love of pleafure, form a character the moft liable to vice. Low vices, pilfering for example, or lying, draw few or no imitators; but vices that indicate a foul above reftraint, produce many admirers. Where a man boldly ftruggles againft unlawful reftraint, he is juftly applauded and imitated; and the vulgar are not apt to diftinguifh nicely between lawful and unlawful reftraint: the boldnefs is vifible, and they pierce no deeper. It is the unruly boy, full of animal fpirits, who at public fchool is admired and imitated; not the virtuous and modeft. Vices accordingly that fhow fpirit, are extremely infectious; virtue very little. Hence the corruption of a great city, which increafes more and more in

proportion

proportion to the number of inhabitants.
But it is fufficient here barely to mention
that objection, becaufe it has been formerly infifted on.

The following bad effects are more of
a political nature. A great town is a profeffed enemy to the free circulation of money. The current coin is accumulated in
the capital : and diftant provinces muft
fink into idlenefs ; for without ready money neither arts nor manufactures can
flourifh. Thus we find lefs and lefs activity, in proportion commonly to the diftance from the capital ; and an abfolute
torpor in the extremities. The city of
Milan affords a good proof of this obfervation. The money that the Emperor of
Germany draws from it in taxes is carried
to Vienna ; not a farthing left but what is
barely fufficient to defray the expence of
government. Manufactures and commerce
have gradually declined in proportion to
the fcarcity of money ; and that city
which the laft century contained 300,000
inhabitants, cannot now mufter above
90,000 *. It may be obferved befide, that

as

* Is not the following inference from thefe pre-
miffes

as horſes in a great city muſt be provided
with provender from a diſtance, the country is robbed of its dung, which goes to
the rich fields round the city. But as manure laid upon poor land, is of more advantage to the farmer, than upon what is
already highly improved, the depriving
diſtant parts of manure is a loſs to the nation in general. Nor is this all : The
dung of an extenſive city, the bulk of it
at leaſt, is ſo remote from the fields to
which it muſt be carried, that the expence
of carriage ſwallows up the profit.

Another bad effect of accumulating money in the capital is, that it raiſes the price
of labour. The temptation of high wages
in the capital, robs the country of its beſt

miſſes well founded, that it would be a ruinous
meaſure to add Bengal to the Britiſh dominions ?
In what manner would the territorial revenues and
other taxes be remitted to London ? If in hard
coin, that country would in time be drained of
money, its manufactures would be annihilated, and
depopulation enſue. If remitted in commodities,
the public would be cheated, and little be added to
the revenue. A land-tax laid on as in Britain would
be preferable in every reſpect ; for It would be paid
by the Eaſt-India company as proprietors of Bengal
without deduction of a farthing.

hands.

hands. And as they who refort to the capital are commonly young people, who
remove as foon as they are fit for work,
diftant provinces are burdened with their
maintenance, without reaping any benefit
by their labour.

But of all, the moft deplorable effect of
a great city, is the preventing of population, by fhortening the lives of its inhabitants. Does a capital fwell in proportion
to the numbers that are drained from the
country ? Far from it. The air of a populous city is infected by multitudes
crouded together; and people there feldom make out the ufual time of life.
With refpect to London in particular, the
fact cannot be diffembled. The burials
in that immenfe city greatly exceed the
births : the difference fome affirm to be no
lefs than ten thoufand yearly : by the moft
moderate computation, not under feven or
eight thoufand. As London is far from
being on the decline, that number muft be
fupplied by the country; and the annual
fupply amounts probably to a greater number, than were needed annually for recruiting our armies and navies in the late
war with France. If fo, London is a

greater

greater enemy to population, than a bloody war would be, suppofing it even to be perpetual. What an enormous tax is Britain thus fubjected to for supporting her capital! The rearing and educating yearly for London 7 or 8000 perfons, re-quire an immenfe fum.

In Paris, if the bills of mortality can be relied on, the births and burials are near-ly equal, being each of them about 19,000 yearly; and according to that computa-tion, Paris fhould need no recruits from the country. But in that city, the bills of mortality cannot be depended on for bu-rials. It is there univerfally the practice of high and low, to have their infants nurfed in the country, till they be three years of age; and confequently thofe who die before that age, are not inlifted. What proportion thefe bear to the whole is un-certain. But a guefs may be made from fuch as die in London before the age of three, which are computed to be one half of the whole that die (*a*). Now gi-ving the utmoft allowance for the healthi-nefs of the country above that of a town, children from Paris that die in the country

(*a*) See Dr Price, p. 362.

before

before the age of three, cannot be brought so low as a third of thofe who die. On the other hand, the London bills of mortality are lefs to be depended on for births than for burials. None are inlifted but infants baptized by clergymen of the Englifh church ; and the numerous children of Papifts, Diffenters, and other fectaries, are left out of the account. Upon the whole, the difference between the births and burials in Paris and in London, is much lefs than it appears to be on comparing the bills of mortality of thefe two cities.

At the fame time, giving full allowance for children who are not brought into the London bills of mortality, there is the higheft probability that a greater number of children are born in Paris than in London ; and confequently, that the former requires fewer recruits from the country, than the latter. In Paris, domeftic fervants are encouraged to marry : they are obferved to be more fettled than when bachelors, and more attentive to their duty. In London, fuch marriages are difcouraged, as rendering a fervant more attentive to his own family than to that of his mafter. But a fervant attentive to his own

2   family,

family, will not, for his own fake, neglect
that of his mafter. At any rate, is he
not more to be depended on, than a fervant who continues fingle? What can
be expected of idle and pampered bachelors, but debauchery and every fort of
corruption ? Nothing reftrains them from
abfolute profligacy, but the eye of the mafter ; who for that reafon is their averfion
not their love. If the poor-laws be named
the folio of corruption, bachelor-fervants
in London may well be confidered as a
large appendix. And this attracts the eye
to the poor-laws, which indeed make the
chief difference between Paris and London, with refpect to the prefent point. In
Paris, certain funds are eftablifhed for the
poor, the yearly produce of which admits
but a limited number. As that fund is
always pre-occupied, the low people who
are not on the lift, have little or no profpect of bread, but from their own induftry ; and to the induftrious, marriage
is in a great meafure neceffary. In London, a parifh is taxed in proportion to the
number of its poor; and every perfon who
is pleafed to be idle, is entitled to maintenance. Moft things thrive by encou-

ragement, and idlenefs above all. Certainty of maintenance, renders the low people in England idle and profligate ; efpecially in London, where luxury prevails, and infects every rank. So infolent are the London poor, that fcarce one of them will condefcend to eat brown bread. There are accordingly in London, a much greater number of idle and profligate wretches, than in Paris, or in any other town in proportion to the number of inhabitants. Thefe wretches, in Doctor Swift's ftyle, never think of pofterity, becaufe pofterity never thinks of them : men who hunt after pleafure, and live from day to day, have no notion of fubmitting to the burden of a family. Thefe caufes produce a greater number of children in Paris than in London ; tho' probably they differ not much in populoufnefs.

I fhall add but one other objection to a great city, which is not flight. An overgrown capital, far above a rival, has, by numbers and riches, a diftreffing influence in public affairs. The populace are ductile, and eafily mifled by ambitious and defigning magiftrates. Nor are there wanting critical times, in which fuch magiftrates,

magiftrates, acquiring artificial influence,
may have power to difturb the public
peace. That an overgrown capital may
prove dangerous to fovereignty, has more
than once been experienced both in Paris
and London.

It would give one the fpleen, to hear the
French and Englifh zealoufly difputing a-
bout the extent of their capitals, as if the
profperity of their country depended on
that circumftance. To me it appears like
one glorying in the king's-evil, or in any
contagious diftemper. Much better employ'd would they be, in contriving means
for leffening thefe cities. There is not a
political meafure, that would tend more to
aggrandize the kingdom of France, or of
Britain, than to fplit its capital into feveral great towns. My plan would be, to
confine the inhabitants of London to
100,000, compofed of the King and his
houfehold, fupreme courts of juftice, go-
vernment-boards, prime nobility and gentry, with neceffary fhopkeepers, artifts,
and other dependents. Let the reft of the
inhabitants be diftributed into nine towns
properly fituated, fome for internal commerce, fome for foreign. Such a plan

R 2   would

would diffufe life and vigour through e-
very corner of the ifland.

To execute fuch a plan, would, I acknowledge, require great penetration and
much perfeverance. I fhall fuggeft what
occurs at prefent. The firft ftep muft be,
to mark proper fpots for the nine towns,
the moft advantageous for trade, or for
manufactures. If any of thefe fpots be
occupied already with fmall towns, fo
much the better. The next ftep is a capi-
tation-tax on the inhabitants of London ;
the fum levied to be appropriated for encouraging the new towns. One encouragement would have a good effect ; which
is, a premium to every man who builds in
any of thefe towns, more or lefs, in proportion to the fize of the houfe. This tax
would banifh from London, every manufacture but of the moft lucrative kind. When
by this means, the inhabitants of London
are reduced to a number not much above
100,000, the near profpect of being relieved from the tax, will make houfeholders
active to banifh all above that number ;
and to prevent a renewal of the tax, a
greater number will never again be permitted. It would require much political
                                    fkill

skill to proportion the sums to be levied and diftributed, so as to have their proper effect, without overburdening the capital on the one hand, or giving too great encouragement for building on the other, which might tempt people to build for the premium merely, without any further view. Much will depend on an advantageous fituation : houfes built there will always find inhabitants.

The two great cities of London and Weftminfter are extremely ill fitted for local union. The latter, the feat of government and of the nobleffe, infects the former with luxury and with love of fhow. The former, the feat of commerce, infects the latter with love of gain. The mixture of thefe oppofite paffions, is productive of every groveling vice.

SKETCH

SKETCH XII.

Origin and Progrefs of American Nations.

HAving no authentic materials for a natural hiftory of all the Americans, the following obfervations are confined to a few tribes, the beft known ; and to the kingdoms of Peru and Mexico, as they were at the date of the Spanifh conqueft.

As there has not been difcovered any paffage by land to America from the old world, no problem has more embarraffed the learned, than to account for the origin of American nations : there are as many different opinions as there are writers. Many attempts have been made for difcovering a paffage by land ; but hitherto in vain. Kamfkatka, it is true, is divided from America by a narrow ftrait, full of iflands : and M. Buffon, to render the paffage ftill more eafy than by thefe iflands, conjectures, that thereabout there may formerly have been a land-paffage, fwallowed up in later times by the ocean.

There

There is indeed great appearance of truth in this conjecture; as all the quadrupeds of the north of Afia feem to have made their way to America; the bear, for example, the roe, the deer, the rain-deer, the beaver, the wolf, the fox, the hare, the rat, the mole. He admits, that in America there is not to be feen a lion, a tiger, a panther, or any other Afiatic quadruped of a hot climate: not, fays he, for want of a land-paffage; but becaufe the cold climate of Tartary, in which fuch animals cannot fubfift, is an effectual bar againft them *.

But to give fatisfaction upon this fubject, more is required than a paffage from Kamfkatka to America, whether by land or fea. An inquiry much more decifive is totally overlooked, relative to the people on the two fides of the ftrait; particularly, whether they have the fame language.

---

* Our author, with fingular candor, admits it as a ftrong objection to his theory, that there are no rain-deer in Afia. But it is doing no more but juftice to fo fair a reafoner, to obferve, that according to the lateft accounts, there are plenty of rain-deer in the country of Kamfkatka, which of all is the neareft to America.

Now

Now by late accounts from Ruffia we are informed, that there is no affinity between the Kamſkatkan tongue, and that of the Americans on the oppoſite ſide of the ſtrait. Whence we may aſſuredly conclude, that the latter are not a colony of the former.

But further. There are ſeveral cogent arguments to evince, that the Americans are not defcended from any people in the north of Aſia or in the north of Europe. Were they defcended from either, Labrador, or the adjacent countries, muſt have been firſt peopled. And as ſavages are remarkably fond of their natal ſoil, they would have continued there, till compelled by over-population to ſpread wider for food. But the fact is directly contrary. When America was difcovered by the Spaniards, Mexico and Peru were fully peopled ; and the other parts leſs and leſs, in proportion to their diſtance from theſe central countries. Fabry reports, that one may travel one or two hundred leagues north-weſt from the Miſſiſippi, without ſeeing a human face, or any veſtige of a houſe. And ſome French officers ſay, that they travelled more than a hundred leagues from the delicious country

I   watered

watered by the Ohio, through Louifiana, without meeting a fingle family of favages. The civilization of the Mexicans and Peruvians, as well as their populoufnefs, make it extremely probable that they were the firft inhabitants of America. In travelling northward, the people are more and more ignorant and favage: the Efquimaux, the moft northern of all, are the moft favage. In travelling fouthward, the Patagonians, the moft fouthern of all, are fo ftupid as to go naked in a bitter cold region.

I venture ftill farther; which is, to indulge a conjecture, that America has not been peopled from any part of the old world. The external appearance of the inhabitants, makes this conjecture approach to a certainty; as they are widely different in appearance from any other known people. Excepting the eye-lafhes, eyebrows, and hair of the head, which is invariably jet black, there is not a fingle hair on the body of any American: no appearance of a beard. Another diftinguifhing mark is their copper colour, uniformly the fame in all climates, hot and cold; and differing from the colour of

every other nation. Ulloa remarks, that
the Americans of Cape Breton, resemble
the Peruvians, in complexion, in manners,
and in customs; the only visible difference
being, that the former are of a larger sta-
ture. A third circumstance no less distin-
guishing is, that American children are
born with down upon the skin, which difappears the eighth or ninth day, and never
grows again. Children of the old world
are born with skins smooth and polished,
and no down appears till puberty.

The Esquimaux are a different race from
the rest of the Americans, if we can have
any reliance on the most striking charac-
teristical marks. Of all the northern nations, not excepting the Laplanders, they
are of the smallest size, few of them exceeding four feet in height. They have a
head extremely gross, hands and feet very
small. That they are tame and gentle
appears from what Ellis says in his
account of a voyage, *anno* 1747, for difcovering a north-west passage, that they
offered their wives to the sailors, with ex-
pressions of satisfaction for being able to
accommodate them. But above all, their
beard and complexion make the strongest
evidence

evidence of a diftinct race. There were lately at London, two Efquimaux men and their wives; and I have the beft authority to affirm, that the men had a beard, thin indeed like that of a Nogayan Tartar; that they were not of a copper colour like the other Americans, but yellow like people in the North of Afia.

It has been lately difcovered, that the language of the Efquimaux is the fame with that of the Greenlanders. A Danifh miffionary, who by fome years refidence in Greenland had acquired the language of that country, made a voyage with Commodore Pallifer to Newfoundland *ann.* 1764. Meeting a company of about two hundred Efquimaux, he was agreeably furprifed to hear the Greenland tongue. They received him kindly, and drew from him a promife to return the next year. And we are informed by Crantz, in his hiftory of Greenland, that the fame Danifh miffionary vifited them the next year, in company with the Rev. Mr Drachart. They agreed, that the difference between the Efquimaux language and that of Greenland, was not greater than between the dialects of North and South Greenland,

land, which differ not fo much as the High and Low Dutch. Both nations call themfelves *Innuit* or *Karalit*, and call the Europeans *Kablunet*. Their ftature, features, manners, drefs, tents, darts, and boats, are entirely the fame. As the language of Greenland refembles not the language of Finland, Lapland, Norway, Tartary, nor that of the Samoides, it is evident, that neither the Efquimaux nor Greenlanders are a colony from any of the countries mentioned. Geographers begin now to conjecture, that Greenland is a part of the continent of North America, without intervention of any fea *.

From the preceding facts it may be concluded with the higheft probability, that the continent of America fouth of the river St Laurence was not peopled from Afia. Labrador on the north fide of that river, is thin of inhabitants; no people having been difcovered there but the Ef-

---

* The Danes had a fettlement in Greenland long before Columbus faw the Weft Indies. Would it not appear paradoxical to fay, that America was difcovered by the Danes long before the time of Columbus, and long before they knew that they had made the difcovery?

quimaux,

quimaux, who are far from being numerous. As they have plenty of food at home, they never could have had any temptation to fend colonies abroad. And there is not the flighteft probability, that any other people more remote would, without neceffity, wander far from home to people Canada or any country farther fouth. But we are fcarce left to a conjecture. The copper colour of the Canadians, their want of beard, and other characteriftical marks above mentioned, demonftrate them to be a race different from the Efquimaux, and different from any people inhabiting a country on the other fide of Labrador. Thefe diftinguifh-ing marks cannot be owing to the climate, which is the fame on both fides of the river St Laurence. I add, that as the copper colour and want of beard continue invariably the fame in every variety of climate, hot and cold, moift and dry, they muft depend on fome invariable caufe acting uniformly; which may be a fingularity in the race of people (*a*), but cannot proceed from the climate.

If we can rely on the conjectures of an

(*a*) Preliminary Difcourfe.

eminent

eminent writer (*a*), America emerged from the fea later than any other part of the known world : and fuppofing the human race to have been planted in America by the hand of God later than the days of Mofes, Adam and Eve might have been the firft parents of mankind, *i. e.* of all who at that time exifted, without being the firft parents of the Americans. The *Terra Auftralis incognita* is feparated from the reft of the world by a wide ocean, which carries a fhip round the earth without interruption *. How has that continent been peopled ? There is not the flighteft probability, that it ever has been joined to any other land. Here a local creation, if it may be termed fo, appears unavoidable ; and if we muft admit more than one act of creation, even the appearance of difficulty, from reiteration of acts, totally vanifheth. M. Buffon in his natural hiftory affirms, that not a fingle American quadruped of a hot climate is

* Late difcoveries have annihilated the *Terra Auftralis incognita.* The argument however remains in force, being equally applicable to many iflands fcattered at a great diftance from the continent in the immenfe South Sea.

(*a*) M. Buffon.

found

found in any other part of the earth: with respect to these we must unavoidably admit a local creation; and nothing seems more natural, than under the same act to comprehend the first parents of the American people.

It is possible, indeed, that a ship with men and women may, by contrary winds, be carried to a very distant shore. But to account thus for the peopling of America, will not be much relished. Mexico and Peru must have been planted before navigation was known in the old world, at least before a ship was brought to such perfection as to bear a long course of bad weather. Will it be thought, that any supposition ought to be embraced, however improbable, rather than admit a separate creation. We are, it is true, much in the dark as to the conduct of creative providence ; but every rational conjecture leans to a separate creation. America and the *Terra Australis* must have been planted by the Almighty with a number of animals and vegetables, some of them peculiar to those vast continents : and when such care has been taken about inferior life, can so wild a thought be admitted,

as

as that man, the nobleft work of terreftrial creation, would be left to chance ?
But it is fcarce neceffary to infift upon
that topic, as the external characters of
the Americans above mentioned reject the
fuppofition of their being defcended from
any people of the old world.

It is highly probable, that the fertile
and delicious plains of Peru and Mexico,
were the firft planted of all the American
countries ; being more populous at the
time of the Spanifh invafion, than any o-
ther part of that great continent. This
conjecture is fupported by analogy : we
believe that a fpot, not centrical only but
extremely fertile, was chofen for the parents of the old world ; and there is not
in America, a fpot more centrical or more
fertile for the parents of the new world,
than Mexico or Peru.

Having thus ventured to ftate what occurred upon the origin of the Americans,
without pretending to affirm any thing as
certain, we proceed to their progrefs. The
North-American tribes are remarkable
with refpect to one branch of their hiftory,
that, inftead of advancing, like other nations, toward the maturity of fociety and
government,

government, they continue to this hour in their original ftate of hunting and fifh-ing. A cafe fo fingular roufes our curio-fity; and we wifh to be made acquainted with the caufe.

It is not the want of animals capable to be domefticated, that obliges them to re-main hunters and fifhers. The horfe, it is true, the fheep, the goat, were import-ed from Europe; but there are plenty of American quadrupeds no lefs docile than thofe mentioned. There is in particu-lar a fpecies of horned cattle peculiar to America, having long wool inftead of hair, and an excrefcence upon the fhoulder like that of the Eaft-India buffalo. Thefe wild cattle multiply exceedingly in the fer-tile countries which the Miffifippi tra-verfes; and Hennepin reports, that the Indians, after killing numbers, take no part away but the tongue, which is reckoned a delicious morfel. Thefe crea-tures are not extremely wild; and, if taken young, are eafily tamed: a calf, when its dam is killed, will follow the hunter, and lick his hand. The wool, the hide, the tallow, would be of great value in the Britifh colonies.

If the shepherd-state be not obstructed in America by want of proper cattle, the only account that can or need be given, is paucity of inhabitants. Confider only the influence of custom, in rivetting men to their local situation and manner of life: once hunters, they will always be hunters, till some cause more potent than custom force them out of that state. Want of food, occasioned by rapid population, brought on the shepherd-state in the old world. That cause has not hitherto existed in North America : the inhabitants, few in number, remain hunters and fishers, because that state affords them a competency of food. I am aware, that the natives have been decreasing in number from the time of the first European settlements. But even at that time, the country was ill peopled : take for example the country above described, stretching northwest from the Mississippi : the Europeans never had any footing there, and yet to this day it is little better than a desert. I give other examples. The Indians who surround the lake Nippifong, from whence the river St Laurence issues, are in whole but five or six thousand; and yet their

country

country is of great extent: they live by hunting and fifhing, having bows and arrows, but no fire-arms; and their cloathing is the fkins of beafts: they are feldom, if ever, engaged in war; have no commerce with any other people, Indian or European, but live as if they had a world to themfelves (*a*). If that country be ill peopled, it is not from fcarcity of food; for the country is extenfive, and well ftored with every fort of game. On the fouth and weft of the lake *Superior*, the country is level and fruitful all the way to the Miffifippi, having large plains covered with rank grafs, and fcarce a tree for hundreds of miles: the inhabitants enjoy the greateft plenty of fifh, fowl, deer, &c.; and yet their numbers are far from being in proportion to their means of fubfiftence. In fhort, it is the conjecture of the ableft writers, that in the vaft extent of North America, when difcovered, there were not as many people, laying afide Mexico, as in the half of Europe.

Paucity of inhabitants explains clearly why the North-American tribes remain

(*a*) Account of North America by Major Robert Rogers.

T 2   hunters

hunters and fifhers, without advancing to
the fhepherd-ftate. But if the foregoing
difficulty be removed, another ftarts up,
no lefs puzzling, viz. By what adverfe fate
are fo rich countries fo ill peopled ? It is a
conjecture of M. Buffon, mentioned above,
that America has been planted later than
the other parts of this globe. But fuppofing the fact, it has however not been
planted fo late as to prevent a great population ; witnefs Mexico and Peru, fully
peopled at the era of the Spanifh invafion.
We muft therefore fearch for another
caufe ; and none occurs but the infecun-
dity of the North-American favages. M.
Buffon, a refpectable author, and for that
reafon often quoted, remarks, that the
males are feeble in their organs of generation, that they have no ardor for the female fex, and that they have few children ; to enforce which remark he adds,
that the quadrupeds of America, both native and tranfplanted, are of a diminutive
fize, compared with thofe of the old world.
A woman never admits her hufband, till
the child fhe is nurfing be three years old ;
and this led Frenchmen to go often aftray
from their Canadian wives. The cafe was
reported

reported by the priefts to their fuperiors in France : what regulation was made has efcaped my memory. Among the males, it is an inviolable law, to abftain from females while they are engaged in a military expedition. This is pregnant evidence of their frigidity ; for among favages the authority of law, or of opinion, feldom prevails over any ftrong appetite : vain would be the attempt to reftrain them from fpirituous liquors, tho' much more debilitating. Neither is there any inftance, of violence offered by any North-American favage, to European women taken captives in war.

Mexico and Peru, when conquered by the Spaniards, afforded to their numerous inhabitants the neceffaries of life in profufion. Cotton was in plenty, more than fufficient for the cloathing needed in warm climates : Indian wheat was univerfal, and was cultivated without much labour. The natural wants of the inhabitants were thus eafily fupplied ; and artificial wants had made no progrefs. But the prefent ftate of thefe countries is very different. The Indians have learned from their conquerors a multitude of artificial wants, good houfes,

houſes, variety of food, and rich cloaths ;
which muſt be imported, becauſe they
are prohibited from exerciſing any art or
calling except agriculture, which ſcarce
affords them neceſſaries ; and this obliges
a great proportion of them to live ſingle.
Even agriculture itſelf is cramped ; for in
moſt of the provinces there is a prohibition
to plant vines or olives.   In ſhort, it is believed that the inhabitants are reduced to a
fourth part of what they were at the time of
the Spaniſh invaſion.   The ſavages alſo of
North America who border on the European ſettlements, are viſibly diminiſhing.
When the Engliſh ſettled in America, the
five nations could raiſe 15,000 fighting
men : at preſent they are not able to raiſe
2000.   Upon the whole, it is computed by
able writers, that the preſent inhabitants
of America amount not to a twentieth part
of thoſe who exiſted when that continent
was diſcovered by Columbus.   This decay
is aſcribed to the intemperate uſe of ſpirits,
and to the ſmall-pox, both of them introduced by the Europeans *.

It

* In all the Weſt-Indian colonies, the ſlaves continually decreaſe ſo as to make frequent recruits
from

It is obfervable, that every fort of plague becomes more virulent by tranfplantation.
The

from Africa neceffary. " This decreafe," fays the author of a late account of Guiana, " is commonly " attributed to oppreffion and hard labour ; tho' " with little reafon, as the flaves are much more " robuft, healthy, and vigorous, than their mafters. " The true caufe is, the commerce of white men " with young Negro wenches, who, to fupport that " commerce, ufe every mean to avoid conception, " and even to procure abortion. By fuch practices " they are incapacitated to bear children when they " fettle in marriage with their own countrymen. " That this is the true caufe, will be evident, from " confidering, that in Virginia and Maryland, the " ftock of flaves is kept up without any importa- " tion ; becaufe in thefe countries commerce with " Negro women is detefted, as infamous and unna- " tural." The caufe here affigned may have fome effect : but there is a ftronger caufe of depopula- tion, viz. the culture of fugar, laborious in the field, and unhealthy in the houfe by boiling, &c. The Negroes employ'd in the culture of cotton, coffee, and ginger, feldom need to be recruited. Add, that where tobacco and rice are cultivated, the ftock of Negroes is kept up by procreation, without ne- ceffity of recruits. Becaufe there, a certain por- tion of work is allotted to the negroes in every plantation ; and when that is performed, they are at liberty to work for themfelves. The manage- ment in Jamaica is very different : no tafk is there affigned ; and the poor flaves know no end of la- bour :

The plague commits lefs ravage in Egypt, its native place, than in any other country. The venereal difeafe was for many ages more violent and deftructive in Europe, than in America where it was firft known. The people who failed with Chriftopher Columbus, brought it to Spain from Hifpaniola. Columbus, with thirty or forty of his failors, went directly to Barcelona, where the King then was, to render an account of his voyage. All the inhabitants, who at that time tripled the prefent number, were immediately feized with the venereal difeafe, which raged fo furioufly as to threaten deftruction to all. The fmall pox comes under the fame obfervation; for it has fwept away many more in America, than ever it did in Europe. In the 1713, the crew of a Dutch veffel infected the Hottentots with the fmall pox; which left fcarce a third of the inhabitants. And the fame fate befel the Laplanders and Greenlanders. In all appearance, that difeafe, if it abate not

bour: they are followed all day long by the lower overfeers with whips. And hence it is, that a plantation in Jamaica, which employs a hundred flaves, requires an annual recruit of no fewer than feven.

foon

foon of its tranfplanted virulence, will ex-
tirpate the natives of North America ; for
they know little of inoculation.

But fpirituous liquors are a ftill more effectual caufe of depopulation.   The American favages, male and female, are inor-
dinately fond of fpirituous liquors; and
favages generally abandon themfelves to
appetite, without the leaft control from
fhame.   The noxious effects of intemperance in fpirits, are too well known, from
fatal experience among ourfelves : before
the ufe of gin was prohibited, the populace of London were debilitated by it to a
degree of lofing, in a great meafure, the
power of procreation.   Lucky it is for the
human fpecies, that the invention of favages never reached the production of gin ;.
for fpirits, in that early period, would
have left not one perfon alive, not a fingle
Noah to reftore the race of men : in order
to accomplifh the plan of Providence, creation muft have been renewed oftner than
once *.

In

---

* Charlevoix fays, that an Indian of Canada will
give all he is worth for a glafs of brandy.   And he
paints thus the effect of drunkennefs upon them.   ·

In the temperate climates of the old world, there is great uniformity in the gradual progrefs of men from the favage ftate to the higheft civilization; beginning with hunting and fifhing, advancing to flocks and herds, and then to agriculture and commerce. One will be much difappointed, if he expect the fame progrefs in America. Among the northern tribes, there is nothing that refembles the fhepherd-ftate: they continue hunters and fifhers as originally; becaufe there is no caufe fo potent as to force them from that ftate to become fhepherds. So far clear. But there is another fact of which we have no example in the old world, that feems not fo eafily explained: thefe people, without paffing through the fhepherd-ftate, have advanced to fome degree of agriculture. Before the feventeenth century, the Iroquois or five nations had villages, and cultivated Indian corn: the Cherokees have many fmall towns; they raife corn

" Even in the ftreets of Montreal are feen the moft
" fhocking fpectacles of ebriety; hufbands, wives,
" fathers, mothers, brothers, and fifters, feizing
" one another by the throat, and tearing one ano-
" ther with their teeth, like fo many enraged
" wolves."

in

in abundance, and enclofe their fields: they breed poultry, and have orchards of peach-trees. The Chickefaws and Creek Indians live pretty much in the fame manner. The Apalachites fow and reap in common; and put up the corn in granaries, to be diftributed among individuals when they want food. The Hurons raife great quantities of corn, not only for their own ufe, but for commerce. Many of thefe nations, particularly the Cherokees, have of late got horfes, fwine, and tame cattle; an improvement borrowed from the Europeans. But corn is of an earlier date: when Sir Richard Greenville took poffeffion of Virginia in the reign of Queen Elifabeth, the natives had corn; and Hennepin affures us, that the nations bordering on the Miffifippi had corn long before they were vifited by any European. Hufbandry, it is true, is among thofe people ftill in its infancy; being left to the women, who fow, who reap, who ftore up in public granaries, and who diftribute as need requires. The inhabitants of Guiana in South America, continue to this day hunters and fifhers. But tho' they have neither flocks nor herds, they have fome

hufbandry;

hufbandry; for the women plant caffava, yams, and plantains. They make a liquor like our ale, termed *piworee*, which they drink with their food. And tho' they are extremely fond of that liquor, their indolence makes them often neglect to provide againft the want of it. To a people having a violent propenfity to intemperance, as all favages have, this improvidence is a blefling; for otherwife they would wallow in perpetual drunkennefs. They are by no means fingular; for unconcern about futurity is the characteriftic of all favages: to forego an immediate for a diftant enjoyment, can only be fuggefted by cultivated reafon. When the Canary iflands were firft vifited by Europeans, which was in the fourteenth century, the inhabitants had corn; for which the ground was prepared in the following manner. They had a wooden inftrument, not unlike a hoe, with a fpur or tooth at the end, on which was fixed a goat's horn. With this inftrument the ground was ftirred; and if rain came not in its proper feafon, water was brought by canals from the rivulets. It was the women's province to reap the corn: they took only the ears; which

which they threſhed with ſticks, or beat with their feet, and then winnowed in their hands. Huſbandry probably will remain in that ſtate among American ſavages; for as they are decreaſing daily, they can have no difficulty about food. The fact however is ſingular, of a people uſing corn before tame cattle : there muſt be a cauſe, which on better acquaintance with that people will probably be diſcovered.

America is full of political wonders. At the time of the Spaniſh invaſion, the Mexicans and Peruvians had made great advances toward the perfection of ſociety ; while the northern tribes, ſeparated from them by diſtance only, were only hunters and fiſhers, and continue ſo to this day. To explain the difference, appears difficult. It is ſtill more difficult to explain, why the Mexicans and Peruvians, inhabitants of the torrid zone, were highly poliſhed in the arts of ſociety and government ; conſidering that in the old world, the inhabitants of the torrid zone are for the moſt part little better than ſavages. We are not ſufficiently acquainted with the natural hiſtory of America, nor with that of

its

its people, to attempt an explanation of these wonders : it is however part of our task, to state the progress of society among the Mexicans and Peruvians; which can-not fail to amuse the reader, as he will find these two nations differing essentially from the North-American tribes, in every article of manners, government, and po-lice.

When the Spaniards invaded America, the Mexicans were skilful in agriculture. Maize was their chief grain, which by good culture produced great plenty, even in the mountainous country of Tlascalla. They had gardening and botany, as well as a-griculture : a physic-garden belonging to the Emperor was open to every one for ga-thering medicinal plants.

The art of cookery was far advanced a-mong that people. Montezuma's table was for ordinary covered with 200 dishes, many of them exquisitely dressed in the o-pinion even of the Spaniards. They used salt, which was made with the sun.

The women were dextrous at spinning; and manufactures of cotton and hair a-bounded every where.

The populousness of Mexico and Peru
at ord

afford irrefragable evidence, that the arts of peace were there carried to a great height. The city of Mexico contained 60,000 families * ; and Montezuma had thirty vaffals who could bring into the field, each of them, 100,000 fighting men. Tlafcalla, a neighbouring republic governed by a fenate, was fo populous as to be almoft a match for the Emperor of Mexico.

The public edifices in the city of Mexico and houfes of the nobility, were of ftone, and well built. The royal palace had thirty gates opening to as many ftreets. The principal front was of jafper, black, red, and white, well polifhed. Three fquares, built and adorned like the front, led to Montezuma's apartment, having large rooms, floors covered with mats of different kinds, walls hung with a mixture of cotton-cloth and rabbit-furs ; the innermoft room adorned with hangings of

---

* We cannot altogether rely on what is reported of this ancient empire with refpect to numbers. The city of Mexico, tho' confiderably enlarged fince the Spanifh conqueft, doth not at prefent contain more than 60,000 fouls, including 20,000 Negroes and Mulattoes.

feathers,

feathers, beautified with various figures in lively colours. In that building, large ceilings were formed fo artificially without nails, as to make the planks fuftain each other. Water was brought into the city of Mexico, from a mountain at a league's diftance.

Gold and filver were in fo high efteem, that veffels made of thefe metals were permitted to none but to the Emperor. Confidering the value put upon gold and filver, the want of current coin would argue great dulnefs in that nation, if inftances did not daily occur of improvements, after being carried to a confiderable height, ftopping fhort at the very threfhold of perfection. The want of current coin made fairs the more neceffary, which were carried on with the moft perfect regularity: judges on the fpot decided mercantile differences; and inferior officers, making conftant circuits, preferved peace and order. The abundance and variety of the commodities brought to market, and the order preferved by fuch multitudes, amazed the Spaniards; a fpectacle deferving admiration, as a teftimony of the grandeur

deur and good government of that extenfive empire.

The fine arts were not unknown in
Mexico. Their goldfmiths were excellent
workmen, particularly in moulding gold
and filver into the form of animals. Their
painters made landfcapes and other imita-
tions of nature, with feathers fo artfully
mixed as to beftow both life and colour-
ing; of.which fort of work, there were
inftances no lefs extraordinary for patience
than for fkill. Their drinking-cups were
of the fineft earth exquifitely made, differing from each other in colour, and even
in fmell. Of the fame materials, they
made great variety of veffels both for ufe
and ornament.

They were not ignorant either of mufic
or of poetry; and one of their capital a-
mufements was fongs fet to mufic relating
the atchievements of their kings and anceftors.

With fuch a progrefs both in the ufeful
and fine arts, is it not furprifing, that tho'
they had meafures, they knew nothing of
weights?

As to the art of writing, it was no farther advanced than the ufing figures com-

pofed of painted feathers, by which they made a fhift to communicate fome fimple thoughts ; and in that manner was Montezuma informed of the Spanifh invafion.

There was great ingenuity fhewn in regulating the calendar : the Mexican year was divided into 365 days ; and into 18 months, containing 20 days each, which made 360 ; the remaining five intercalary days were added at the end of the year, for making it correfpond to the courfe of the fun. They religioufly employ'd thefe five days upon diverfions, being of opinion that they were appropriated to that end by their anceftors.

Murder, theft, and corruption in officers of ftate, were capital crimes. Adultery alfo was capital ; for female chaftity was in high eftimation. At the fame time, confent was deemed a fufficient caufe of divorce, the law leaving it to the parties concerned, who ought to be the beft judges. In cafe of a divorce, the father took care of the male children, leaving the female children with the mother. But to prevent rafh feparations, it was capital for them to unite again.

It may be gathered from what has been

said,

faid, that there was a diftinction of rank among the Mexicans. So ftrictly was it obferved, as to be difplay'd even in their buildings : the city of Mexico was divided into two parts, one appropriated to the Emperor and nobility, and one left to plebeians.

Education of children was an important article in the Mexican police. Public fchools were allotted for plebeian children; and colleges well endowed for the fons of the nobility, where they continued till they were fit for bufinefs. The mafters were confidered as officers of ftate; not without reafon, as their office was to qualify young men for ferving their king and country. Such of the young nobles as made choice of a military life, were fent to the army, and made to fuffer great hardfhips before they could be inlifted. They had indeed a powerful motive for perfeverance, the moft honourable of all employments being that of a foldier. Young women of quality were educated with no lefs care, by proper matrons chofen with the utmoft circumfpection.

As hereditary nobility and an extenfive empire, lead both of them to monarchy,

the

the government of Mexico was monarchical; and as the progrefs of monarchy is from being elective to be hereditary, Mexico had advanced no farther than to be an elective monarchy, of which Montezuma was the eleventh king. And it was an example of an elective monarchy that approaches the neareft to hereditary; for the power of election, as well as the privilege of being elected, were confined to the princes of the blood-royal. As a talent for war was chiefly regarded in chufing a fucceffor to the throne, the Mexican kings always commanded their own armies. The Emperor-elect, before his coronation, was obliged to make fome conqueft, or perform fome warlike exploit; a cuftom that fupported the military fpirit, and enlarged the kingdom. From every king was exacted a coronation-oath, to adhere to the religion of his anceftors, to maintain the laws and cuftoms of the empire, and to be a father to his people.

Matters of government were diftributed among different boards with great propriety. The management of the royal patrimony was allotted to one board; appeals from inferior tribunals, to another; the
levying

levying of troops and the providing of ma-
gazines, to a third : affairs of fupreme importance were referved to a council of
ftate, held commonly in the King's pre-
fence. Thefe boards, all of them, were
compofed of men experienced in the arts
of war and of peace : the council of ftate
was compofed of thofe who elected the
Emperor.

Concerning the patrimony of the crown,
mines of gold and filver belonged to the
Emperor ; and the duty on falt brought
in a great revenue. But the capital duty
was a third of the land-rents, the eftates
of the nobles excepted ; upon whom no
tribute was impofed, but to ferve in the
army with a number of their vaffals, and
to guard the Emperor's perfon. Goods
manufactured and fold were fubjected to a
duty ; which was not prejudicial to their
manufactures, becaufe there was no rival
nation within reach.

Montezuma introduced a multitude of
ceremonies into his court, tending to infpire veneration for his perfon ; an excellent artifice in rude times, of however
little fignificancy among nations enlightened and rational. Veneration and humi-
lity

lity were fo much the tone of the court, that it was even thought indecent in the Mexican lords, to appear before the King in their richeft habits. Veffels of gold and filver were appropriated to his table, and not permitted even to the princes of the blood. The table-cloths and napkins, made of the fineft cotton, with the earthen ware, never made a fecond appearance at the Emperor's table, but were diftributed among the fervants.

In war, their offenfive weapons were bows and arrows; and as iron was not known in America, their arrows were headed with bones fharpened at the point. They ufed alfo darts and long wooden fwords, in which were fixed fharp flints; and men of more than ordinary ftrength fought with clubs. They befide had flingers, who threw ftones with great force and dexterity. Their defenfive arms, ufed only by commanders and perfons of diftinction, were a coat of quilted cotton, a fort of breaft-plate, and a fhield of wood or tortoife-fhell, adorned with plates of fuch metal as they could procure. The private men fought naked; their faces and bodies being deformed with paint, in order

order to ſtrike terror. They had warlike
inſtruments of muſic, ſuch as ſea-ſhells,
flutes made of large canes, and a ſort of
drum made of the trunk of a tree hollow'd. Their battalions conſiſted of great
numbers crouded together, without even
the appearance of order. They attacked
with terrible outcries in order to intimi-
date the enemy ; a practice prompted by
nature, and formerly uſed by many nations. It was not deſpiſed even by the
Romans ; for Cato the elder was wont to
ſay, that he had obtained more victories
by the throats of his ſoldiers, than by their
ſwords ; and Cæſar applauds his own ſoldiers, above thoſe of Pompey, for their
warlike ſhouts. Eagerneſs to engage is
vented in loud cries : and the effects are
excellent : they redouble the ardor of thoſe
who attack, and ſtrike terror into the e-
nemy.

Their armies were formed with eaſe :
the princes of the empire, with the cacics
or governors of provinces, were obliged to
repair to the general rendezvous, each
with his quota of men.

Their fortifications were trunks of large
trees, fixed in the ground like paliſades,
                                    leaving

leaving no intervals but what were barely
fufficient for difcharging their arrows upon the enemy.

Military orders were inftituted, with
peculiar habits as marks of diftinction and
honour ; and each cavalier bore the device
of his order, painted upon his robe, or
fixed to it. Montezuma founded a new
order of knighthood, into which princes
only were admitted, or nobles defcended
from the royal ftock; and as a token of its
fuperiority, he became one of its members.
The knights of that order had part of their
hair bound with a red ribbon, to which a
taffel was fixed hanging down to the
fhoulder. Every new exploit was honoured with an additional taffel ; which made
the knights with ardor embrace every opportunity to fignalize themfelves. As nothing can be better contrived than fuch a
regulation for fupporting a military fpirit,
the Mexicans would have been invincible
had they underftood the order of battle :
for want of which that potent empire fell
a prey to a handful of ftrangers. I differ
from thofe who afcribe that event to the
fire-arms of the Spaniards, and to their
horfes. Thefe could not be more terrible

I   to

to the Mexicans, than elephants were at firft to the Romans : but familiarity with thefe unwieldy animals, reftored to the Romans their wonted courage ; and the Mexicans probably would have behaved like the Romans, had they equalled the Romans in the art of war.

When that illuftrious people, by their own genius without borrowing from o- thers, had made fuch proficiency in the arts of peace, as well as of war ; is it not ftrange, that with refpect to religion they were no better than favages ? They not only practifed human facrifices, but dreff- ed and ate the flefh of thofe that were fa- crificed. Their great temple was contri- ved to raife horror : upon the walls were crouded the figures of noxious ferpents : the heads of perfons facrificed were ftuck up in different places, and carefully re- newed when wafted by time. There were eight temples in the city, nearly of the fame architecture ; 2000 of a fmaller fize, dedicated to different idols ; fcarce a ftreet without a tutelar deity ; nor a calamity that had not an altar, to which the di- ftreffed might have recourfe for a remedy. Unparallelled ignorance and ftupidity,

obliged every Emperor, at his coronation, to fwear, that there fhould be no
unfeafonable rains, no overflowing of rivers, no fields affected with fterility, nor
any man hurt with the bad influences of
the fun. In fhort, it was a flavifh religion, built upon fear, not love. At the
fame time, they believed the immortality
of the foul, and rewards and punifhments
in a future ftate; which made them bury
with their dead, quantities of gold and filver for defraying the expence of their
journey ; and alfo made them put to death
fome of their fervants to attend them.
Women fometimes, actuated with the
fame belief, were authors of their own
death, in order to accompany their hufbands.

The author we chiefly rely on for an
account of Peru is Garcilaffo de la Vega:
tho' he may be juftly fufpected of partiality; for, being of the Inca race, he be-
ftows on the Peruvian government, improvements of later times. The articles
that appear the leaft fufpicious are what
follow.

The principle of the Peruvian conftitution feems to have been an Agrarian law

of

of the ſtricteſt kind. To the ſovereign was firſt allotted a large proportion of land, for defraying the expences of government; and the remainder was divided among his ſubjects, in proportion to the number of each family. Theſe portions were not alienable: the ſovereign was held proprietor of the whole, as in the feudal ſyſtem; and from time to time the diſtribution was varied according to the circumſtances of families. 'This Agrarian law contributed undoubtedly to the populouſneſs of the kingdom of Peru.

It is a ſure ſign of improved agriculture, that aqueducts were made by the Peruvians for watering their land. Their plough was of wood, a yard long, flat before, round behind, and pointed at the end for piercing the ground. Agriculture ſeems to have been carried on by united labour: lands appropriated for maintaining the poor were firſt ploughed; next the portion allotted to ſoldiers performing duty in the field; then every man ſeparately ploughed his own field; after which he aſſiſted his neighbour: they proceeded to the portion of the curaca or lord; and laſtly to the King's portion. In the month

of

of March they reaped their maize, and celebrated the harveſt with joy and feaſting.

There being no artiſt nor manufacturer
by profeſſion, individuals were taught to
do every thing for themſelves. Every one
knew how to plough and manure the land:
every one was a carpenter, a maſon, a
ſhoemaker, a weaver, &c.; and the women were the moſt ingenious and diligent
of all. Blas Valera mentions a law, named *the law of brotherhood*, which, without
the profpect of reward, obliged them to
be mutually aiding and aſſiſting in ploughing, ſowing, and reaping, in building
their houſes, and in every ſort of occupation.

As the art was unknown of melting
down metals by means of bellows, long
copper pipes were contrived, contracted at
the end next the fire, that the breath might
act the more forcibly on it; and they uſed
ten or twelve of theſe pipes together, when
they wanted a very hot fire. Having no
iron, their hatchets and pick-axes were of
copper; they had neither ſaw nor augre,
nor any inſtrument that requires iron:
ignorant of the uſe of nails, they tied their
timber with cords of hemp. The tool
they

they had for cutting ftone, was a fharp flint; and with that tool they fhaped the ftone by continual rubbing, more than by cutting. Having no engines for raifing ftones, they did all by ftrength of arm. Thefe defects notwithftanding, they erected great edifices ; witnefs the fortrefs of Cufco, a ftupenduous fabric. It paffes all underftanding, by what means the ftones, or rather great rocks, employ'd in that building, were brought from the quarry. One of thefe ftones, meafured by Acofta, was thirty feet in length, eighteen in breadth, and fix in thicknefs.

Having neither fciffars nor needles of metal, they ufed a certain long thorn for a needle. The mirrors ufed by ladies of quality were of burnifhed copper: but fuch implements of drefs were reckoned too effeminate for men.

With refpect to mufic, they had an inftrument of hollow canes glew'd together, the notes of which were like thofe of an organ. They had love-fongs accompanied with a pipe ; and war-fongs, which were their feftival entertainment. They compofed and acted comedies and tragedies. The art of writing was unknown: but
filken

filken threads, with knots caft upon them of divers colours, enabled them to keep exact accounts, and to fum them up with a readinefs that would have rivalled an expert European arithmetician. They had alfo attained to as much geometry as to meafure their fields.

In war, their offenfive arms were the bow and arrow, lance, dart, club, and bill. Their defenfive arms, were the helmet and target. The army was provided from the King's ftores, and no burden was laid on the people.

In philofophy, they had made no progrefs. An eclipfe of the moon was attributed to her being fick; and they fancied the milky way to be a ewe giving fuck to a lamb. With regard to the fetting fun, they faid, that he was a good fwimmer, and that he pierced through the waves, to rife next morning in the eaft. But fuch ignorance is not wonderful; for no branch of fcience can make a progrefs without writing.

The people were divided into fmall bodies of ten families each : every divifion had a head, and a regifter was kept of the whole; a branch of public police, that

very

very much refembles the Englifh decen-
naries.

They made but two meals, one between
eight and nine in the morning, the other
before funfet.   Idlenefs was punifhed with
infamy : 'even children were employ'd according to their capacity.   Public vifitors
or monitors were appointed, having accefs to every houfe, for infpecting the
manners of the inhabitants ; who were
rewarded or punifhed according to their
behaviour.   Moderation and induftry were
fo effectually enforc'd by this article of
police, that few were reduced to indigence ; and thefe got their food and
cloathing out of the King's ftores.

With refpect to their laws and cuftoms,
children were bound to ferve their parents
until the age of twenty-five ; and marriage contracted before that time, without
confent of parents, was null.   Polygamy
was prohibited, and perfons were confined
to marry within their own tribe.   The
tradition, that the Inca family were children of the fun, introduced inceft among
them ; for it was a matter of religion to
preferve their divine blood pure, without
mixture.

It

It was the chief article of the Peruvian creed, upon which every other article of their religion depended, that the Inca family were children of their great god the fun, and fent by him to fpread his worfhip and his laws among them. Nothing could have a greater influence upon an ignorant and credulous people, than fuch a doctrine. The fanctity of the Inca family was fo deeply rooted in the hearts of the Peruvians, that no perfon of that family was thought capable of committing a crime. Such blind veneration for a family, makes it probable, that the government of Peru under the Incas had not fubfifted many years; for a government founded upon deceit and fuperftition, cannot long fubfift in vigour. However that be, fuch belief of the origin of the Incas, is evidence of great virtue and moderation in that family; for any grofs act of tyranny or injuftice, would have opened the eyes of the people to fee their error. Moderation in the fovereign and obedience without referve in the fubjects, cannot fail to produce a government mild and gentle; which was verified in that of Peru; fo mild and gentle, that to manure

2   and

and cultivate the lands of the Inca and to lay up the produce in ſtorehouſes, were the only burdens impoſed upon the people, if it was not ſometimes to make cloaths and weapons for the army. At the ſame time, their kings were ſo revered, that theſe articles of labour were performed with affection and alacrity.

The government was equally gentle with regard to puniſhments. Indeed very few crimes were committed, being conſidered as a ſort of rebellion againſt their great god the ſun. The only crime that ſeems to have been puniſhed with ſeverity, is the marauding of ſoldiers; for death was inflicted, however inconſiderable the damage.

In this empire, there appears to have been the moſt perfect union between law and religion; which could not fail to produce obedience, order, and tranquillity, among that people, tho' extremely numerous. The Inca family was fam'd for moderation: they made conqueſts in order to civilize their neighbours; and as they ſeldom if ever tranſgreſſed the bounds of morality, no other art was neceſſary to preſerve the government entire, but to keep the people ignorant of true religion. They had virgins dedicated to the fun, who, like the veftal virgins in Rome, were under a vow of perpetual chaftity.

This fubject fhall be concluded with fome flight obfervations on the two governments I have been defcribing. Comparing them together, the Mexican government feems to have been fupported by arms ; that of Peru by religion.

The kings of Peru were hereditary and abfolute : thofe of Mexico elective. In contradiction however to political principles, the government of Peru was by far the milder. It is mentioned above, that the electors of the Mexican kings were hereditary princes ; and the fame electors compofed the great council of ftate. Montefquieu therefore has been mifinformed when he terms this a defpotic monarchy (a) : a monarchy can never be defpotic, where the fovereign is limited by a great council, the members of which are independent of him. As little reafon has he to term Peru defpotic. An abfolute monarchy it was, but the fartheft in the world from being defpotic : on the con-

(a) L'Efprit des loix, liv. 17. ch. 7.

trary,

trary, we find not in hiſtory any government ſo well contrived for the good of the people.   An Agrarian law, firmly rooted, was a firm bar againſt ſuch inequality of rank and riches, as lead to luxury and diſſolution of manners : a commonwealth is naturally the reſult of ſuch a conſtitution ; but in Peru it was prevented by a theocratical government under a family ſent from heaven to make them happy. This wild opinion, ſupported by ignorance and ſuperſtition, proved an effectual bar againſt tyranny in the monarch ; a moſt exemplary conduct on his part being neceſſary for ſupporting the opinion of his divinity.   Upon the whole, comprehending king and ſubject, there perhaps never exiſted more virtue in any other government, whether monarchical or republican.

In Peru there are traces of ſome diſtinction of ranks, ariſing probably from office merely, which, as in France, was a bulwark to the monarch againſt the peaſants. The great ſuperiority of the Peruvian Incas, as demi-gods, did not admit a hereditary nobility.

With reſpect to the progreſs of arts and
Z 2   manufactures,

manufactures, the two nations differed
widely: in Mexico, arts and manufactures were carried to a furprifing height,
confidering the tools they had to work
with: in Peru, they had made no progrefs; every man, as among mere favages,
providing the neceffaries of life for himfelf. As the world goes at prefent, our
multiplied wants require fuch numbers,
that not above one of a hundred can be
fpared for war. In ancient times, when
thefe wants were few and not much enlarged beyond nature, it is computed that an
eighth part could be fpared for war: and
hence the numerous armies we read of in
the hiftory of ancient nations. The Peruvians had it in their power to go ftill
farther: it was poffible to arm the whole
males capable of fervice: leaving the women to fupply the few neceffaries that
might be wanted during a fhort campaign; and accordingly we find that the
Incas were great conquerors.

The religion of the Peruvians, confidered in a political light, was excellent. The
veneration they paid their fovereign upon
a falfe religious principle, was their only
fuperftition; and that fuperftition contributed

buted greatly to improve their morals and their manners : on the other hand, the religion of Mexico was execrable.

Upon the whole, there never was a country deftitute of iron, where arts feem to have been carried higher than in Mexico : and, bating their religion, there never was a country deftitute of writing, where government feems to have been more perfect. I except not the government of Peru, which, not being founded on political principles, but on fuperftition, might be more mild, but was far from being fo folidly founded.

SKETCHES

SKETCHES

OF THE

HISTORY OF MAN.

BOOK III.

Progress of SCIENCES.

PREFACE.

*M*Orality, theology, and the art of reasoning, are three great branches of a learned education; and justly held to be so, being our only sure guides in passing through the intricate paths of life. They are indeed not essential to those termed men of the world: the most profound philosopher makes but an insipid figure in fashionable company; would be somewhat ridiculous at a court-ball; and an absolute absurdity among the gamesters at Arthur's,

I

. thur's, or jockeys at *Newmarket.* But, *these cogent objections notwithstanding, I venture to pronounce such studies to be not altogether unsuitable to a gentleman.* Man *is a creature full of curiosity ; and to gratify that appetite, many roam through the world, submitting to heat and cold, nay to hunger and thirst, without a sigh.* Could *indeed that troublesome guest be expelled, we might hug ourselves in ignorance ; and, like true men of the world, undervalue knowledge that cannot procure money, nor a new sensual pleasure.* But, alas ! *the expulsion is not in the power of every one ; and those who must give vent to their curiosity, will naturally employ it upon studies that make them good members of society, and endear them to every person of virtue.*

And *were we even men of ·the world in such perfection, as to regard nothing but our own interest ; yet does not ignorance lay us open to the crafty and designing ? and does not the art of reasoning guard many an honest man from being misled by subtile sophisms ?* With *respect to right and wrong, not even passion is more dangerous than error.* And *as to religion, better it were ·to settle in a conviction that there is no God, than to be in*

· *a*

a state of wavering and fluctuation; sometimes indulging every loose desire, as if we were not accountable beings; and sometimes yielding to superstitious fears, as if there were no god but the devil. To a well-disposed mind, the existence of a supreme benevolent Deity, appears highly probable: and if by the study of theology that probability be improved into a certainty, the conviction of a supreme Deity who rules with equity and mildness, will be a source of constant enjoyment, which I boldly set above the titillating pleasures of external sense. Possibly there may be less present amusement in abstract studies, than in newspapers, in party-pamphlets, or in *Hoyl* upon *Whist:* but let us for a moment anticipate futurity, and imagine that we are reviewing past transactions, — how pleasant the retrospect of those who have maintained the dignity of their nature, and employ'd their talents to the best purposes!

Contradictory opinions that have influence on practice, will be regretted by every person of a sound heart; and as erroneous opinions are commonly the result of imperfect education, I would gladly hope, that a remedy is not altogether out of reach. At the revival of arts and sciences, the learned languages

were

were our fole ftudy, becaufe in them were
locked up all the treafures of ufeful knowledge. This ftudy has long ago ceafed to be
the chief object of education; and yet the o-
riginal plan is handed down to us with very
little variation. Wifhing to contribute to a
more perfect fyftem of education, I prefent to
the public the following fketches. The books
that have been publifhed on morality, theology, and the art of reafoning, are not eminent either for fimplicity, or for perfpicuity.
To introduce thefe into the fubjects mentioned,
is my aim; with what fuccefs, is with deference fubmitted to the judgement of others.
The hiftorical part, hitherto much neglected,
is neceffary as a branch of my general plan;
and I am hopeful, that, befide inftruction, it
will contribute to recreation, which, in abftract ftudies, is no lefs neceffary than pleafant.

SKETCH I.

Principles and Progress of Reason.

SECTION I.

Principles of Reason.

EVery affirmation, whatever be the subject, is termed a *proposition.*

Truth and error are qualities of propositions. A proposition that says a thing is what it is in reality, is termed a *true proposition.* A proposition that says a thing is what it is not in reality, is termed an *erroneous proposition.*

Truth is so essential in conducting affairs, that man would be a disjointed being were it not agreeable to him. Truth accordingly is agreeable to every human being, and falsehood or error disagreeable.

The

The purſuit of truth is no leſs pleaſant than the purſuit of any other good *.

Our knowledge of what is agreeable and diſagreeable in objects is derived from the ſenſe of beauty, handled in Elements of Criticiſm. Our knowledge of right and wrong in actions, is derived from the moral ſenſe, to be handled in the ſketch immediately following. Our knowledge of truth and error is derived from various ſources.

Our external ſenſes are one ſource of knowledge : they lay open to us external ſubjects, their qualities, their actions, with events produced by theſe actions. The internal ſenſes are another ſource of knowledge : they lay open to us things paſſing in the mind ; thinking, for example, deliberating, inclining, reſolving, willing, conſenting, and other acts ; and they alſo lay open to us our emotions and paſſions. There is a ſenſe by which we perceive the truth of many propoſitions ; ſuch as, That every thing which begins

* It has been wiſely obſerved, that truth is the ſame to the underſtanding that muſic is to the ear, or beauty to the eye.

to

to exiſt muſt have a cauſe; That every effect adapted to ſome end or purpoſe, proceeds from a deſigning cauſe; and, That
every effect adapted to a good end or purpoſe, proceeds from a deſigning and benevolent cauſe. A multitude of axioms in
every ſcience, particularly in mathematics, are equally perceived to be true. By
a peculiar ſenſe, of which afterward, we
know that there is a Deity. There is a
ſenſe by which we know, that the external ſigns of paſſion are the ſame in all
men; that animals of the ſame external
appearance, are of the ſame ſpecies; and
that animals of the ſame ſpecies, have the
ſame properties (*a*). There is a ſenſe
that dives into futurity: we know that
the ſun will riſe to-morrow; that the
earth will perform its wonted courſe
round the ſun; that winter and ſummer
will follow each other in ſucceſſion; that
a ſtone dropt from the hand will fall to
the ground; and a thouſand other ſuch
propoſitions.

There are many propoſitions, the truth
of which is not ſo apparent: a proceſs of

(*a*) Preliminary Diſcourſe.

reaſoning

reafoning is neceffary, of which afterward.

Human teftimony is another fource of
knowledge. So framed we are by nature,
as to rely on human teftimony; by which
we are informed of beings, attributes, and
events, that never came under any of our
fenfes.

The knowledge that is derived from the
fources mentioned, is of different kinds.
In fome cafes, our knowledge includes abfolute certainty, and produces the higheft
degree of conviction : in other cafes, probability comes in place of certainty, and
the conviction is inferior in degree.
Knowledge of the latter kind is diftinguifhed into belief, which concerns facts;
and opinion, which concerns relations,
and other things that fall not under the
denomination of 'facts. In contradiftinc-
tion to opinion and belief, that fort of
knowledge which includes abfolute certainty and produces the higheft degree of
conviction, retains its proper name. To
explain what is here faid, I enter into particulars.

The fenfe of feeing, with very few exceptions, affords knowledge properly fo
                              termed :

termed: it is not in our power to doubt of the exiftence of a perfon we fee, touch, and converfe with. When fuch is our conftitution, it is a vain attempt to call in queftion the authority of our fenfe of feeing, as fome writers pretend to do. No one ever called in queftion the exiftence of internal actions and paffions, laid open to us by internal fenfe; and there is as little ground for doubting of what we fee. The fenfe of feeing, it is true, is not always correct: through different mediums the fame object is feen differently: to a jaundic'd eye every thing appears yellow; and to one intoxicated with liquor, two candles fometimes appear four. But we are never left without a remedy in fuch a cafe: it is the province of the reafoning faculty, to correct every error of that kind.

An object of fight recalled to mind by the power of memory, is termed an *idea* or fecondary perception. An original perception, as faid above, affords knowledge in its proper fenfe; but a fecondary perception affords belief only. And Nature in this, as in all other inftances, is faithful to truth; for it is evident, that we

‘ cannot

cannot be so certain of the existence of an object in its absence, as when present.

With respect to many abstract propositions, of which instances are above given, we have an absolute certainty and conviction of their truth, derived to us from various senses. We can, for example, entertain as little doubt that every thing which begins to exist must have a cause, as that the sun is in the firmament; and as little doubt that he will rise to-morrow, as that he is now set. There are many other propositions, the truth of which is probable only, not absolutely certain; as, for example, that winter will be cold and summer warm. That natural operations are performed in the simplest manner, is an axiom of natural philosophy: it may be probable, but is far from being certain *.

In

* I have given this proposition a place, because it is assumed as an axiom by all writers on natural philosophy. And yet there appears some room for doubting, whether our conviction of it do not proceed from a bias in our nature, rather than from an original sense. Our taste for simplicity, which undoubtedly is natural, renders simple operations more agreeable than what are complex, and consequently makes them appear more natural. It deserves

In every one of the inftances given, conviction arifes from a fingle act of perception : for which reafon, knowledge acquired by means of that perception, not
only knowledge in its proper fenfe but alfo opinion and belief, are termed *intuitive
knowledge*. But there are many things,
the knowledge of which is not obtained
with fo much facility. Propofitions for
the moft part require a procefs or operation in the mind, termed *reafoning* ; leading, by certain intermediate fteps, to the
propofition that is to be demonftrated or
made evident ; which, in oppofition to intuitive knowledge, is termed *difcurfive
knowledge*. This procefs or operation muft
be explained, in order to underftand the
nature of reafoning. And as reafoning is
moftly employ'd in difcovering relations,
I fhall draw my examples from them. E-
very propofition concerning relations, is
an affirmation of a certain relation between two fubjects. If the relation affirmed appear not intuitively, we muft fearch

ferves a moft ferious difcuffion, whether the operations of nature be always carried on with the greateft fimplicity, or whether we be not mifled by our
tafte for fimplicity to be of that opinion.

for a third fubject, intuitively connected
with each of the others by the relation affirmed : and if fuch a fubject be found,
the propofition is demonftrated ; for it is
intuitively certain, that two fubjects connected with a third by any particular relation, muft be connected together by the
fame relation. The longeft chain of reafoning may be linked together in this
manner. Running over fuch a chain, e-
very one of the fubjects muft appear intuitively to be connected with that immediately preceding, and with that immediately fubfequent, by the relation affirmed in the propofition ; and from the whole
united, the propofition, as above mentioned, muft appear intuitively certain. The
laft ftep of the procefs is termed *a conclufion*, being the laft or concluding perception.

No other reafoning affords fo clear a
notion of the foregoing procefs, as that
which is mathematical. Equality is the
only mathematical relation ; and comparifon therefore is the only means by which
mathematical propofitions are afcertained.
To that fcience belong a number of intuitive propofitions, termed *axioms*, which

are all founded on equality. For example:
Divide two equal lines, each of them, into
a thousand equal parts, a single part of
the one line muſt be equal to a single part
of the other. Second: Take ten of theſe
parts from the one line, and as many
from the other, and the remaining parts
muſt be equal; which is more ſhortly expreſſed thus: From two equal lines take e-
qual parts, and the remainders will be e-
qual; or add equal parts, and the ſums
will be equal. Third: If two things be,
in the ſame reſpect, equal to a third, the
one is equal to the other in the ſame reſpect. I proceed to ſhow the uſe of theſe
axioms. Two things may be equal without being intuitively ſo; which is the caſe
of the equality between the three angles
of a triangle and two right angles. To
demonſtrate that truth, it is neceſſary to
ſearch for ſome other angles that intuitively are equal to both. If this property
cannot be diſcovered in any one ſet of
angles, we muſt go more leiſurely to
work, and try to find angles that are equal
to the three angles of a triangle. Theſe
being diſcovered, we next try to find o-
ther angles equal to the angles now diſcovered;

vered; and fo on in the comparifon, till at laft we difcover a fet of angles, equal not only to thofe thus introduced, but alfo to two right angles. We thus connect the two parts of the original propofition, by a number of intermediate equalities; and by that means perceive, that thefe two parts are equal among themfelves; it being an intuitive propofition, as mentioned above, That two things are equal, each of which, in the fame refpect, is equal to a third.

I proceed to a different example, which concerns the relation between caufe and effect. The propofition to be demonftrated is, " That there exifts a good and in-
" telligent Being, who is the caufe of all
" the wife and benevolent effects that are
" produced in the government of. this
" world." That there are fuch effects, is in the prefent example the fundamental propofition; which is taken for granted, becaufe it is verified by experience. In order to difcover the caufe of thefe effects, I begin with an intuitive propofition mentioned above, " That every effect adapted
" to a good end or purpofe, proceeds
" from a defigning and benevolent caufe."

The

The next ftep is, to examine whether man can be the caufe: he is provided indeed with fome fhare of wifdom and benevolence; but the effects mentioned are far above his power, and no lefs above his wifdom. Neither can this earth be the caufe, nor the fun, the moon, the ftars; for, far from being wife and benevolent, they are not even fenfible. If thefe be excluded, we are unavoidably led to an invifible being, endowed with boundlefs power, goodnefs, and intelligence; and that invifible being is termed *God*.

Reafoning requires two mental powers, namely, the power of invention, and the power of perceiving relations. By the former are difcovered intermediate propofitions, equally related to the fundamental propofition and to the conclufion: by the latter we perceive, that the different links which compofe the chain of reafoning, are all connected together by the fame relation.

We can reafon about matters of opinion and belief, as well as about matters of knowledge properly fo termed. Hence reafoning is diftinguifhed into two kinds; demonftrative, and probable. Demon-
                                        ftrative

ftrative reafoning is alfo of two kinds : in the firft, the conclufion is drawn from the nature and inherent properties of the fubject : in the other, the conclufion is drawn from fome principle, of which we are certain by intuition. With refpect to the firft, we have no fuch knowledge of the nature or inherent properties of any being, material or immaterial, as to draw conclufions from it with certainty. I except not even figure confidered as a quality of matter, tho' it is the object of mathematical reafoning. As we have no ftandard for determining with precifion the figure of any portion of matter, we cannot with precifion reafon upon it : what appears to us a ftraight line may be a curve, and what appears a rectilinear angle may be curvilinear. How then comes mathematical reafoning to be demonftrative? This queftion may appear at firft fight puzzling; and I know not that it has any where been diftinctly explained. Perhaps what follows may be fatisfactory.

The fubjects of arithmetical reafoning are numbers. The fubjects of mathematical reafoning are figures. But what figures? Not fuch as I fee; but fuch as I

form

form an idea of, abftracting from every imperfection. I explain myfelf. There is a power in man to form images of things that never exifted; a golden mountain, for example, or a river running upward. This power operates upon figures: there is perhaps no figure exifting the fides of which are ftraight lines; but it is eafy to form an idea of a line that has no waving or crookednefs, and it is eafy to form an idea of a figure bounded by fuch lines. Such ideal figures are the fubjects of mathematical reafoning; and thefe being perfectly clear and diftinct, are proper fubjects for demonftrative reafoning of the firft kind. Mathematical reafoning however is not merely a mental entertainment: it is of real ufe in life, by directing us to operate upon matter. There poffibly may not be found any where a perfect globe, to anfwer the idea we form of that figure: but a globe may be made fo near perfection, as to have nearly the properties of a perfect globe. In a word, tho' ideas are, properly fpeaking, the fubject of mathematical evidence; yet the end and purpofe of that evidence is, to direct us with refpect to figures as they really exift; and

the

the nearer any real figure approaches to its ideal perfection, with the greater accuracy will the mathematical truth be applicable.

The component parts of figures, viz. lines and angles, are extremely fimple, requiring no definition. Place before a child a crooked line, and one that has no appearance of being crooked : call the former a *crooked line*, the latter a *ftraight line ;* and the child will ufe thefe terms familiarly, without hazard of a miftake. Draw a perpendicular upon paper : let the child advert, that the upward line leans neither to the right nor the left, and for that reafon is termed *a perpendicular :* the child will apply that term familiarly to a tree, to the wall of a houfe, or to any other perpendicular. In the fame manner, place before the child two lines diverging from each other, and two that have no appearance of diverging : call the latter *parallel lines*, and the child will have no difficulty of applying the fame term to the fides of a door or of a window. Yet fo accuftomed are we to definitions, that even thefe fimple ideas are not fuffered to efcape. A ftraight line, for example, is defined to be
the

the fhorteft that can be drawn between two
given points. Is it fo, that even a man,
not to talk of a child, can have no idea of
a ftraight line till he be told that the
fhorteft line between two points is a
ftraight line? How many talk familiarly
of a ftraight line who never happened to
think of that fact, which is an inference
only, not a definition. If I had not beforehand an idea of a ftraight line, I fhould
never be able to find out, that it is the
fhorteft that can be drawn between two
points. D'Alembert ftrains hard, but
without fuccefs, for a definition of a
ftraight line, and of the others mentioned.
It is difficult to avoid fmiling at his definition of parallel lines. Draw, fays he,
a ftraight line: erect upon it two perpendiculars of the fame length: upon their
two extremities draw another ftraight line;
and that line is faid to be parallel to the
firft mentioned; as if, to underftand what
is meant by the expreffion *two parallel
lines*, we muft firft underftand what is
meant by a ftraight line, by a perpendicular, and by two lines equal in length.
A very flight reflection upon the operations of his own mind, would have taught

I   this

this author, that he could form the idea of parallel lines without running through fo many intermediate fteps : fight alone is fufficient to explain the term to a boy, and even to a girl. At any rate, where is the neceffity of introducing the line laft mentioned ? If the idea of parallels cannot be obtained from the two perpendiculars alone, the additional line drawn through their extremities will certainly not make it more clear.

·Mathematical figures being in their nature complex, are capable of being defined ; and from the foregoing fimple ideas, it is eafy to define every one of them. For example, a circle is a figure having a point within it, named the *centre*, through which all the ftraight lines that can be drawn, and extended to the circumference, are equal; a furface bounded by four equal ftraight lines, and having four right angles, is termed a *fquare;* and a cube is a folid, of which all the fix furfaces are fquares.

In the inveftigation of mathematical truths, we affift the imagination, by drawing figures upon paper that refemble our ideas. There is no neceffity for a perfect refemblance: a black fpot, which in reality is a fmall round furface, ferves to reprefent a mathematical point; and a black line, which in reality is a long narrow furface, ferves to reprefent a mathematical line. When we reafon about the figures compofed of fuch lines, it is fufficient that thefe figures have fome appearance of regularity: lefs or more is of no importance; becaufe our reafoning is not founded upon them, but upon our ideas. Thus, to demonftrate that the three angles of a triangle are equal to two right angles, a triangle is drawn upon paper, in order to keep the mind fteady to its object. After tracing the fteps that lead to the conclufion, we are fatisfied that the propofition is true; being confcious that the reafoning is built upon the ideal figure, not upon that which is drawn upon the paper. And being alfo confcious, that the enquiry is carried on independent of any particular length of the fides; we are fatisfied of the univerfality of the propofition, and of its being applicable to all triangles whatever.

Numbers confidered by themfelves, abftractedly from things, make the fubject
of

of arithmetic. And with refpect both to mathematical and arithmetical reafonings, which frequently confift of many fteps, the procefs is fhortened by the invention of figns, which, by a fingle dafh of the pen, exprefs clearly what would require many words. By that means, a very long chain of reafoning is expreffed by a few fymbols; a method that contributes greatly to readinefs of comprehenfion. If in fuch reafonings words were neceffary, the mind, embarraffed with their multitude, would have great difficulty to follow any long chain of reafoning. A line drawn upon paper reprefents an ideal line, and a few fimple characters reprefent the abftract ideas of number.

Arithmetical reafoning, like mathematical, depends entirely upon the relation of equality, which can be afcertained with the greateft certainty among many ideas. Hence, reafonings upon fuch ideas afford the higheft degree of conviction. I do not fay, however, that this is always the cafe; for a man who is confcious of his own fallibility, is feldom without fome degree of diffidence, where the reafoning confifts of many fteps. And tho' on a re-

view no error be difcovered, yet he is confcious that there may be errors, tho' they
have efcaped him.

As to the other kind of demonftrative
reafoning, founded on propofitions of
which we are intuitively certain; I juftly
call it *demonftrative*, becaufe it affords the
fame conviction that arifes from mathematical reafoning. In both, the means of
conviction are the fame, viz. a clear perception of the relation between two ideas :
and there are many relations of which we
have ideas no lefs clear than of equality;
witnefs fubftance and quality, the whole
and its parts, caufe and effect, and many
others. From the intuitive propofition,
for example, That nothing which begins
to exift can exift without a caufe, I can
conclude, that fome one being muft have
exifted from all eternity, with no lefs certainty, than that the three angles of a triangle are equal to two right angles.

What falls next in order, is that inferior fort of knowledge which is termed *o-
pinion*; and which, like knowledge properly fo termed, is founded in fome inftances upon intuition, and in fome upon
reafoning. But it differs from knowledge
properly

properly fo termed in the following particular, that it produces different degrees of conviction, fometimes approaching to certainty, fometimes finking toward the verge of improbability. The conftancy and uniformity of natural operations, is a fit fubject for illuftrating that difference. The future fucceffive changes of day and night, of winter and fummer, and of other fucceffions which have hitherto been conftant and uniform, fall under intuitive knowledge, becaufe of thefe we have the higheft conviction. As the conviction is inferior of fucceffions that hitherto have varied in any degree, thefe fall under intuitive opinion. We expect fummer after winter with the utmoft confidence; but we have not the fame confidence in expecting a hot fummer or a cold winter. And yet the probability approaches much nearer to certainty, than the intuitive opinion we have, that the operations of nature are extremely fimple, a propofition that is little rely'd on.

As to opinion founded on reafoning, it is obvious, that the conviction produced by reafoning, can never rife above what is produced by the intuitive propofition up-

on

on which the reafoning is founded. And
that it may be weaker, will appear from
confidering, that even where the fundamental propofition is certain, it may lead
to the conclufive opinion by intermediate
propofitions, that are probable only, not
certain. In a word, it holds in general
with refpect to every fort of reafoning,
that the conclufive propofition can never
rife higher in point of conviction, than
the very loweft of the intuitive propofitions employ'd as fteps in the reafoning.

The perception we have of the contin-
gency of future events, opens a wide field
to our reafoning about probabilities. That
perception involves more or lefs doubt according to its fubject. In fome inftances,
the event is perceived to be extremely
doubtful; in others, it is perceived to be
lefs doubtful. It appears altogether doubtful, in throwing a dye, which of the fix
fides will turn up; and for that reafon,
we cannot juftly conclude for one rather
than for another. If one only of the fix
fides be marked with a figure, we conclude, that a blank will turn up; and five
to one is an equal wager that fuch will be
the effect. In judging of the future behaviour

haviour of a man who has hitherto been governed by intereſt, we may conclude with a probability approaching to certainty, that intereſt will continue to prevail.

Belief comes laſt in order, which, as defined above, is knowledge of the truth of facts that falls below certainty, and involves in its nature ſome degree of doubt. It is alſo of two kinds ; one founded upon intuition, and one upon reaſoning. Thus, knowledge, opinion, belief, are all of them equally diſtinguiſhable into intuitive and diſcurſive. Of intuitive belief, I diſcover three different ſources or cauſes. Firſt, A preſent object. Second, An object formerly preſent. Third, The teſtimony of others.

To have a clear conception of the firſt cauſe, it muſt be obſerved, that among the ſimple perceptions that compoſe the complex perception of a preſent object, a perception of real and preſent exiſtence is one. This perception riſes commonly to certainty ; in which caſe it is a branch of knowledge properly ſo termed ; and is handled as ſuch above. But this perception falls below certainty in ſome inſtances ; as where an object, ſeen at a

great

great diſtance or in a fog, is perceived to be a horſe, but ſo indiſtinctly as to make it a probability only. The perception in ſuch a caſe is termed *belief*. Both perceptions are fundamentally of the ſame nature; being ſimple perceptions of real exiſtence. They differ only in point of diſtinctneſs: the perception of reality that makes a branch of knowledge, is ſo clear and diſtinct as to exclude all doubt or heſitation: the perception of reality that occaſions belief, being leſs clear and diſtinct, makes not the exiſtence of the object certain to us, but only probable.

With reſpect to the ſecond cauſe; the exiſtence of an abſent object, formerly ſeen, amounts not to a certainty; and therefore is the ſubject of belief only, not of knowledge. Things are in a continual flux from production to diſſolution; and our ſenſes are accommodated to that variable ſcene: a preſent object admits no doubt of its exiſtence; but after it is removed, its exiſtence becomes leſs certain, and in time ſinks down to a ſlight degree of probability.

Human teſtimony, the third cauſe, produces belief, more or leſs ſtrong, accor-

ding

ding to circumftances. In general, nature leads us to rely upon the veracity of each other; and commonly the degree of reliance is proportioned to the degree of veracity. Sometimes belief approaches to certainty, as when it is founded on the evidence of perfons above exception as to veracity. Sometimes it finks to the loweft degree of probability, as when a fact is told by one who has no great reputation for truth. The nature of the fact, common or uncommon, has likewife an influence : an ordinary incident gains credit upon very flight evidence ; but it requires the ftrongeft evidence to overcome the improbability of an event that deviates from the ordinary courfe of nature. At the fame time, it muft be obferved, that belief is not always founded upon rational principles. There are biaffes and weakneffes in human nature that fometimes difturb the operation, and produce belief without fufficient or proper evidence : we are difpofed to believe on very flight evidence, an interefting event, however rare or fingular, that alarms and agitates the mind ; becaufe the mind in agitation is remarkably fufceptible of impreffions : for

VOL. III.   D d   which

which reafon, ftories of ghofts and apparitions pafs current with the vulgar. E-
loquence alfo has great power over the
mind; and, by making deep impreffions,
enforces the belief of facts upon evidence
that would not be regarded in a cool moment.

The dependence that our perception of
real exiftence, and confequently belief,
hath upon oral evidence, enlivens focial
intercourfe, and promotes fociety. But
the perception of real exiftence has a ftill
more extenfive influence; for from that
perception is derived a great part of the
entertainment we find in hiftory, and in
hiftorical fables (a). At the fame time, a
perception that may be raifed by fiction as
well as by truth, would often miflead were
we abandoned to its impulfe: but the
God of nature hath provided a remedy for
that evil, by erecting within the mind a
tribunal, to which there lies an appeal
from the rafh impreffions of fenfe. When
the delufion of eloquence or of dread fub-
fides, the perplexed mind is uncertain
what to believe. A regular procefs com-
mences, counfel is heard, evidence pro-

(a) Elements of Criticifin, ch. 2. part 1. § 7.

duced,

duced, and a final judgement pronounced, fometimes confirming, fometimes varying, the belief impreffed upon us by the lively perception of reality. Thus, by a wife appointment of nature, intuitive belief is fubjected to rational difcuffion : when confirmed by reafon, it turns more vigorous and authoritative ; when contradicted by reafon, it difappears among fenfible people. In fome inftances, it is too headftrong for reafon ; as in the cafe of hobgoblins and apparitions, which pafs current among the vulgar in fpite of reafon.

We proceed to the other kind of belief, that which is founded on reafoning ; to which, when intuition fails us, we muft have recourfe for afcertaining certain facts. Thus, from known effects, we infer the exiftence of unknown caufes. That an effect muft have a caufe, is an intuitive propofition ; but to afcertain what particular thing is the caufe, requires commonly a procefs of reafoning. This is one of the means by which the Deity, the primary caufe, is made known to us, as mentioned above. Reafon, in tracing caufes from known effects, produces different degrees of conviction. It fometimes

D d 2   produces

produces certainty, as in proving the existence of the Deity; which on that account is handled above, under the head of knowledge. For the moſt part it produces belief only, which, according to the ſtrength of the reaſoning, ſometimes approaches to certainty, ſometimes is ſo weak as barely to turn the ſcale on the ſide of probability. Take the following examples of different degrees of belief founded on probable reaſoning. When Inigo Jones flouriſhed and was the only architect of note in England; let it be ſuppoſed, that his model of the palace of Whitehall had been preſented to a ſtranger, without mentioning the author. The ſtranger, in the firſt place, would be intuitively certain, that this was the work of ſome Being, intelligent and ſkilful. Secondly, He would have a conviction approaching to certainty, that the operator was a man. And, thirdly, He would have a conviction that the man was Inigo Jones; but leſs firm than the former. Let us next ſuppoſe another Engliſh architect little inferior in reputation to Jones: the ſtranger would ſtill pronounce in favour of the latter; but his belief would be in the loweſt degree.

When

When we inveſtigate the cauſes of certain effects, the reaſoning is often founded
upon the known nature of man. In the
high country, for example, between E-
dinburgh and Glaſgow, the people lay
their coals at the end of their houſes,
without any fence to ſecure them from
theft : whence it is rationally inferred,
that coals are there in plenty. In the weſt
of Scotland, the corn-ſtacks are covered
with great care and nicety : whence it is
inferred, that the climate is rainy. Pla-
centia is the capital town of Biſcay : the
only town in Newfoundland bears the
ſame name ; from which circumſtance it
is conjectured, that the Biſcayners were
the firſt Europeans who made a ſettlement
in that iſland.

Analogical reaſoning, founded upon the
uniformity of nature, is frequently employ'd in the inveſtigation of facts ; and
we infer, that facts of which we are uncertain, muſt reſemble thoſe of the ſame
kind that are known. The reaſonings in
natural philoſophy are moſtly of that kind.
Take the following examples. We learn
from experience, that proceeding from the
humbleſt vegetable to man, there are numberleſs

berlefs claffes of beings rifing one above
another by differences fcarce perceptible,
and leaving no where a fingle gap or interval : and from conviction of the uniformity of nature we infer, that the line
is not broken off here, but is carried on
in other worlds, till it end in the Deity.
I proceed to another example. Every man
is confcious of a felf-motive power in
himfelf ; and from the uniformity of nature, we infer the fame power in every
one of our own fpecies. The argument
here from analogy carries great weight,
becaufe we entertain no doubt of the uniformity of nature with refpect to beings
of our own kind. We apply the fame argument to other animals ; tho' their refemblance to man appears not fo certain,
as that of one man to another. But why
not alfo apply the fame argument to infer
a felf-motive power in matter ? When we
fee matter in motion without an external
mover, we naturally infer, that, like us,
it moves itfelf. Another example is borrow'd from Maupertuis. " As there is no
" known fpace of the earth covered with
" water fo large as the *Terra Auftralis in-*
" *cognita*, we may reafonably infer, that
                                    " fo

" fo great a part of the earth is not alto-
" gether fea, but that there muft be fome
" proportion of land." The uniformity
of nature with refpect to the intermixture
of fea and land, is an argument that affords but a very flender degree of conviction ; and from late voyages it is difcovered, that the argument holds not in fact.
The following argument of the fame kind,
tho' it cannot be much rely'd on, feems
however better founded. " The inhabi-
" tants of the northern hemifphere, have,
" in arts and fciences, excelled fuch of the
" fouthern as we have any knowledge of:
" and therefore among the latter we ought
" not to expect many arts, nor much cul-
" tivation."

After a fatiguing inveftigation of numberlefs particulars which divide and fcatter
the thought, it may not be unpleafant to
bring all under one view by a fuccinct re-
capitulation.

We have two means for difcovering
truth and acquiring knowledge, viz. intuition and reafoning. By intuition we difcover fubjects and their attributes, paffions,
internal action, and in fhort every thing
that is matter of fact. By intuition we
alfo

alfo difcover feveral relations. There are fome facts and many relations, that cannot be difcovered by a fingle act of intuition, but require feveral fuch acts linked together in a chain of reafoning.

Knowledge acquired by intuition, includes for the moft part certainty : in fome inftances it includes probability only. Knowledge acquired by reafoning, frequently includes certainty; but more frequently includes probability only.

Probable knowledge, whether founded on intuition or on reafoning, is termed *opinion* when it concerns relations ; and is termed *belief* when it concerns facts. Where knowledge includes certainty, it retains its proper name.

.Reafoning that produces certainty, is termed *demonftrative ;* and is termed *probable*, when it only produces probability.

Demonftrative reafoning is of two kinds. The firft is, where the conclufion is derived from the nature and inherent properties of the fubject : mathematical reafoning is of that kind ; and perhaps the only inftance. The fecond is, where the conclufion is derived from fome propofition, of which we are certain by intuition.

I

Probable

Probable reasoning is endless in its varieties; and affords different degrees of conviction, depending on the nature of the subject upon which it is employ'd.

S E C T.   II.

Progress of Reason.

A Progress from infancy to maturity in the mind of man, similar to that in his body, has been often mentioned. The external senses, being early necessary for self-preservation, arrive quickly at maturity. The internal senses are of a flower growth, as well as every other mental power: their maturity would be of little or no use while the body is weak, and unfit for action. Reasoning, as observed in the first section, requires two mental powers, the power of invention, and that of perceiving relations. By the former are discovered intermediate propositions, having the same relation to the fundamental proposition and to the con-

clufion; and that relation is verified by
the latter. Both powers are neceffary to
the perfon who frames an argument, or a
chain of reafoning : the latter only, to the
perfon who judges of it. Savages are
miferably deficient in both. With refpect
to the former, a favage may have from his
nature a talent for invention ; but it will
ftand him in little ftead without a ftock of
ideas enabling him to felect what may anfwer his purpofe; and a favage has no
opportunity to acquire fuch a ftock. With
refpect to the latter, he knows little of relations. And how fhould he know, when
both ftudy and practice are neceffary for
diftinguifhing between relations ? The
underftanding, at the fame time, is a-
mong the illiterate obfequious to paffion
and prepoffeffion ; and among them the
imagination acts without control, forming conclufions often no better than mere
dreams. In fhort, confidering the many
caufes that miflead from juft reafoning,
in days efpecially of ignorance, the erroneous and abfurd opinions that have prevailed in the world, and that continue in
fome meafure to prevail, are far from being furprifing. Were reafon our only

guide

guide in the conduct of life, we fhould have caufe to complain; but our Maker has provided us with the moral fenfe, a guide little fubject to error in matters of importance. In the fciences, reafon is effential; but in the conduct of life, which is our chief concern, reafon may be an ufeful affiftant; but to be our director is not its province.

The national progrefs of reafon has been flower in Europe, than that of any other art: ftatuary, painting, architecture, and other fine arts, approach nearer perfection, as well as morality and natural hiftory. Manners and every art that appears externally, may in part be acquired by imitation and example: in reafoning there is nothing external to be laid hold of. But there is befide a particular caufe that regards Europe, which is the blind deference that for many ages was paid to Ariftotle; who has kept the reafoning faculty in chains more than two thoufand years. In his logic, the plain and fimple mode of reafoning is rejected, that which Nature dictates; and in its ftead is introduced an artificial mode, fhowy but unfubftantial, of no ufe for difcovering truth; but con-

trived with great art for wrangling and
difputation. Confidering that reafon for
fo many ages has been immured in the
enchanted caftle of fyllogifm, where phan-
toms pafs for realities ; the flow progrefs
of reafon toward maturity is far from being furprifing. The taking of Conftantinople by the Turks *ann.* 1453, unfolded
a new fcene, which in time relieved the
world from the ufurpation of Ariftotle,
and reftored reafon to her privileges. All
the knowledge of Europe was centred in
Conftantinople ; and the learned men of
that city, abhorring the Turks and their
government, took refuge in Italy. The
Greek language was introduced among the
weftern nations of Europe ; and the ftudy
of Greek and Roman claffics became fafhionable. Men, having acquired new i-
deas, began to think for themfelves : they
exerted their native faculty of reafon : the
futility of Ariftotle's logic became apparent to the penetrating ; and is now apparent to all. Yet fo late as the year 1621,
feveral perfons were banifhed from Paris
for contradicting that philofopher, about
matter and form, and about the number
of the elements. And fhortly after, the
parliament

parliament of Paris prohibited, under pain
of death, any thing to be taught contrary
to the doctrines of Ariftotle. Julius II.
and Leo X, Roman Pontiffs, contributed
zealoufly to the reformation of letters;
but they did not forefee that they were alfo contributing to the reformation of religion, and of every fcience that depends on
reafoning. Tho' the fetters of fyllogifm
have many years ago been fhaken off;
yet, like a limb long kept from motion,
the reafoning faculty has fcarcely to this
day attained its free and natural exercife.
Mathematics is the only fcience that never
has been cramped by fyllogifm, and we
find reafoning there in great perfection at
an early period. The very flow progrefs
of reafoning in other matters, will appear
from the following induction.

  To exemplify erroneous and abfurd reafonings of every fort, would be endlefs.
The reader, I prefume, will be fatisfied
with a few inftances; and I fhall endeavour to felect what are amufing. For the
fake of order, I divide them into three
heads. Firft, Inftances fhowing the imbecillity of human reafon during its nonage.
Second, Erroneous reafoning occafioned by

natural

natural biaffes. Third, Erroneous reafoning occafioned by acquired biaffes. With re-fpect to the firft, inftances are endlefs of reafonings founded on erroneous premifes. It was an Epicurean doctrine, That the gods have all of them a human figure; moved by the following argument, that no being of any other figure has the ufe of reafon. Plato, taking for granted the following erroneous propofition, That e-very being which moves itfelf muft have a foul, concludes that the world muft have a foul, becaufe it moves itfelf (*a*). Ari-ftotle taking it for granted, without the leaft evidence and contrary to truth, that all heavy bodies tend to the centre of the univerfe, proves the earth to be the centre of the univerfe by the fol-lowing argument. " Heavy bodies natu-" rally tend to the centre of the univerfe : " we know by experience that heavy " bodies tend to the centre of the earth : " therefore the centre of the earth is the " centre of the univerfe." Appion ridi-cules the Jews for adhering literally to the precept of refting on their fabbath, fo as to fuffer Jerufalem to be taken that day by

(*a*) Cicero, De natura Deorum, lib. 2. § 12.

Ptolomy

Ptolomy fon of Lagus.   Mark the anfwer
of Jofephus : " Whoever paffes a fober
" judgement on this matter, will find our
" practice agreeable to honour and vir-
" tue ; for what can be more honourable
" and virtuous, than to poftpone our
" country, and even life itfelf, to the fer-
" vice of God, and of his holy religion ?"
A ftrange idea of religion, to put it in direct oppofition to every moral principle !
A fuperftitious and abfurd doctrine, That
God will interpofe by a miracle to declare
what is right in every controverfy, has
occafioned much erroneous reafoning and
abfurd practice.   The practice of determining controverfies by fingle combat,
commenced about the feventh century,
when religion had degenerated into fuperftition, and courage was efteemed the only moral virtue.   The parliament of Paris,
in the reign of Charles VI. appointed a
fingle combat between two gentlemen, in
order to have the judgement of God whether the one had committed a rape on the
other's wife.   In the 1454, John Picard
being accufed by his fon-in-law for too
great familiarity with his wife, a duel between them was appointed by the fame
parliament.

parliament. Voltaire juftly obferves, that the parliament decreed a parricide to be committed, in order to try an accufation of inceft, which poffibly was not committed. The trials by water and by fire, reft on the fame erroneous foundation. In the former, if the perfon accufed funk to the bottom, it was a judgement pronounced by God that he was innocent: if he kept above, it was a judgement that he was guilty. Fleury (a) remarks, that if ever the perfon accufed was found guilty, it was his own fault. In Sicily, a woman accufed of adultery, was compelled to fwear to her innocence: the oath, taken down in writing, was laid on water; and if it did not fink, the woman was innocent. We find the fame practice in Japan, and in Malabar. One of the articles infifted on by the reformers in Scotland, was, That public prayers be made and the facraments adminiftered in the vulgar tongue. The anfwer of a provincial council was in the following words: " That to " conceive public prayers or adminifter " the facraments in any language but La- " tin, is contrary to the traditions and

(a) Hiftoire Ecclefiaftique.

2   " practice

" practice of the Catholic church for
" many ages paft; and that the demand
" cannot be granted, without impiety to
" God and difobedience to the church."
Here it is taken for granted, that the practice of the church is always right; which
is building an argument on a very rotten
foundation.   The Caribbeans abftain
from fwines flefh; taking it erroneoufly
for granted, that fuch food would make
them have fmall eyes, held by them a
great deformity.   They alfo abftain from
eating turtle; which they think would in-
fect them with the lazinefs and ftupidity
of that animal.   Upon the fame erroneous
notion, the Brafilians abftain from the
flefh of ducks, and of every creature that
moves flowly.   It is obferved of northern
nations, that they do not open the mouth
fufficiently for diftinct articulation; and
the reafon given is, that the coldnefs of
the air makes them keep the mouth as
clofe as poffible.   This reafon is indolently
copied by writers one from another: people enured to a cold climate feel little cold
in the mouth; befide that a caufe fo weak
could never operate equally among fo
many different nations.   The real caufe is,

that northern tongues abound with confo-
nants, which admit but a fmall aperture
of the mouth. (See Elements of Criticifm,
chap. Beauty of language). A lift of German names to be found in every catalogue
of books, will make this evident, *Rutger-
fius*, for example, *Faefch*. To account for
a fact that is certain, any reafon commonly fuffices.

A talent for writing feems in Germany
to be eftimated by weight, as beauty is
faid to be in Holland. Cocceius for writing three weighty folio volumes on law,
has obtained among his countrymen the
epithet of *Great*. This author, handling
the rules of fucceffion in land-eftates, has
with moft profound erudition founded all
of them upon the following very fimple
propofition : In a competition, that de-
fcendent is entitled to be preferred who
has the greateft quantity of the predeceffor's blood in his veins. *Quæritur*, has a
man any of his predeceffor's blood in his
veins, otherwife than metaphorically ?
Simple indeed ! to build an argument in
law upon a pure metaphor.

Next of reafonings where the conclufion
follows not from the premifes, or fundamental

mental propofition. Plato endeavours to prove, that the world is endowed with wifdom, by the following argument. " The world is greater than any of its " parts: therefore it is endowed with wif- " dom ; for otherwife a man who is en- " dowed with wifdom would be greater " than the world (*a*)." The conclufion here does not follow ; for tho' man is en- dowed with wifdom, it follows not, that he is greater than the world in point of fize. Zeno endeavours to prove, that the world has the ufe of reafon, by an argu- ment of the fame kind. To convince the world of the truth of the four gofpels, I- reneus (*b*) urges the following arguments, which he calls demonftration. " There " are four quarters of the world and four " cardinal winds, confequently there are " four gofpels in the church, as there are " four pillars that fupport it, and four " breaths of life that render it immortal." Again, " The four animals in Ezekiel's " vifion mark the four ftates of the Son " of God. The lion is his royal dignity :

(*a*) Cicero, De natura Deorum, lib 2. § 12.

(*b*) Lib. 3. cap. 11.

" the

" the calf, his priefthood : the beaft with
" the face of man, his human nature :
" the eagle, his fpirit which defcends on
" the church. To thefe four animals cor-
" refpond the four gofpels, on which our
" Lord is feated. John, who teaches his
" celeftial origin, is the lion, his gofpel
" being full of confidence ; Luke, who
" begins with the priefthood of Zachariah,
" is the calf : Matthew, who defcribes
" the genealogy of Chrift according to the
" flefh, is the animal refembling a man :
" Mark, who begins with the prophetic
" fpirit coming from above, is the eagle.
" This gofpel is the fhorteft of all, becaufe
" brevity is the character of prophecy."
Take a third demonftration of the truth of the
four gofpels. " There have been four cove-
" nants ; the firft under Adam, the fecond
" under Noah, the third under Mofes, the
" fourth under Jefus Chrift." Whence
Irenæus concludes, that they are vain,
rafh, and ignorant, who admit more or
lefs than four gofpels. St Cyprian in his
exhortation to martyrdom, after having
applied the myfterious number feven, to
the feven days of the creation, to the feven
thoufand years of the world's duration, to
the

the feven fpirits that ftand before God, to the feven lamps of the tabernacle, to the feven candlefticks of the Apocalypfe, to the feven pillars of wifdom, to the feven children of the barren woman, to the feven women who took one man for their hufband, to the feven brothers of the Maccabees; obferves, that St Paul mentions that number as a privileged number; which, fays he, is the reafon why he did not write but to feven churches. Pope Gregory, writing in favour of the four councils, viz. Nice, Conftantinople, Ephefus, and Calcedon, reafons thus: " That as there " are four evangelifts, there ought alfo to " be four councils." What would he have faid, if he had lived 100 years later, when there were many more than four? In adminiftering the facrament of the Lord's fupper, it was ordered, that the hoft fhould be covered with a clean linen cloth; becaufe, fays the Canon law, the body of our Lord Jefus Chrift was buried in a clean linen cloth. Jofephus, in his anfwer to Appion, urges the following argument for the temple of Jerufalem: " As there " is but one God, and one world, it holds " in analogy, that there fhould be but one " temple."

" temple." At that rate, there fhould be but one worfhipper. And why fhould that one temple be at Jerufalem rather than at Rome, or at Pekin? The Syrians and Greeks did not for a long time eat fifh. Two reafons are affigned: one is, that fifh is not facrificed to the gods; the other, that being immerfed in the fea, they look not up to heaven (a). The firft would afford a more plaufible argument for eating fifh. And if the other have any weight, it would be an argument for facrificing men, and neither fifh nor cattle. In juftification of the Salic law, which prohibits female fucceffion, it was long held a conclufive argument, That in the fcripture the lilies are faid neither to work nor to fpin. Vieira, termed by his countrymen *the Lufitanian Cicero*, publifhed fermons, one of which begins thus, " Were " the Supreme Being to fhow himfelf vi- " fibly, he would chufe the circle rather " than the triangle, the fquare, the pen- " tagon, the duodecagon, or any other " figure." But why appear in any of thefe figures? And if he were obliged to appear in fo mean a fhape, a globe is un-

(a) Sir John Marfham, p. 221.

doubtedly

doubtedly more beautiful than a circle. Peter Hantz of Horn, who lived in the laft century, imagined that Noah's ark is the true conftruction of a fhip; " which," faid he, " is the workmanfhip of God, " and therefore perfect;" as if a veffel made merely for floating on the water, were the beft alfo for failing. Sixty or feventy years ago, the fashion prevailed, in imitation of birds, to fwallow fmall ftones for the fake of digeftion; as if what is proper for birds, were equally proper for men. The Spaniards, who laid wafte a great part of the Weft Indies, endeavoured to excufe their cruelties, by maintaining, that the natives were not men, but a fpecies of the Ouran Outang; for no better reafon, than that they were of a copper colour, fpoke an unknown language, and had no beard. The Pope iffued a bull, declaring, that it pleafed him and the Holy Ghoft to acknowledge the Americans to be of the human race. This bull was not received cordially; for in the council of Lima, *ann.* 1583, it was violently difputed, whether the Americans had fo much underftanding as to be admitted to the facraments of the church.

In

In the 1440, the Portuguefe folicited the Pope's permiffion to double the Cape of Good Hope, and to reduce to perpetual fervitude the negroes, becaufe they had the colour of the damned, and never went to church. In the Frederician Code, a propofition is laid down, That by the law of nature no man can make a teftament. And in fupport of that propofition the following argument is urged, which is faid to be a demonftration: " No deed " can be a teftament while a man is alive, " becaufe it is not neceffarily his *ultima* " *voluntas ;* and no man can make a te- " ftament after his death." Both pre- mifes are true, but the negative conclu- fion does not follow: it is true a man's deed is not his *ultima voluntas*, while he is alive: but does it not become his *ultima voluntas*, when he dies without altering the deed ?

Many reafonings have paffed current in the world as good coin, where the premi- fes are not true; nor, fuppofing them true, would they infer the conclufion. Plato in his Phœdon relies on the follow- ing argument for the immortality of the foul. " Is not death the oppofite of life ?

I   " Certainly.

" Certainly. And do they not give birth
" to each other? Certainly. What then
" is produced from life? Death. And
" what from death? Life. It is then
" from the dead that all things living
" proceed; and confequently fouls exift
" after death." God, fays Plato, made
but five worlds, becaufe according to his
definition there are but five regular bodies
in geometry. Is that a reafon for confi-
ning the Almighty to five worlds, not one
lefs or more. Ariftotle, who wrote a book
upon mechanics, was much puzzled about
the equilibrium of a balance, when un-
equal weights are hung upon it at different
diftances from the centre. Having obferved, that the arms of the balance defcribe portions of a circle, he accounted
for the equilibrium by a notable argument: " All the properties of the circle are
" wonderful: the equilibrium of the two
" weights that defcribe portions of a circle
" is wonderful. *Ergo,* the equilibrium
" muft be one of the properties of the
" circle." What are we to think of Ariftotle's logic, when we find him capable
of fuch childifh reafoning? And yet that
work has been the admiration of all the

world for centuries upon centuries. Nay, that foolish argument has been espoused and commented upon by his disciples, for the same length of time. To proceed to another instance: 'Marriage within the fourth degree of consanguinity, as well as of affinity, is prohibited by the Lateran council; and the reason given is, That the body being made up of the four elements, has four different humours in it *. The Roman Catholics began with beheading heretics, hanging them, or stoning them to death. But such punishments were discovered to be too slight, in matters of faith. It was demonstrated, that heretics ought to be burnt in a slow fire: it being taken for granted, that God punishes them in the other world with a slow fire; it was inferred, " That as every prince

---

* The original is curious: " Quaternarius enim
" numerus bene congruit prohibitioni conjugii cor-
" poralis; de quo dicit Apostolus, Quod vir non
" habet potestatem sui corporis, sed mulier; neque
" mulier habet potestatem sui corporis, sed vir;
" quia quatuor sunt humores in corpore, quod
" constat ex quatuor elementis." Were men who could be guilty of · such nonsense, qualified to be our leaders in the most important of all concerns, that of eternal salvation ?

" and

" and every magiftrate is the image of
" God in this world, they ought to follow
" his example." Here is a double error in
reafoning: firft, the taking for granted
the fundamental propofition, which is
furely not felf-evident ; and next, the
drawing a conclufion from it without any
connection. The heat of the fun, by the reflection of its rays from the earth, is greatly
encreafed in paffing over the great country
of Africa. Hence rich mines of gold,
and the black complexion of the inhabitants. In paffing over the Atlantic it is
cooled : and by the time it reaches the
continent of America, it has loft much of
its vigour. Hence no gold on the eaft fide
of America. But being heated again in
paffing over a great fpace of land, it produces much gold in Peru. Is not this reafoning curious ? What follows is no lefs
fo. Huetius Bifhop of Auvranches, de-
claiming againft the vanity of eftablifhing
a perpetual fucceffion of defcendents, obferves, that other writers had expofed it
upon moral principles, but that he would
cut it down with a plain metaphyfical argument. " Father and fon are relative
" ideas ; and the relation is at an end by

G g 2   " the

" the death of either.   My will therefore
" to leave my eſtate to my ſon, is abſurd;
" becauſe after my death, he is no longer
" my ſon."   By the ſame ſort of argument he demonſtrates the vanity of fame.
" The relation that ſubſiſts between a man
" and his character, is at an end by his
" death : and therefore, that the charac-
" ter given him by the world, belongs not
" to him nor to any perſon."   Huetius is
not the only writer who has urged meta-
phyſical arguments contrary to common
ſenſe.

It once was a general opinion among
thoſe who dwelt near the ſea, that people
never die but during the ebb of the tide.
And there were not wanting plauſible reaſons.   The ſea, in flowing, carries with
it vivifying particles that recruit the ſick.
The ſea is ſalt, and ſalt preſerves from
rottenneſs.   When the ſea ſinks in ebbing,
every think ſinks with it : nature lan-
guiſhes : the ſick are not vivified : they
die.

What ſhall be ſaid of a reaſoning where
the concluſion is a flat contradiction to the
premiſes ? If a man ſhooting at a wild
pigeon happen unfortunately to kill his
neighbour,

neighbour, it is in the Englifh law excu-
fable homicide ; becaufe the fhooting an
animal that is no man's property, is a lawful act. If the aim be at a tame fowl for
amufement, which is a trefpafs on the
property of another, the death of the man
is manflaughter. If the tame fowl be fhot
in order to be ftolen, it is murder, by
reafon of the felonious intent. From this
laft the following confequence is drawn,
that if a man, endeavouring to kill another, miffes his blow and happeneth to kill
himfelf, he is in judgement of law guilty
of wilful and deliberate felf-murder (a).
Strange reafoning ! to conftrue an act to
be wilful and deliberate felf-murder, contrary to the very thing that is fuppofed.

A plentiful fource of inconclufive reafoning, which prevails greatly during the
infancy of the rational faculty, is the making of no proper diftinction between
ftrong and weak relations. Minutius Fe-
lix, in his apology for the Chriftians, endeavours to prove the unity of the Deity
from a moft diftant analogy or relation,
" That there is but one king of the bees,

(a) Hale, Pleas of the Crown, cap. 1. 413.

" and

" and that more than one chief magiſtrate
" would breed confuſion." It is a proſti-
tution of reaſon to offer ſuch an argument
for the unity of the Deity. But any argument paſſes current, in ſupport of a
propoſition that we know beforehand to
be true. Plutarch ſays, " that it ſeemed
" to have happened by the peculiar direc-
" tion of the gods, that Numa was born
" on the 21ſt of April, the very day in
" which Rome was founded by Romu-
" lus ;" a very childiſh inference from a
mere accident. Suppoſing Italy to have
been tolerably populous, as undoubtedly
it was at that period, the 21ſt of April, or
any day of April, might have given birth
to thouſands. In many countries, the
furgeons and barbers are claſſed together,
as members of the ſame trade, from a
very ſlight relation, that both of them o-
perate upon the human body. The Jews
enjoy'd the reputation, for centuries, of
being ſkilful phyſicians. Francis I. of
France, having long laboured under a diſeaſe that eluded the art of his own phyſicians, apply'd to the Emperor Charles V.
for a Jewiſh phyſician from Spain. Finding that the perſon ſent had been converted

ed to Chriſtianity, the King refuſed to employ him; as if a Jew were to loſe his
ſkill upon being converted to Chriſtianity.
Why did not the King order one of his
own phyſicians to be converted to Juda-
iſm? The following childiſh argument is
built upon an extreme ſlight relation, that
between our Saviour and the wooden croſs
he ſuffered on. " Believe me," ſays Julius Firmicus, " that the devil omits no-
" thing to deſtroy miſerable mortals;
" converting himſelf into every different
" form, and employing every ſort of arti-
" fice. He appoints wood to be uſed in
" ſacrificing to him, knowing that our
" Saviour, fixed to the croſs, would be-
" ſtow immortality upon all his followers.
" A pine-tree is cut down, and uſed in
" ſacrificing to the mother of the gods.
" A wooden image of Oſiris is buried in
" ſacrificing to Iſis. A wooden image of
" Proſerpina is bemoaned for forty nights,
" and then thrown into the flames. De-
" luded mortals, theſe flames can do you
" no ſervice. On the contrary, the fire
" that is deſtined for your puniſhment
" rages without end. Learn from me to
" know that divine wood which will ſet
                                    " you

" you free. A wooden ark faved the hu-
" man race from the univerfal deluge.
" Abraham put wood upon the fhoulders
" of his fon Ifaac. The wooden rod
" ftretched out by Aaron brought the
" children of Ifrael out of the land of E-
" gypt. Wood fweetened the bitter wa-
" ters of Marah, and comforted the chil-
" dren of Ifrael after wandering three
" days without water. A wooden rod
" ftruck water out of the rock. The rod
" of God in the hand of Mofes overcame
" Amalek. The patriarch dreamed, that
" he faw angels defcending and afcending
" upon a wooden ladder: and the law of
" God was inclofed in a wooden ark.
" Thefe things were exhibited, that, as if
" it were by certain fteps, we might a-
" fcend to the wood of the crofs, which
" is our falvation. The wood of the
" crofs fuftains the heavenly machine,
" fupports the foundations of the earth,
" and leads men to eternal life. The
" wood of the devil burns and perifhes,
" and its afhes carries down finners to the
" loweft pit of hell." The very flighteft
relations make an impreffion on a weak
underftanding. It was a fancy of Anto-

2   ninus

ninus Geta, in ordering his table, to have
fervices compofed of difhes beginning with
the fame letter; fuch as lamb and lobfter;
broth, beef, blood-pudding; pork, plumb-
cake, pigeons, potatoes. The name of
John king of Scotland was changed into
Robert, for no better reafon than that the
Johns of France and of England had been
unfortunate.

In reafoning, inftances are not rare, of
miftaking the caufe for the effect, and the
effect for the caufe. When a ftone is
thrown from the hand, the continuance
of its motion in the air, was once univerfally accounted for as follows : " That the
" air follows the ftone at the heels, and
" pufhes it on." The effect here is miftaken for the caufe : the air indeed follows
the ftone at the heels; but it only fills the
vacuity made by the ftone, and does not
pufh it on. It has been flyly urged a-
gainft the art of phyfic, that phyficians are
rare among temperate people, fuch as have
no wants but thofe of nature; and that
where phyficians abound, difeafes abound.
This is miftaking the caufe for the effect,
and the effect for the caufe : people in
health have no occafion for a phyfician;

but indolence and luxury beget difeafes, and difeafes beget phyficians.

During the nonage of reafon, men are fatisfied with words merely, inftead of an argument. A fea-profpect is charming; but we foon tire of an unbounded profpect. It would not give fatisfaction to fay, that it is too extenfive; for why fhould not a profpect be relifhed, however extenfive? But employ a foreign term and fay, that it is *trop vafte*, we enquire no farther: a term that is not familiar, makes an impreffion, and captivates weak reafon. This obfervation accounts for a mode of writing formerly in common ufe, that of ftuffing our language with Latin words and phrafes. Thefe are now laid afide as ufelefs; becaufe a proper emphafis in reading, makes an impreffion deeper than any foreign term can do.

There is one proof of the imbecillity of human reafon in dark times, which would fcarce be believed, were not the fact fupported by inconteftable evidence. Inftead of explaining any natural appearance by fearching for a caufe, it has been common to account for it by inventing a fable, which gave fatisfaction without enquiring farther.

farther. For example, inftead of giving
the true caufe of the fucceffion of day and
night, the facred book of the Scandinavians,
termed *Edda*, accounts for that fucceffion
by a tale : " The giant Nor had a daugh-
" ter named *Night*, of a dark complexion.
" She was wedded to Daglingar, of the
" family of the gods. They had a male
" child, which they named *Day*, beauti-
" ful and fhining like all of his father's
" family. The univerfal father took
" Night and Day, placed them in heaven,
" and gave to each a horfe and a car, that
" they might travel round the world, the
" one after the other. Night goes firft
" upon her horfe named *Rimfaxe*, [Frofty
" Mane], who moiftens the earth with the
" foam that drops from his bit, which is
" the dew. The horfe belonging to Day is
" named *Skinfaxe*, [Shining Mane], who by
" his radiant mane illuminates the air and
" the earth." It is obferved by the tranf-
lator of the Edda, that this way of accounting for things is well fuited to the
turn of the human mind, endowed with
curiofity that is keen ; but eafily fatisfied,
often with words inftead of ideas. Zoroa-
fter, by a fimilar fable, accounts for the

growth of evil in this world.   He invents
a good and an evil principle named *Oromazes* and *Arimanes*, who are in continual
conflict for preference.   At the laft day,
Oromazes will be reunited to the fupreme
God, from whom he iffued. Arimanes
will be fubdued, darknefs deftroyed ; and
the world, purified by an univerfal confla-
gration, will become a luminous and fhining abode, from which evil will be excluded.   I return to the Edda, which is
ftored with fables of this kind.   The higheft notion favages can form of the gods, is
that of men endowed with extraordinary
power and knowledge.   The only puzzling
circumftance is, how they differ fo much
from other men as to be immortal.   The
Edda accounts for it by the following
fable.   " The gods prevented the effect of
" old age and decay, by eating certain
" apples, trufted to the care of *Iduna*.
" *Loke*, the Momus of the Scandinavians,
" craftily convey'd away *Iduna*, and con-
" cealed her in a wood, under the cufto-
" dy of a giant.   The gods, beginning
" to wax old and gray, detected the au-
" thor of the theft ; and, by terrible me-
" naces, compelled him to employ his ut-
" moft

" moft cunning, for regaining Iduna and
" her apples, in which he was fuccefsful."
The origin of poetry is thus accounted for
in the fame work: " The gods formed
" *Cuafer*, who traverfed the earth, teach-
" ing wifdom to men. He was treacher-
" oufly flain by two dwarfs, who mixed
" honey with his blood, and compofed a
" liquor that renders all who drink of it
" poets. Thefe dwarfs having incurred
" the refentment of a certain giant, were
" expofed by him upon a rock, furround-
" ed on all fides with the fea. They gave
" for their ranfom the faid liquor, which
" the giant delivered to his daughter *Gun-*
" *loda.* The precious potion was eagerly
" fought for by the gods ; but how were
" they to come at it ? *Odin*, in the fhape
" of a worm, crept through a crevice in-
" to the cavern where the liquor was con-
" cealed. Then refuming his natural
" fhape, and obtaining Gunloda's confent
" to take three draughts, he fucked up
" the whole ; and, transforming himfelf
" into an eagle, flew away to *Afgard.* The
" giant, who was a magician, flew with
" all fpeed after Odin, and came up with
" him near the gate of *Afgard.* The gods
                              " iffued

" iffued out of their palaces to affift their
" mafter ; and prefented to him all the
" pitchers they could lay hands on, which
" he inftantly filled with the precious li-
" quor. But in the hurry of difcharging
" his load, Odin poured only part of the
" liquor through his beak, the reft being
" emitted through a lefs pure vent. The
" former is beftow'd by the gods upon
" good poets, to infpire them with divine
" enthufiafm. The latter, which is in
" much greater plenty, is beftow'd libe-
" rally on all who apply for it ; by which
" means the world is peftered with an
" endlefs quantity of wretched verfes."
Ignorance is equally credulous in all ages.
Albert, furnamed *the Great*, flourifhed in
the thirteenth century, and was a man of
real knowledge. During the courfe of his
education he was remarkably dull ; and
fome years before he died became a fort of
changeling. That fingularity produced
the following ftory. The holy Virgin,
appearing to him, demanded, whether he
would excel in philofophy or in theology :
upon his chufing the former, fhe promifed,
that he fhould become an incomparable
philofopher ; but added, that to punifh
him

him for not preferring theology, he fhould become ftupid again as at firft.

Upon a flight view, it may appear un-accountable, that even the groffeft favages fhould take a childifh tale for a folid rea-fon. But nature aids the deception: where things are related in a lively man-ner, and every circumftance appears as paffing in our fight, we take all for grant-ed as true (*a*). Can an ignorant ruftic doubt of infpiration, when he fees as it were the poet fipping the pure celeftial li-quor? And how can that poet fail to produce bad verfes, who feeds on the ex-crements that drop from the fundament even of a deity?

In accounting for natural appearances, even good writers have betray'd a weak-nefs in reafoning, little inferior to that a-bove mentioned. They do not indeed put off their difciples with a tale; but they put them off with a mere fuppofition, not more real than the tale. Defcartes afcribes the motion of the planets to a vortex of ether whirling round and round. He thought not of enquiring whether there really be fuch a vortex, nor what makes

(*a*) Elements of Criticifm, vol. 1. p. 100. edit. 5.

it move. M. Buffon forms the earth out of a fplinter of the fun, ftruck off by a comet. May not one be permitted humbly to enquire at that eminent philofopher, what formed the comet? This paffes for folid reafoning; and yet we laugh at the poor Indian, who fupports the earth from falling by an elephant, and the elephant by a tortoife.

It is ftill more ridiculous to reafon upon what is acknowledged to be a fiction, as if it were real. Such are the fictions admitted in the Roman law. A Roman taken captive in war, loft his privilege of being a Roman citizen; for freedom was held effential to that privilege. But what if he made his efcape after perhaps an hour's detention? The hardfhip in that cafe ought to have fuggefted an alteration of the law, fo far as to fufpend the privilege no longer than the captivity fubfifted. But the ancient Romans were not fo ingenious. They remedied the hardfhip by a fiction, that the man never had been a captive. The Frederician code banifhes from the law of Pruffia an endlefs number of fictions found in the Roman law (a). Yet

(a) Preface, § 28.

afterward,

afterward, treating of perfonal rights, it is laid down as a rule, That a child in the womb is feigned or fuppofed to be born when the fiction is for its advantage (*a*). To a weak reafoner, a fiction is a happy contrivance for refolving intricate queftions. Such is the conftitution of England, that the Englifh law-courts are merely territorial; and that no fact happening abroad comes under their cognifance. An Englifhman, after murdering his fellow-traveller in France, returns to his native country. What is to be done, for guilt ought not to pafs unpunifhed? The crime is feigned to have been committed in England.

Ancient hiftories are full of incredible facts that paffed current during the infancy of reafon, which at prefent would be rejected with contempt. Every one who is converfant in the hiftory of ancient nations, can recall inftances without end. Does any perfon believe at prefent, tho' gravely reported by hiftorians, that in old Rome there was a law, for cutting into pieces the body of a bankrupt, and diftri-

(*a*) Part 1. book 1. title 4. § 4.

buting the parts among his creditors?
The ſtory of Porſenna and Scevola is
highly romantic; and the ſtory of Vam-
pires in Hungary, ſhamefully abſurd.
There is no reaſon to believe, there ever
was ſuch a ſtate as that of the Amazons;
and the ſtory of Thaleſtris and Alexander
the Great is certainly a fiction. Scotch
hiſtorians deſcribe gravely and circum-
ſtantially the battle of Luncarty, as if they
had been eye-witneſſes. A peaſant and
his two ſons, it is ſaid, were ploughing in
an adjacent field, during the heat of the
action. Enraged at their countrymen for
turning their backs, they broke the plough
in pieces; and each laying hold of a part,
ruſhed into the midſt of the battle, and
obtained a complete victory over the
Danes. This ſtory has every mark of
fiction: A man following out unconcern-
edly his ordinary occupation of ploughing,
in ſight of a battle, on which depended
his wife and children, his goods, and perhaps his own life: three men, without
rank or figure, with only a ſtick in the
hand of each, ſtemming the tide of victory, and turning the fate of battle. I
mention not that a plough was unknown

in

in Scotland for a century or two after that battle; for that circumftance could not create a doubt in the hiftorian, if he was ignorant of it.

Reafon, with refpect to its progrefs, is fingular. Morals, manners, and every thing that appears externally, may in part be acquired by imitation and example; which have not the flighteft influence upon the reafoning faculty. The only means for advancing that faculty to maturity, are indefatigable ftudy and practice; and even thefe will not carry a man one ftep beyond the fubjects he is converfant about: examples are not rare of men extremely expert in one fcience, and grofsly deficient in others. Many able mathematicians are novices in politics, and even in the common arts of life: ftudy and practice have ripened them in every relation of equality, while they remain ignorant, like the vulgar, about other relations. A man, in like manner, who has beftow'd much time and thought in political matters, may be a child as to other branches of knowledge *.

I

---

* Pafcal, the celebrated author of *Lettres Pro-*

I proceed to the fecond article, containing erroneous reafoning occafioned by natural biaffes.   The firft bias I fhall, mention has an extenfive influence.   What is
feen, makes a deeper impreffion than what
is reported, or difcovered by reflection.
Hence it is, that in judging of right and
wrong, the ignorant and illiterate are
ftruck with the external act only, without
penetrating into will or intention which
lie out of fight.   Thus with refpect to co-
venants, laws, vows, and other acts that
are completed by words, the whole weight
in days of ignorance is laid upon the external expreffion, with no regard to the
meaning of the fpeaker or writer.   The
bleffing beftow'd by Ifaac upon his fon

vinciales, in order to explain the infinity and indivifi-
bility of the Deity, has the following words. " I will
" fhow you a thing both infinite and indivifible.   It
" is a point moving with infinite celerity: that point
" is in all places at once, and entire in every place."
What an abfurdity, fays Voltaire, to afcribe motion
to a mathematical point, that has no exiftence but
in the mind of the geometer ! that it can be every
where at the fame inftant, and that it can move with
infinite celerity I as if infinite celerity could actually
exift.   Every word, adds he, is big with abfurdity ;
and yet he was a great man who uttered that ftuff.

Jacob,

Jacob, miftaking him for Efau, is an illuftrious inftance.   Not only was the bleffing intended for Efau, but Jacob, by de-
ceiving his father, had rendered himfelf
unworthy of it (*a*);   yet Ifaac had pronounced the founds, and it was not in his
power to unfay them : *Nefcit vox emiſſa
reverti* *.   Joſhua, grofsly impofed on
by the Gibeonites denying that they were
Canaanites, made a covenant with them ;
and yet, tho' he found them to be Canaanites, he held himfelf to be bound.   Led
by the fame bias, people think it fufficient
to fulfil the words of a vow, however
fhort of intention.   The Duke of Lanca-
fter, vexed at the obftinate refiftance of
Rennes, a town in Britany, vowed in
wrath not to raife the fiege till he had
planted the Englifh colours upon one of
the gates.   He found it neceſſary to raife
the fiege ; but his vow ftood in the way.
The governor relieved him from his

---

* Many more are killed by a fall from a horfe or
by a fever, than by thunder.   Yet we are much
more afraid of the latter.   It is the found that ter-
rifies ; tho' every man knows that the danger is o-
ver when he hears the found.

(*a*) Genefis, chap. 27.

fcruple,

scruple, permitting him to plant his colours upon one of the gates ; and he was
satisfied that his vow was fulfilled. The
following is an example of an absurd conclusion deduced from a precept taken literally, against common sense. We are ordered by the Apostle, to pray always ;
from which Jerom, one of the fathers, argues thus : " Conjugal enjoyment is in-
" consistent with praying ; *ergo*, conjugal
" enjoyment is a sin." By the same argument it may be proved, that eating and
drinking are sins ; and that sleeping is a
great sin, being a great interruption to
praying. With respect to another text,
" That a bishop must be blameless, the
" husband of one wife" taken literally, a
very different conclusion is drawn in A-
byssinia, That no man can be ordained a
presbyter till he be married. Prohibitions
have been interpreted in the same shallow
manner. Lord Clarendon gives two instances, both of them relative to the great
fire of London. The mayor proposing to
pull down a house in order to stop the progress of the fire, was opposed by the lawyers, who declared the act to be unlawful ;
and the house was burnt without being
pulled

pulled down. About the fame time it was propofed to break open fome houfes in the temple for faving the furniture, the poffeffors being in the country; but it was declared burglary to force open a door without confent of the poffeffor. Such literal interpretation, contrary to common fenfe, has been extended even to inflict punifhment. Ifadas was bathing when the alarm was given in Lacedemon, that Epaminondas was at hand with a numerous army. Naked as he was, he rufhed againft the enemy with a fpear in one hand and a fword in the other, bearing down all before him. The Ephori fined him for going to battle unarmed; but honoured him with a garland for his gallant behaviour. How abfurd to think that the law was intended for fuch a cafe! and how much more abfurd to think, that the fame act ought to be both punifhed and rewarded! The King of Caftile being carried off his horfe by a hunted hart, was faved by a perfon at hand, who cut his belt. The judges thought a pardon abfolutely requifite, to relieve from capital punifhment a man who had lifted a fword

againft

againſt his, ſovereign *. It is a ſalutary regulation, that a man who is abſent cannot be tried for his life. Pope Formoſus died ſuddenly without ſuffering any puniſhment for his crimes. He was raiſed from his grave, dreſſed in his pontifical habit; and in that ſhape a criminal procefs went on againſt him. Could it ſeriouſly be thought, that a rotten carcaſe brought into court was ſufficient to fulfil the law? The ſame abſurd farce was play'd in Scotland, upon the body of Logan of Reſtalrig, ſeveral years after his interment. The body of Tancred King of Sicily was raiſed from the grave, and the head cut off for ſuppoſed rebellion. Henry IV. of Caſtile was depoſed in abſence; but, for a colour of juſtice, the following ridiculous ſcene was acted. A wooden ſtatue dreſſed in a royal habit, was placed on a theatre; and the ſentence of depoſition was ſolemnly

* A perſon unacquainted with the hiſtory of law, will imagine that Swift has carried beyond all bounds his ſatire againſt lawyers, in ſaying, that Gulliver had incurred a capital puniſhment, for ſaving the Emperor's palace by piſſing out the fire; it being capital in any perſon of what quality ſoever, to make water within the precincts of the palace.

read to it, as if it had been the King himfelf.   The Archbifhop of Toledo feized
the crown, another the fceptre, a third
the fword ; and the ceremony was concluded with proclaiming another king.
How humbling are fuch fcenes to man,
who values himfelf upon the faculty of
reafon as his prime attribute !   An expedient of that kind would now be rejected
with difdain, as fit only to amufe children ;   and yet it grieves me to obferve
that law-proceedings are not yet totally
purged of fuch abfurdities.   By a law in
Holland, the criminal's confeffion is effential to a capital punifhment, no other
evidence being held fufficient : and yet if
he infift on his innocence, he is tortured
till he pronounce the words of confeffion ;
as if founds merely were fufficient, without will or intention.   The practice of
England in a fimilar cafe, is no lefs abfurd.   Confeffion is not there required ;
but it is required, that the perfon accufed
fhall plead, and fay whether he be innocent or guilty.   But what if he ftand
mute ?   He is preffed down by weights
till he plead ; and if he continue mute, he
is preffed till he give up the ghoft, a tor-

ture known by the name of *Peine forte et dure* *. Further, law copying religion, has exalted ceremonies above the fubftantial part. In England, fo ftrictly has form been adhered to, as to make the moft trivial defect in words fatal, however certain the meaning be. *Murdredavit* for *murdravit*, *feloniter* for *felonice*, have been adjudged to vitiate an indictment. *Burgariter* for *burglariter* hath been a fatal objection ; but *burgulariter* hath been holden good. Webfter being indicted for murder, and the ftroke being laid " finiftro " *bracio*" inftead of " *brachio*," he was difmiffed. *A. B. alias dictus A. C. Butcher*, was found to vitiate the indictment ; becaufe it ought to have been *A. B. Butcher*, *alias dictus A. C. Butcher*. So *gladium in dextra fua*, without *manu*.

No bias in human nature is more prevalent than a defire to anticipate futurity, by being made acquainted beforehand

---

* Since the above was written, the parliament has enacted, That perfons arraigned for felony or piracy, who ftand mute, or refufe to anfwer directly to the indictment, fhall be held as confeffing, and judgement fhall pafs againft them, as if they had been convicted by verdict or confeffion.

with

with what will happen. It was indulged without referve in dark times; and hence omens, auguries, dreams, judicial aftrology, oracles, and prophecies, without end. It fhows ftrange weaknefs not to fee, that fuch foreknowledge would be a gift more pernicious to man than Pandora's box: it would deprive him of every motive to action; and leave no place for fagacity, nor for contriving means to bring about a defired event. Life is an enchanted caftle, opening to interefting views that inflame the imagination and excite induftry. Remove the vail that hides futurity. —To an active, buftling, animating fcene, fucceeds a dead ftupor, men converted into ftatues; paffive like inert matter, becaufe there remains not a fingle motive to action. Anxiety about futurity roufes our fagacity to prepare for what may happen; but an appetite to know what fagacity cannot difcover, is a weaknefs in nature inconfiftent with every rational principle *.

---

* Foreknowledge of future events, differs widely from a conviction, that all events are fixed and immutable: the latter leaves us free to activity; the former annihilates all activity.

Propenfity to things rare and wonderful, is a natural bias no lefs univerfal than the former. Any ftrange or unaccountable e- vent roufes the attention, and enflames the mind: we fuck it in greedily, wifh it to be true, and believe it to be true upon the flighteft evidence (a). A hart taken in the foreft of Senlis by Charles VI. of France, bore a collar upon which was infcribed, *Cæfar hoc me donavit* *. Every one belie- ved that a Roman Emperor was meant, and that the beaft muft have lived at leaft a thoufand years; overlooking that the Emperor of Germany is alfo ftyled *Cæfar*, and that it was not neceffary to go back fifty years. This propenfity difplays it- felf even in childhood: ftories of ghofts and apparitions are anxioufly liftened to; and firmly believed, by the terror they oc- cafion: the vulgar accordingly have been captivated with fuch ftories, upon evi- dence that would not be fufficient to afcer- tain the fimpleft fact. The abfurd and childifh prodigies that are every where fcattered through the hiftory of Titus Li-

* " Cæfar gave me this."

(a) See Elements of Criticifm, vol. 1. p. 163. ed. 5.

vius,

vius, not to mention other ancient hiftorians, would be unaccountable in a writer of fenfe and gravity, were it not for
the propenfity mentioned. But human belief is not left at the mercy of every irre-
gular bias : our maker has fubjected belief
to the correction of the rational faculty ;
and accordingly, in proportion as reafon
advances toward maturity, wonders, prodigies, apparitions, incantations, witchcraft,
and fuch ftuff, lofe their influence. That
reformation however has been exceedingly
flow, becaufe the propenfity is exceedingly
ftrong. Such abfurdities found credit a-
mong wife men, even as late as the laft
age. I am ready to verify the charge, by
introducing two men of the firft rank for
underftanding : were a greater number
neceffary, there would be no difficulty of
making a very long catalogue. The celebrated Grotius fhall lead the van. Procopius in his Vandal hiftory relates, that
fome orthodox Chriftians, whofe tongues
were cut out by the Arians, continued
miraculoufly to fpeak as formerly. And
to vouch the fact, he appeals to fome of
thofe miraculous perfons, alive in Conftantinople at the time of his writing. In
the

the dark ages of Chriftianity, when different fects were violently enflamed againft
each other, it is not furprifing that grofs
abfurdities were fwallowed as real miracles: but is it not furprifing, and alfo mortifying, to find Grotius, the greateft genius of the age he lived in, adopting fuch
abfurdities? For the truth of the foregoing miracle, he appeals not only to Procopius, but to feveral other writers (a); as
if the hearfay of a few writers were fufficient to make us believe an impoffibility.
Could it ferioufly be his opinion, that the
great God who governs by general laws,
permitting the fun to fhine alike upon men
of whatever religion, would miraculoufly
fufpend the laws of nature, in order to
teftify his difpleafure at an honeft fect of
Chriftians, led innocently into error? Did
he alfo believe what Procopius adds, that
two of thefe orthodox Chriftians were a-
gain deprived of fpeech, as a punifhment
inflicted by the Almighty for cohabiting
with proftitutes?

I proceed to our famous hiftorian, the
Earl of Clarendon, the other perfon I had
in view. A man long in public bufinefs,

(a) Prolegomena to his Hiftory of the Goths.

a

a confummate politician and well ftored with knowledge from books as well as from experience, might be fortified a- gainft foolifh miracles, if any man can be fortified : and 'yet behold his fuperftiti- ous credulity in childifh ftories ; no lefs weak in that particular, than was his cotemporary Grotius. He gravely relates an incident concerning the affaffination of the Duke of Buckingham, the fum of which follows. " There were many " ftories fcattered abroad at that time, of " prophecies and predictions of the Duke's " untimely and violent death ; one of " which was upon a better foundation of " credit, than ufually fuch difcourfes are " founded upon. There was an officer in " the King's wardrobe in Windfor caftle, " of reputation for honefty and difcretion, " and at that time about the age of fifty. " About fix months before the miferable " end of the Duke, this man being in bed " and in good health, there appeared to " him at midnight a man of a venerable " afpect, who drawing the curtains and " fixing his eye upon him, faid, Do you " know me, Sir. The poor man, half " dead with fear, anfwered, That he " thought

" thought him to be Sir George Villiers,
" father to the Duke. Upon which he
" was ordered by the apparition, to go to
" the Duke and tell him, that if he did
" not fomewhat to ingratiate himfelf with
" the people, he would be fuffered to live
" but a fhort time. The fame perfon ap-
" peared to him a fecond and a third time,
" reproaching him bitterly for not per-
" forming his promife. The poor man
" pluck'd up as much courage as to excufe
" himfelf, that it was difficult to find ac-
" cefs to the Duke, and that he would be
" thought a madman. The apparition
" imparted to him fome fecrets, which he
" faid would be his credentials to the
" Duke. The officer, introduced to the
" Duke by Sir Ralph Freeman, was recei-
" ved courteoufly. They walked together
" near an hour; and the Duke fometimes
" fpoke with great commotion, tho' his
" fervants with Sir Ralph were at fuch a
" diftance that they could not hear a
" word. The officer, returning from the
" Duke, told Sir Ralph, that when he
" mentioned the particulars that were to
" gain him credit, the Duke's colour chan-
" ged; and he fwore the officer could

I   " come

" come to that knowledge only by the de-
": vil; for that theſe particulars were
" known only to himſelf, and to one per-
" ſon more, of whoſe fidelity he was ſe-
" cure. The Duke, who went to accom-
" pany the King at hunting, was obſer-
" ved to ride all the morning in deep
" thought; and before the morning was
" ſpent, left the field and alighted at his
" mother's houſe, with whom he was
" ſhut up for two or three hours. When
" the Duke left her, his countenance ap-
": peared full of trouble, with a mixture
" of anger, which never appeared before
" in converſing with her: and ſhe was
" found overwhelmed with tears, and in
" great agony. ¡Whatever there was of
" all this, it is a notorious truth, that
" when ſhe heard of the Duke's murder,
" ſhe ſeemed not in the leaſt ſurpriſed,
" nor did expreſs much ſorrow."

The name of Lord Clarendon calls for
more attention to the foregoing relation
than otherwiſe it would deſerve. It is no
article of the Chriſtian faith, that the dead
preſerve their connection with the living,
or are ever ſuffered to return to this world:
we have no ſolid evidence for ſuch a fact;

and rarely hear of it, except in tales for a-
mufing or terrifying children.   Secondly,
The ftory is inconfiftent with the fyftem
of Providence ; which, for the beft purpofes, has drawn an impenetrable veil between us and futurity.   Thirdly, This
apparition, tho' fuppofed to be endowed
with a miraculous knowledge of future e-
vents, is however deficient in the fagacity
that belongs to a perfon of ordinary underftanding.   It appears twice to the officer,
without thinking of giving him proper
credentials ; nor does it think of them till
fuggefted by the officer.   Fourthly, Why
did not the apparition go directly to the
Duke himfelf ; what neceffity for employing a third perfon ?   The Duke muft have
been much more affected with an apparition to himfelf, than with the hearing it
at fecond hand.   The officer was afraid of
being taken for a madman ; and the Duke
had fome reafon to think him fuch.
Laftly, The apparition happened above
three months before the Duke's death ;
and yet we hear not of a fingle ftep taken
by him, in purfuance of the advice he
got.   The authority of the hiftorian and
the regard we owe him, have drawn from
                                                me

me the foregoing reflections, which with refpect to the ftory itfelf are very little neceffary; for the evidence is really not fuch as to verify any ordinary occurrence. His Lordfhip acknowledges, that he had no evidence but common report, faying, that it was one of the many ftories fcattered abroad at that time. He does not fay, that the ftory was related to him by the officer, whofe name he does not even mention, or by Sir Ralph Freeman, or by the Duke, or by the Duke's mother. If any thing happened like what is related, it may with good reafon be fuppofed, that the officer was crazy or enthufiaftically mad : nor have we any evidence beyond common report, that he communicated any fecret to the Duke. Here are two remarkable inftances of an obfervation made above, that a man may be high in one fcience and very low in another. Had Grotius, or had Clarendon, ftudied the fundamentals of reafon and religion coolly and impartially, as they did other fciences, they would never have given faith to reports fo ill vouched, and fo contradictory to every found principle of theology.

Another fource of erroneous reafoning,

is a fingular tendency in the mind of man
to myfteries and hidden meanings. Where
an object makes a deep impreffion, the
bufy mind is feldom fatisfied with the
fimple and obvious intendment: invention is roufed to allegorize, and to pierce
into hidden views and purpofes. I have
a notable example at hand, with refpect
to forms and ceremonies in religious worfhip. Jofephus (a), talking of the tabernacle, has the following paffage. " Let
" any man confider the ftructure of the
" tabernacle, the facerdotal veftments,
" the veffels dedicated to the fervice of the
" altar; and he muft of neceffity be con-
" vinced, that our lawgiver was a pious
" man, and that all the clamours againft
" us and our profeffion, are mere calum-
" ny. For what are all of thefe but the
" image of the whole world? This will
" appear to any man who foberly and im-
" partially examines the matter. The ta-
" bernacle of thirty cubits is divided into
" three parts; two for the priefts in ge-
" neral, and as free to them as the earth
" and the fea; the third, where no mor-
" tal muft be admitted, is as the heaven,

(a) Jewifh Antiquities, book 3.

" referved

" referved for God himfelf. The twelve
" loaves of fhew-bread fignify the twelve
" months of the year. The candleftick,
" compofed of feven branches, refers to
" the twelve figns of the zodiac, through
" which the feven planets fhape their
" courfe; and the feven lamps on the top
" of the feven branches bear an analogy
" to the planets themfelves. The curtains
" of four colours reprefent the four ele-
" ments. The fine linen fignifies the
" earth, as flax is raifed there. By the
" purple is underftood the fea, from the
" blood of the murex, which dies that
" colour. The violet colour is a fymbol
" of the air; and the fcarlet of the fire.
" By the linen garment of the high-
" prieft, is defigned the whole body of the
" earth: by the violet colour the heavens.
" The pomegranates fignify lightning:
" the bells tolling fignify thunder. The
" four-coloured ephod bears a refem-
" blance to the very nature of the uni-
" verfe, and the interweaving it with gold
" has a regard to the rays of light. The
" girdle about the body of the prieft is as
" the fea about the globe of the earth.
" The two fardonyx ftones are a kind of
                                " figure

" figure of the fun and moon; and the
" twelve other ftones may be underftood,
" either of the twelve months, or of the
" twelve figns in the zodiac. The vio-
" let-coloured tiara is a refemblance of
" heaven; and it would be irreverent to
" have written the facred name of God
" upon any other colour. The triple
" crown and plate of gold give us to un-
" derftand the glory and majefty of Al-
" mighty God. ' This is a plain illuftra-
" tion of thefe matters; and I would not
" lofe any opportunity of doing juftice to
" the honour and wifdom of our incom-
" parable lawgiver." How wire-drawn
and how remote from any appearance of
truth, are the foregoing allufions and i-
magined refemblances ! But religious
forms and ceremonies, however arbitrary,
are never held to be fo. If an ufeful purpofe do not appear, it is taken for granted that there muft be a hidden meaning;
and any meaning, however childifh, will
ferve when a better cannot be found.
Such propenfity there is in dark ages for
allegorizing, that even our Saviour's miracles have not efcaped. Where-ever any
feeming difficulty occurs in the plain fenfe,

the

the fathers of the church, Origen, Augu-
ftine, and Hilary, are never at a lofs for a
myftic meaning. " Sacrifice to the cele-
" ftial gods with an odd number, and to
" the terreftrial gods with an even num-
" ber," is a precept of Pythagoras. Another is, " Turn round in adoring the
" gods, and fit down when thou haft wor-
" fhipped." The learned make a ftrange
pother about the hidden meaning of thefe
precepts. But, after all, have they any
hidden meaning? Forms and ceremonies
are ufeful in external worfhip, for occupy-
ing the vulgar ; and it is of no importance
what they be, provided they prevent the
mind from wandering. Why fuch partiality to ancient ceremonies, when no hidden
meaning is fuppofed in thofe of Chriftians,
fuch as bowing to the eaft, or the prieft performing the liturgy, partly in a black up-
per garment, partly in a white ? No ideas
are more fimple than of numbers, nor lefs
fufceptible of any hidden meaning; and
yet the profound Pythagoras has imagined
many fuch meanings. The number *one*,
fays he, having no parts, reprefents the
Deity : it reprefents alfo order, peace, and
tranquillity, which refult from unity of
                                    fentiment.

fentiment. The number *two* reprefents
diforder, confufion, and change. He difcovered in the number *three* the moft
fublime myfteries: all things are compofed, fays he, of three fubftances. The
number *four* is holy in its nature, and con-
ftitutes the divine effence, which confifts
in unity, power, benevolence, and wifdom. Would one believe, that the great
philofopher, who demonftrated the 47th
propofition of the firft book of Euclid,
was the inventor of fuch childifh conceits?
Perhaps Pythagoras meant only to divert
himfelf with them. Whether fo or not,
it feems difficult to be explained, how fuch
trifles were preferved in memory, and
handed down to us through fo many generations. All that can be faid is, that
during the infancy of knowledge, every
novelty makes a figure, and that it requires
a long courfe of time to feparate the corn
from the chaff *. A certain writer, fmitten

---

* The following precepts of the fame philofopher, tho' now only fit for the *Child's Guide*, were
originally cherifhed, and preferved in memory, as
emanations of fuperior wifdom. " Do not enter a
" temple for worfhip, but with a decent air. Ren-

2   " der

ten with the conceit of hidden meanings,
has applied his talent to the conftellations
of the zodiac. The *lion* typifies the force
or heat of the fun in the month of July,
when he enters that conftellation. The
conftellation where the fun is in the month
of Auguft is termed the *virgin*, fignifying
the time of harveft. He enters the *balance*
in September, denoting the equality of
day and night. The *fcorpion*, where he is
found in October, is an emblem of the
difeafes that are frequent during that
month, &c. The *balance*, I acknowledge,
is well hit off; but I fee not clearly the refemblance of the force of a lion to the heat
of the fun; and ftill lefs that of harveft
to a virgin: the fpring would be more
happily reprefented by a virgin, and the
harveft by a woman in the act of delivery.

Our tendency to myftery and allegory,

" der not life painful by undertaking too many af-
" fairs. Be always ready for what may happen.
" Never bind yourfelf by a vow, nor by an oath.
" Irritate not a man who is angry." The feven
wife men of Greece made a figure in their time;
but it would be unreafonable to expect, that what
they taught during the infancy of knowledge, fhould
make a figure in its maturity.

diſplays itſelf with great vigour in thinking of our forefathers and of the ancients
in general, by means of the veneration
that is paid them. Before writing was
known, ancient hiſtory is made up of tra-
ditional fables. A Trojan Brutus peopled
England; and the Scots are deſcended
from Scota, daughter to an Egyptian king.
Have we not equally reaſon to think, that
the hiſtories of the heathen gods are in-
volved in fable? We pretend not to draw
any hidden meaning from the former:
why ſhould we ſuſpect any ſuch meaning
in the latter? Allegory is a ſpecies of writing too refined for a ſavage or barbarian:
it is the fruit of a cultivated imagination;
and was a late invention even in Greece.
The allegories of Æſop are of the ſimpleſt
kind: yet they were compoſed after learning began to flouriſh; and Cebes, whoſe
allegory about the life of man is juſtly celebrated, was a diſciple of Socrates. Pre-
poſſeſſion however in favour of the ancients makes us conclude, that there muſt
be ſome hidden meaning or allegory in
their hiſtorical fables; for no better reaſon
than that they are deſtitute of common
ſenſe. In the Greek mythology, there
are

are numberlefs fables related as hiftorical facts merely; witnefs the fable of gods mixing with women, and procreating giants, like what we find in the fabulous hiftories of many other nations. Thefe giants attempt to dethrone Jupiter: Apollo keeps the fheep of Admetus: Minerva fprings from the head of Jove *: Bacchus is cut out of his thigh: Orpheus goes to hell for his wife: Mars and Venus are caught by Vulcan in a net; and a thoufand other fuch childifh ftories. But the Greeks, many centuries after the invention of fuch foolifh fables, became illuftrious for arts and fciences; and nothing would fatisfy writers in later times, but to dub them profound philofophers, even when mere favages. Hence endlefs attempts to

---

* However eafy it may be to draw an allegorical meaning out of that fable, I cannot admit any fuch meaning to have been intended. An allegory is a fable contrived to illuftrate fome acknowledged truth, by making a deeper impreffion than the truth would make in plain words; of which we have feveral beautiful inftances in the Spectator (Elements of Criticifm, chap. 20. § 6.). But the fable here was underftood to be a matter of fact, Minerva being worfhipped by the Greeks as a real goddefs, the daughter of Jupiter without a mother.

detect

detect myſteries and hidden meanings in
their fables.   Let other interpreters of
that kind paſs : they give me no concern.
But I cannot, without the deepeſt concern,
behold our illuſtrious philoſopher Bacon
employing his talents ſo abſurdly.   What
imbecillity muſt there be in human nature, when ſo great a genius is capable of
ſuch puerilities ! As a ſubject ſo humbling
is far from being agreeable, I confine my-
ſelf to a few inſtances.   In an ancient
fable, Prometheus formed man out of
clay ; and kindling a bundle of birch rods
at the chariot of the ſun, brought down
fire to the earth for the uſe of his creature
man.   And tho' ungrateful man complain-
ed to Jupiter of that theft, yet the god,
pleaſed with the ingenuity of Prometheus,
not only confirmed to man the uſe of fire,
but conferred on him a gift much more
conſiderable : the gift was perpetual
youth, which was laid upon an aſs to be
carried to the earth.   The aſs, wanting to
drink at a brook, was oppoſed by a ſer-
pent, who inſiſted to have the burden,
without which, no drink for the poor aſs.
And thus, for a draught of plain water,
was perpetual youth transferred from man

to

to the ferpent. This fable has a ftriking refemblance to many in the Edda; and, in the manner of the Edda, accounts for the invention of fire, and for the mortality of man. Nor is there in all the Edda one more childifh, or more diftant from any appearance of a rational meaning. It is handled however by our philofopher with much folemn gravity, as if every fource of wifdom were locked up in it. The explanation he gives, being too long to be copied here, fhall be reduced to a few particulars. After an elogium upon fire, his Lordfhip proceeds thus. " The " manner wherein Prometheus ftole his " fire, is properly defcribed from the na- " ture of the thing; he being faid to have " done it by applying a rod of birch to the " chariot of the fun: for birch is ufed in " ftriking and beating; which clearly de- " notes fire to proceed from violent per- " cuffions and collifions of bodies, where- " by the matters ftruck are fubtilized, " rarefied, put into motion, and fo pre- " pared to receive the heat of the celeftial " bodies. And accordingly they, in a " clandeftine and fecret manner, fnatch " fire, as it were by ftealth, from the
                              " chariot

" chariot of the fun." He goes on as follows. " The next is a remarkable part of
" the fable; which reprefents, that men,
" inftead of gratitude, accufed both Pro-
" metheus and his fire to Jupiter : and yet
" the accufation proved fo pleafant to Ju-
" piter, that he not only indulged man-
" kind the ufe of fire, but conferred upon
" them perpetual youth. Here it may
" feem ftrange, that the fin of ingratitude
" fhould meet with approbation or reward.
" But the allegory has another view ; and
" denotes, that the accufation both of hu-
" man nature and human art, proceeds
" from a noble and laudable temper of
" mind, viz. modefty ; and alfo tends to
" a very good purpofe, viz. to ftir up
" frefh induftry and new difcoveries."
Can any thing be more wire-drawn ?

Vulcan, attempting the chaftity of Minerva, had recourfe to force. In the
ftruggle, his *femen*, falling upon the ground,
produced Ericthonius ; whofe body from
the middle upward was comely and well
proportioned, his thighs and legs fmall
and deformed like an eel. Confcious of
that defect, he was the inventer of cha-
riots ; which fhowed the graceful part of

his

his body, and concealed what was deformed.   Liften to the explanation of this
ridiculous fable.   " Art, by the various
" ufes it makes of fire, is here reprefented
" by Vulcan : and Nature is reprefented
" by Minerva, becaufe of the induftry
" employ'd in her works.   Art, when it
" offers violence to Nature in order to
" bend her to its purpofe, feldom attains
" the end propofed.   Yet, upon great
" ftruggle and application, there proceed
" certain imperfect births, or lame abor-
" tive works ; which however, with great
" pomp and deceitful appearances, are
" triumphantly carried about, and fhown
" by impoftors."   I admit the ingenuity
of that forc'd meaning ; but had the inventer of that fable any latent meaning ?
If he had, why did he conceal it ?   The ingenious meaning would have merited
praife ; the fable itfelf none at all.

I fhall add but one other inftance, for
they grow tirèfome.   Sphinx was a monfter, having the face and voice of a virgin,
the wings of a bird, and the talons of a
gryphin.   She refided on the fummit of a
mountain, near the city Thebes.   Her
manner was, to lie in ambufh for travellers,

lers, to propofe dark riddles which fhe received from the Mufes, and to tear thofe
to pieces who could not folve them. The
Thebans having offered their kingdom to
the man who fhould interpret thefe riddles,
Oedipus prefented himfelf before the monfter, and he was required to explain the
following riddle : What creature is that,
which being born four-footed, becomes
afterwards two-footed, then three-footed,
and laftly four-footed again. Oedipus
anfwered, It was man, who in his infancy
crawls upon his hands and feet, then
walks upright upon his two feet, walks in
old age with a ftick, and at laft lies four-
footed in bed. Oedipus having thus obtained the victory, flew the monfter; and
laying the carcafe upon an afs, carried it
off in triumph. Now for the explanation.
" This is an elegant and inftructive fable,
" invented to reprefent fcience: for Sci-
" ence may be called a monfter, being
" ftrangely gazed at and admired by the
" ignorant. Her figure and form is va-
" rious, by reafon of the vaft variety of
" fubjects that fcience confiders. Her
" voice and countenance are reprefented
" female, by reafon of her gay appear-
I   " ance,

" ance, and volubility of fpeech. Wings
" are added, becaufe the fciences and their
" inventions fly about in a moment; for
" knowledge, like light communicated
" from torch to torch, is prefently catch-
" ed, and copioufly diffufed. Sharp and
" hooked talons are elegantly attributed to
" her; becaufe the axioms and arguments
" of fcience fix down the mind, and keep
" it from moving or flipping away." A-
gain: " All fcience feems placed on
" high, as it were on the tops of moun-
" tains that are hard to climb: for fci-
" ence is juftly imagined a fublime and
" lofty thing, looking down upon igno-
" rance, and at the fame time taking an
" extenfive view on all fides, as is ufual
" on the tops of mountains. Sphinx is
" faid to propofe difficult queftions and
" riddles, which fhe received from the
" Mufes. Thefe queftions, while they re-
" main with the Mufes, may be pleafant,
" as contemplation and enquiry are when
" knowledge is their only aim: but after
" they are delivered to Sphinx, that is, to
" practice, which impels to action, choice,
" and determination; then it is that they
" become fevere and torturing; and un-

" lefs folved, ftrangely perplex the hu-
" man mind, and tear it to pieces. It is
" with the utmoft elegance added in the
" fable, that the carcafs of Sphinx was laid
" upon an afs; for there is nothing fo fub-
" tile and abftrufe, but after being made
" plain, may be conceived by the floweft
" capacity." According to fuch latitude
of interpretation, there is nothing more
eafy than to make *quidlibet ex quolibet.*

> " *Who would not laugh if fuch a man there be?*
> " *Who would not weep if Atticus were he?*"

I will detain the reader but a moment
longer, to hear what our author fays in
juftification of fuch myfterious meaning.
Out of many reafons, I felect the two following. " It may pafs for a farther in-
" dication of a concealed and fecret mean-
" ing, that fome of thefe fables are fo ab-
" furd and idle in their narration, as to
" proclaim an allegory even afar off. A
" fable that carries probability with it, may
" be fuppofed invented for pleafure, or in
" imitation of hiftory; but what could
" never be conceived or related in this
" way, muft furely have a different ufe.
" For example, what a monftrous fiction
" is

" is this, That Jupiter fhould take *Metis*
" to wife; and as foon as he found her
" pregnant eat her up; whereby he alfo
" conceived, and out of his head brought
" forth *Pallas* armed! Certainly no mor-
" tal could, but for the fake of the moral
" it couches, invent fuch an abfurd dream
" as this, fo much out of the road of
" thought." At that rate, the more ridiculous or abfurd a fable is, the more inftructive it muft be. This opinion refembles that of the ancient Germans with
refpect to mad women, who were held to
be fo wife, as that every thing they uttered was prophetic. Did it never occur to
our author, that in the infancy of the reafoning faculty, the imagination is fuffered
to roam without control, as in a dream;
and that the vulgar in all ages are delight-
ed with wonderful ftories; the more out
of nature, the more to their tafte?

We proceed to the other reafon. " The
" argument of moft weight with me is,
" That many of thefe fables appear not
" to have been invented by the perfons
" who relate and divulge them, whether
" Homer, Hefiod, or others; for if I were
" affured they firft flowed from thofe la-

" ter

" ter times and authors, I fhould never
" expect any thing fingularly great or
" noble from fuch an origin. But who-
" ever attentively confiders the thing, will
" find, that thefe fables are delivered
" down by thofe writers, not as matters
" then firft invented, but as received and
" embraced in earlier ages. And this
" principally raifes my efteem of thofe fa-
" bles ; which I receive, not as the pro-
" duct of the age, or invention of the po-
" ets, but as facred relics, gentle whif-
" pers, and the breath of better times,
" that from the traditions of more an-
" cient nations, came at length into the
" flutes and trumpets of the Greeks."
Was it our author's fincere opinion, that
the farther back we trace the hiftory of
man, the more of fcience and knowledge
is found ; and confequently that favages
are the moft learned of all men ?

The following fable of the favage Canadians ought to be myfterious, if either
of the reafons urged above be conclufive.
" There were in the beginning but fix
" men in the world, (from whence fprung
" is not faid) : one of thefe afcended to
" heaven

" heaven in queft of a woman named *A-*
" *tahentfic*, and had carnal knowledge of
" her. She being thrown headlong from
" the height of the empyrean, was recei-
" ved on the back of a tortoife, and de-
" livered of two children, one of whom
" flew the other." This fable is fo abfurd, that it muft have a latent meaning ;
and one needs but copy our author to
pump a deep myftery out of it, however
little intended by the inventer. And if
either abfurdity or antiquity entitle fables
to be held facred relics, gentle whifpers,
and the breath of better times, the following Japanefe fables are well entitled to
thefe diftinguifhing epithets. " Bunfio,
in wedlock, having had no children for
many years, addreffed her prayers to the
gods, was heard, and was delivered of
500 eggs. Fearing that the eggs might
produce monfters, fhe packed them up in
a box, and threw them into the river. An
old fifherman finding the box, hatched
the eggs in an oven, every one of which
produced a child. The children were fed
with boiled rice and mugwort-leaves; and
being at laft left to fhift for themfelves,
they fell a-robbing on the highway.
                                    Hearing

Hearing of a man famous for great wealth, they told their ſtory at his gate, and beged ſome food. This happening to be the houſe of their mother, ſhe own'd them for her children, and gave a great entertainment to her friends and neighbours. She was afterward inliſted among the goddeſſes by the name of *Benſaiten:* her 500 ſons were appointed to be her attendants; and to this day ſhe is worſhipped in Japan as the goddeſs of riches." Take another fable of the ſame ſtamp. The Japaneſe have a table of lucky and unlucky days, which they believe to have been compoſed by Abino Seimei, a famous aſtrologer, and a ſort of demi-god. They have the following tradition of him. " A young fox, purſued by hunters, fled into a temple, and took ſhelter in the boſom of A- bino Jaſſima, ſon and heir to the king of the country. Refuſing to yield the poor creature to the unmerciful hunters, he defended himſelf with great bravery, and ſet the fox at liberty. The hunters, through reſentment againſt the young prince, murdered his royal father; but Jaſſima revenged his father's death, killing the traitors with his own hand. Upon

on this fignal victory, a lady of incomparable beauty appeared to him, and made fuch an impreffion on his heart, that he took her to wife. Abino Seimei, procreated of that marriage, was endowed with divine wifdom, and with the precious gift of prophecy. Jaffima was ignorant that his wife was the very fox whofe life he had faved, till fhe refumed by degrees her former fhape." If there be any hidden myftery in this tale, I fhall not defpair of finding a myftery in every fairy-tale invented by Madam Gomez.

It is lamentable to obferve the flow progrefs of human underftanding and the faculty of reafon. If this reflection be verified in our celebrated philofopher Bacon, how much more in others? It is comfortable, however, that human underftanding is in a progrefs toward maturity, however flow. The fancy of allegorizing ancient fables, is now out of fafhion : enlightened reafon has unmafked thefe fables, and left them in their nakednefs, as the invention of illiterate ages when wonder was the prevailing paffion.

Having difcuffed the firft two heads, I proceed to the third, viz. Erroneous reafoning

foning occafioned by acquired biaffes.
And one of thefe that has the greateft influence in perverting the rational faculty,
is blind religious zeal. There is not in
nature ·a fyftem more fimple or perfpicu-
ous than that of pure religion; and yet
what a complication do we find in it of
metaphyfical fubtilties and unintelligible
jargon! That fubject being too well
known to need illuftration, I fhall confine
myfelf to a few inftances of the influence
that religious fuperftition has on other
fubjects.

A hiftory-painter and a player require
the fame fort of genius. The one by colours, the other by looks and geftures, exprefs various modifications of paffion, even
what are beyond the reach of words; and
to accomplifh thefe ends, great fenfibility
is requifite, as well as judgement. Why
then is not a player equally refpected with
a hiftory-painter? It was thought by zea-
lots, that a play is an entertainment too
fplendid for a mortified Chriftian; upon
which account players fell under church-
cenfure, and were even held unworthy of
Chriftian burial. A hiftory-painter, on
the contrary, being frequently employ'd

in

in painting for the church, was always in high efteem. It is only among Proteftants that players are beginning to be reftored to their privileges as free citizens ; and there perhaps never exifted a hiftory-painter more juftly efteemed, than Garrick, a player, is in Great Britain. Ariftarchus, having taught that the earth moves round the fun, was accufed by the Heathen priefts, for troubling the repofe of their houfehold-gods. Copernicus, for the fame doctrine, was accufed by Chriftian priefts, as contradicting the fcriptures, which talk of the fun's moving. And Galileo, for adhering to Copernicus, was condemned to prifon and penance : he found it neceffary to recant upon his knees. A bias acquired from Ariftotle, kept reafon in chains for centuries. Scholaftic divinity in particular, founded on the philofophy of that author, was more hurtful to the reafoning faculty than the Goths and Huns. Tycho Brachè fuffered great perfecution for maintaining, that the heavens were fo far empty of matter as to give free courfe to the comets ; contrary to Ariftotle, who taught, that the heavens are harder than a diamond : it was extremely ill taken, that a fimple mortal fhould pretend to give Ariftotle the lie. During the infancy of reafon, authority is the prevailing argument *.

Reafon is eafily warped by habit. In the difputes among the Athenians about adjufting the form of their government, thofe who lived in the high country were for democracy; the inhabitants of the plains were for oligarchy; and the feamen for monarchy. Shepherds are all equal: in a corn-country, there are a few mafters and many fervants: on fhipboard, there is one commander, and all the reft fubjects. Habit was their advifer: none of them thought of confulting reafon, in order to judge what was the beft form

* Ariftotle, it would appear, was lefs regarded by his cotemporaries than by the moderns. Some perfons having travelled from Macedon all the way to Perfia with complaints againft Antipater; Alexander obferved, that they would not have made fo long a journey had they received no injury. And Caffander, fon of Antipater, replying, that their long journey was an argument againft them, trufting that witneffes would not be brought from fuch a diftance to give evidence of their calumny. Alexander, fmiling, faid, " Your argument is one " of Ariftotle's fophifms, which will ferve either " fide equally."

upon the whole. Habit of a different kind has an influence no lefs powerful. Perfons who are in the habit of reafoning, require demonftration for every thing: even a felf-evident propofition is not fuffered to efcape. Such demonftrations occur more than once in the Elements of Euclid, nor has Ariftotle, with all his fkill in logic, entirely avoided them. Can any thing be more felf-evident, than the difference between pleafure and motion? Yet Ariftotle attempts to demonftrate, that they are different. " No mo- " tion," fays he, " except circular mo- " tion, is perfect in any one point of " time: there is always fomething want- " ing during its courfe, and it is not per- " fected till it arrive at its end. But plea- " fure is perfect in every point of time ; " being the fame from the beginning to " the end." The difference is clear from perception : but inftead of being clear from this demonftration, it fhould rather follow from it, that pleafure is the fame with motion in a circle. Plato alfo attempts to demonftrate a felf-evident propofition, that a quality is not a body. " Every body," fays he, " is a fubject

O o 3   " quality

" quality is not a fubject, but an acci-
" dent; *ergo*, quality is not a body. A-
" gain, A body cannot be in a fubject :
" every quality is in a fubject; *ergo*, qua-
" lity is not a body." But Defcartes affords
the moft illuftrious inftance of the kind.
He was the greateft geometer of the age he
lived in, and one of the greateft of any age;
which infenfibly led him to overlook intuitive knowledge, and to admit no propofition but what is demonftrated or proved in the regular form of fyllogifm. He
took a fancy to doubt even of his own exiftence, till he was convinced of it by the
following argument. *Cogito, ergo fum :
I think, therefore I exift.* And what fort
of a demonftration is this after all ? In
the very fundamental propofition he acknowledges his exiftence by the term *I;*
and how abfurd is it, to imagine a proof
neceffary of what is admitted in the fundamental propofition ? In the next place,
How does our author know that he
thinks ? If nothing is to be taken for
granted, an argument is no lefs neceffary
to prove that he thinks, than to prove that
he exifts. It is true, that he has intuitive
knowledge of his thinking; but has he
                                              not

not the fame of his exifting? Would not
a man deferve to be laughed at, who, after warming himfelf at a fire, fhould imagine the following argument neceffary to
prove its exiftence, " The fire burns, *ergo*
" it exifts?" Liften to an author of high
reputation attempting to demonftrate a
felf-evident propofition. " The *labour* of
" B cannot be the labour of C; becaufe it
" is the application of the organs and
" powers of B, not of C, to the effecting
" of fomething; and therefore the labour
" is as much B's, as the *limbs* and *faculties*
" made ufe of are his. Again, the *effect*
" or *produce* of the labour of B, is not
" the effect of the labour of C: and there-
" fore this effect or produce is B's, not
" C's; as much B's, as the *labour* was
" B's, and not C's: Becaufe, what the la-
" bour of B caufes or produces, B pro-
" duces by his labour; or it is the pro-
" duct of B by his labour: that is, it is
" B's product, not C's, or any other's.
" And if C fhould pretend to any *property*
" in that which B can truly call *his*, he
" would act contrary to truth (*a*)."

In every fubject of reafoning, to define

(*a*) Religion of Nature delineated, fect. 6. paragr. 2.

terms is neceſſary in order to avoid miſ-
takes : and the only poſſible way of defining a term, is to expreſs its meaning in
more ſimple terms. Terms expreſſing i-
deas that are ſimple without parts, admit
not of being defined, becauſe there are no
terms more ſimple to expreſs their meaning. To ſay that every term is capable of
a definition, is in effect to ſay, that terms
reſemble matter ; that as the ·latter is di-
viſible without end, ſo the former is reducible into ſimpler terms without end.
The habit however of defining is ſo inveterate in ſome men, that they will attempt
to define words ſignifying ſimple ideas.
Is there any neceſſity to define motion : do
not children underſtand the meaning of
the word ? And how is it poſſible to define it, when there are not words more
ſimple to define it by ? Yet Worſter (*a*)
attempts that bold taſk. " A continual
" change of place," ſays he, " or leàving
" one place for another, without remain-
" ing for any ſpace of time in the ſame
" place, is called *motion*." That every
body in motion is continually changing
place, is true : but change of place is not

(*a*) Natural Philoſophy, p. 31.

motion ;

motion; it is the effect of motion. Gravefend (*a*) defines motion thus, " Mo-
" tus eft tranflatio de loco in locum, five
" continua loci mutatio * ;" which is the
fame with the former. Yet this very author admits *locus* or *place* to fignify a fimple
idea, incapable of a definition. Is it more
fimple or more intelligible than motion?
But, of all, the moft remarkable definition of motion is that of Ariftotle, famous
for its impenetrability, or rather abfurdity, " Actus entis in potentia, quatenus in
" potentia †." His definition of time is
numerus motus fecundum prius ac pofterius.
This definition as well as that of motion,
may more properly be confidered as riddles
propounded for exercifing invention. Not
a few writers on algebra define negative
quantities to be quantities lefs than nothing.

Extenfion enters into the conception of
every particle of matter; becaufe every

(*a*) Elements of Phyfics, p. 23.

* " Motion is, the removing from one place to
" another, or a continual change of place."

† " The action of a being in power, fo far as it
" is in power."

particle

particle of matter has length, breadth, and thicknefs. Figure in the fame manner enters into the conception of every particle of matter; becaufe every particle of matter is bounded. By the power of abftraction, figure may be conceived independent of the body that is figured; and extenfion may be conceived independent of the body that is extended. Thefe particulars are abundantly plain and obvious; and yet obferve what a heap of jargon is employ'd by the followers of Leibnitz, in their fruitlefs endeavours to define extenfion. They begin with *fimple exiftences*, which they fay are unextended, and without parts. According to that definition, fimple exiftences cannot belong to matter, becaufe the fmalleft particle of matter has both parts and extenfion. But to let that pafs, they endeavour to fhow as follows, how the idea of extenfion arifes from thefe fimple exiftences. " We " may look upon fimple exiftences, as ha- " ving mutual relations with refpect to " their internal ftate : relations that form " a certain order in their manner of exift- " ence. And this order or arrangement " of things, coexifting and linked toge-

I   " ther

" ther but fo as we do not diftinctly un-
" derftand how, caufes in us a confufed
" idea, from whence arifes the appearance
" of extenfion." A Peripatetic philofopher
being afked, What fort of things the fenfible fpecies of Ariftotle are, anfwered,
That they are neither entities nor nonen-
tities, but fomething intermediate between
the two.   The famous aftronomer Ifmael
Bulialdus lays down the following propofition, and attempts a mathematical demonftration of it, " That light is a mean-
" proportional between corporeal fub-
" ftance and incorporeal."

I clofe with a curious fort of reafoning,
fo fingular indeed as not to come under
any of the foregoing heads.   The firft e-
ditions of the lateft verfion of the Bible
into Englifh, have the following preface.
" Another thing we think good to admo-
" nifh thee of, gentle reader, that we have
" not tied ourfelves to an uniformity of
" phrafing, or to an identity of words,
" as fome peradventure would wifh that
" we had done, becaufe they obferve, that
" fome learned men fomewhere have been
" as exact as they could be that way. Truly,
" that we might not vary from the fenfe

" of that which we have tranflated before,
" if the word fignified the fame in both
" places, (for there be fome words that
" be not of the fame fenfe every where),
" we were efpecially careful, and made a
" confcience according to our duty. But
" that we fhould exprefs the fame notion
" in the fame particular word; as, for
" example, if we tranflate the Hebrew or
" Greek word once by *purpofe*, never to
" call it *intent*; if one where *journeying*,
" never *travelling*; if one where *think*,
" never *fuppofe*; if one where *pain*, never
" *ache*; if one where *joy*, never *gladnefs*,
" &c.; thus to mince the matter, we
" thought to favour more of curiofity than
" wifdom, and that rather it would breed
" fcorn in the Atheift, than bring profit
" to the godly reader. For is the king-
" dom of God become words or fyllables?
" Why fhould we be in bondage to them,
" if we may be free; ufe one precifely,
" when we may ufe another, no lefs fit,
" as commodioufly? We might alfo be
" charged by fcoffers, with fome unequal
" dealing toward a great number of good
" Englifh words. For as it is written by
" a certain great philofopher, that he
" fhould

" fhould fay, that thofe logs were happy
" that were made images to be worfhip-
" ped ; for their fellows, as good as they,
" lay for blocks behind the fire : fo if we
" fhould fay, as it were, unto certain
" words, Stand up higher, have a place
" in the Bible always ; and to others of
" like quality, Get ye hence, be banifhed
" for ever, we might be taxed peradven-
" ture with St James his words, namely,
" to be partial in ourfelves, and judges of
" evil thoughts." *Quæritur,* Can this
tranflation be fafely rely'd on as the
rule of faith, when fuch are. the tranfla-
tors ?

APPENDIX.

IN reviewing the foregoing sketch, it occurred, that a fair analysis of Aristotle's logic, would be a valuable addition to the historical branch. A distinct and candid account of a system that for many ages governed the reasoning part of mankind, cannot but be acceptable to the public. Curiosity will be gratified, in seeing a phantom delineated that so long fascinated the learned world; a phantom, which shows infinite genius, but like the pyramids of Egypt or hanging gardens of Babylon, is absolutely useless unless for raising wonder. Dr Reid, professor of moral philosophy in the college of Glasgow, relished the thought; and his friendship to me prevailed on him, after much solicitation, to undertake the laborious task. No man is better acquainted with Aristotle's writings; and, without any enthusiastic attachment, he holds that philosopher to be a first-rate genius.

The

The logic of Ariſtotle has been on the decline more than a century; and is at preſent relegated to ſchools and colleges. It has occaſionally been criticiſed by different writers; but this is the firſt attempt to draw it out of its obſcurity into day-light. From what follows, one will be enabled to paſs a true judgement on that work, and to determine whether it ought to make a branch of education. The Doctor's eſſay, as a capital article in the progreſs and hiſtory of the ſciences, will be made welcome, even with the fatigue of ſqueezing through many thorny paths, before a diſtinct view can be got of that ancient and ſtupendous fabric.

It will at the ſame time ſhow the hurt that Ariſtotle has done to the reaſoning faculty, by drawing it out of its natural courſe into devious paths. His artificial mode of reaſoning, is no leſs ſuperficial than intricate: I ſay, ſuperficial; for in none of his logical works, is a ſingle truth attempted to be proved by ſyllogiſm that requires a proof: the propoſitions he undertakes to prove by ſyllogiſm, are all of them ſelf-evident. Take for inſtance the following propoſition, That man has a
                                            power

power of felf-motion. To prove this, he
aſſumes the following axiom, upon which
indeed every one of his ſyllogiſms are
founded, That whatever is true of a number of particulars joined together, holds
true of every one ſeparately; which is
thus expreſſed in logical terms, Whatever
is true of the genus, holds true of every
ſpecies. Founding upon that axiom, he
reaſons thus : " All animals have a power
" of ſelf-motion : man is an animal : *ergo*,
" man has a power of ſelf-motion." Now
if all animals have a power of ſelf-motion,
it requires no argument to prove, that
man, an animal, has that power : and
therefore, what he gives as a concluſion or
conſequence, is not really ſo ; it is not *inferred* from the fundamental propoſition,
but is *included* in it. At the ſame time,
the ſelf-motive power of man, is a faċt
that cannot be known but from experience ; and it is more clearly known from
experience than that of any other animal.
Now, in attempting to prove man to be a
ſelf-motive animal, is it not abſurd, to
found the argument on a propoſition leſs
clear than that undertaken to be demonſtrated ? What is here obſerved, will be

found

found applicable to the greater part, if not the whole, of his fyllogifms.

Unlefs for the reafon now given, it would appear fingular, that Ariftotle never attempts to apply his fyllogiftic mode of reafoning to any fubjeƈt handled by himfelf: on ethics, on rhetoric, and on poetry, he argues like a rational being, without once putting in praƈtice any of his own rules. It is not fuppofable that a man of his capacity could be ignorant, how infufficient a fyllogifm is for difcovering any latent truth. He certainly intended his fyftem of logic, chiefly if not folely, for difputation: and if fuch was his purpofe, he has been wonderfully fuccefsful; for nothing can be better contrived for wrangling and difputing without end. He indeed in a manner profeffes this to be his aim, in his books *De Sophifticis elenchis*.

Some ages hence, when the goodly fabric of the Romifh fpiritual power fhall be laid low in the duft, and fcarce a veftige remain; it will among antiquaries be a curious enquiry, What was the nature and extent of a tyranny, more oppreffive to the minds of men, than the tyranny of ancient

ancient Rome was to their perfons. During every ftep of the enquiry, pofterity
will rejoice over mental liberty, no lefs
precious than perfonal liberty. The defpotifm of Ariftotle with refpect to the faculty of reafon, was no lefs complete, than
that of the Bifhop of Rome with refpect to
religion ; and it is now a proper fubject
of curiofity, to enquire into the nature and
extent of that defpotifm. One cannot per-
ufe the following fheets, without fympa-
thetic pain for the weaknefs of man with
refpect to his nobleft faculty ; but that
pain will redouble his fatisfaction, in now
being left free to the dictates of reafon
and common fenfe.

In my reveries, I have more than once
compared Ariftotle's logic to a bubble made
of foap-water for amufing children ; a
beautiful figure with fplendid colours ; fair
on the outfide, empty within. It has for
more than two thoufand years been the hard
fate of Ariftotle's followers, Ixion like, to
embrace a cloud for a goddefs.—But this
is more than fufficient for a preface : and
I had almoft forgot, that I am detaining
my readers from better entertainment, in
liftening to Dr Reid.

A Brief Account of Aristotle's Logic. With Remarks.

CHAP. I.

Of the First Three Treatises.

SECT. 1. *Of the Author.*

ARiftotle had very uncommon advantages : born in an age when the philofophical fpirit in Greece had long flourifhed, and was in its greateft vigour; brought up in the court of Macedon, where his father was the King's phyfician; twenty years a favourite fcholar of Plato, and tutor to Alexander the Great; who both honoured him with his friendfhip, and fupplied him with every thing neceffary for the profecution of his enquiries.

Thefe advantages he improved by indefatigable ftudy, and immenfe reading. He was the firft, we know, fays Strabo,

who compofed a library.   And in this the
Egyptian and Pergamenian kings, copied
his example.   As to his genius, it would
be difrefpectful to mankind, not to allow
an uncommon fhare to a man who governed the opinions of the moft enlightened part of the fpecies near two thoufand
years.

   If his talents had been laid out folely
for the difcovery of truth and the good of
mankind, his laurels would have remained for ever frefh : but he feems to have
had a greater paffion for fame than for
truth, and to have wanted rather to be
admired as the prince of philofophers than
to be ufeful : fo that it is dubious, whether there be in his character, moft of the
philofopher or of the fophift.   The opinion of Lord Bacon is not without probability, That his ambition was as boundlefs as that of his royal pupil ; the one a-
fpiring at univerfal monarchy over the bodies and fortunes of men, the other over
their opinions.   If this was the cafe, it
cannot be faid, that the philofopher purfued his aim with lefs induftry, lefs abi-
lity, or lefs fuccefs than the hero.

   His writings carry too evident marks

of

of that philofophical pride, vanity, and envy, which have often fullied the charac- ter of the learned. He determines boldly things above all human knowledge; and enters upon the moft difficult queftions, as his pupil entered on a battle, with full affurance of fuccefs. He delivers his de- cifions oracularly, and without any fear of miftake. Rather than confefs his igno- rance, he hides it under hard words and ambiguous expreffions, of which his in- terpreters can make what they pleafe. There is even reafon to fufpect, that he wrote often with affected obfcurity, either that the air of myftery might procure greater veneration, or that his books might be underftood only by the adepts who had been initiated in his philofophy.

His conduct towards the writers that went before him has been much cenfured. After the manner of the Ottoman princes, fays Lord Verulam, he thought his throne could not be fecure unlefs he killed all his brethren. Ludovicus Vives charges him with detracting from all philofophers, that he might derive that glory to himfelf, of which he robbed them. He rarely quotes an author but with a view to cenfure, and is not very fair in reprefenting the opinions which he cenfures.

The faults we have mentioned are fuch as might be expected in a man, who had the daring ambition to be tranfmitted to all future ages, as the prince of philofophers, as one who had carried every branch of human knowledge to its utmoft limit; and who was not very fcrupulous about the means he took to obtain his end.

We ought, however, to do him the juftice to obferve, that although the pride and vanity of the fophift appear too much in his writings in abftract philofophy; yet in natural hiftory the fidelity of his narrations feems to be equal to his induftry; and he always diftinguifhes between what he knew and what he had by report. And even in abftract philofophy, it would be unfair to impute to Ariftotle all the faults, all the obfcurities, and all the contradictions, that are to be found in his writings. The greateft part, and perhaps the beft part, of his writings is loft. There is reafon to doubt whether fome of thofe we afcribe to him be really his; and whether what are his be not much vitiated and interpolated.

interpolated. Thefe fufpicions are jufti-
fied by the fate of Ariftotle's writings,
which is judicioufly related, from the beft
authorities, in Bayle's dictionary, under
the article *Tyrannion*, to which I refer.

His books in logic which remain, are,
1. One book of the Categories. 2. One of
interpretation. 3. Firft Analytics, two
books. 4. Laft Analytics, two books.
5. Topics, eight books. 6. Of Sophifms, one book. Diogenes Laertius
mentions many others that are loft. Thofe
I have mentioned have commonly been
publifhed together, under the name of *A-
riftotle's Organon*, or *his Logic;* and for
many ages, Porphyry's Introduction to
the Categories has been prefixed to them.

SECT. 2. *Of Porphyry's Introductino.*

In this Introduction, which is addreffed
to Chryfoarius, the author obferves, That
in order to underftand Ariftotle's doctrine
concerning the categories, it is neceffary
to know what a *genus* is, what a *fpecies*,
what a *fpecific difference*, what a *property*,
and what an *accident;* that the knowledge
of thefe is alfo very ufeful in definition, in
divifion,

divifion, and even in demonftration :
therefore he propofes, in this little tract,
to deliver fhortly and fimply the doctrine
of the ancients, and chiefly of the Peripatetics, concerning thefe five *predicables ;* a-
voiding the more intricate queftions concerning them ; fuch as, Whether *genera*
and *fpecies* do really exift in nature ? or,
Whether they are only conceptions of the
human mind ? If they exift in nature,
Whether they are corporeal or incorporeal?
and, Whether they are inherent in the
objects of fenfe, or disjoined from them ?
Thefe, he fays, are very difficult queftions,
and require accurate difcuffion ; but that
he is not to meddle with them.

After this preface, he explains very minutely each of the five words above mentioned, divides and fubdivides each of
them, and then purfues all the agreements
and differences between one and another
through fixteen chapters.

SECT. 3. *Of the Categories.*

The book begins with an explication of
what is meant by univocal words, what
by

by equivocal, and what by denominative.
Then it is obferved, that what we fay is
either fimple, without compofition or
ftructure, as *man, horfe*; or, it has compofition and ftructure, as, *a man fights, the
horfe runs.* Next comes a diftinction between a fubject of predication ; that is, a
fubject of which any thing is affirmed or
denied, and a fubject of inhefion. Thefe
things are faid to be inherent in a fubject,
which although they are not a part of the
fubject, cannot poffibly exift without it,
as figure in the thing figured. Of things
that are, fays Ariftotle, fome may be predicated of a fubject, but are in no fubject;
as *man* may be predicated of James or
John, but is not in any fubject. Some a-
gain are in a fubject, but can be predicated of no fubject. Thus, my knowledge
in grammar is in me as its fubject, but it
can be predicated of no fubject; becaufe
it is an individual thing. Some are both
in a fubject, and may be predicated of a
fubject, as fcience; which is in the mind
as its fubject, and may be predicated of
geometry. Laftly, Some things can neither be in a fubject, nor be predicated of
any fubject. Such are all individual fub-

ftances,

stances, which cannot be predicated, because they are individuals ; and cannot be
in a subject, because they are substances.
After some other subtilties about predicates and subjects, we come to the categories themselves ; the things above mentioned being called by the schoolmen the
antepredicamenta. It may be observed,
however, that notwithstanding the distinc-
tion now explained, the *being in a subject,*
and the *being predicated truly of a subject,*
are in the Analytics used as synonymous
phrases ; and this variation of style has led
some persons to think that the Categories
were not written by Aristotle.

Things that may be expressed without
composition or structure, are, says the author, reducible to the following heads.
They are either *substance,* or *quantity,* or
quality, or *relatives,* or *place,* or *time,* or
having, or *doing,* or *suffering.* These are
the predicaments or categories. The first
four are largely treated of in four chapters ;
the others are slightly passed over, as suffi-
ciently clear of themselves. As a speci-
men, I shall give a summary of what he
says on the category of substance.

Substances are either primary, to wit,

I   individual

individual fubftances, or fecondary, to
wit, the genera and fpecies of fubftances.
Primary fubftances neither are in a fubject, nor can be predicated of a fubject;
but all other things that exift, either are
in primary fubftances, or may be predicated of them. For whatever can be predicated of that which is in a fubject, may
alfo be predicated of the fubject itfelf.
Primary fubftances are more fubftances
than the fecondary; and of the fecondary,
the fpecies is more a fubftance than the
genus. If there were no primary, there
could be no fecondary fubftances.

The properties of fubftance are thefe :
1. No fubftance is capable of intenfion or
remiffion. 2. No fubftance can be in any
other thing as its fubject of inhefion. 3.
No fubftance has a contrary; for one fubftance cannot be contrary to another; nor
can there be contrariety between a fubftance and that which is no fubftance.
4. The moft remarkable property of fubftance, is, that one and the fame fubftance may, by fome change in itfelf, become the fubject of things that are contrary. Thus, the fame body may be at
one time hot, at another cold.

Let this ferve as a fpecimen of Ariftotle's manner of treating the categories. After them, we have fome chapters, which the fchoolmen call *poftprædicamenta*; wherein, firft, the four kinds of oppofition of terms are explained; to wit, *relative, privative*, of *contrariety*, and of *contradiction*. This is repeated in all fyftems of logic. Laft of all we have diftinctions of the four Greek words which anfwer to the Latin ones, *prius, fimul, motus*, and *habere*.

SECT. 4. *Of the book concerning Interpretation.*

We are to confider, fays Ariftotle, what a noun is, what a verb, what affirmation, what negation, what fpeech. Words are the figns of what paffeth in the mind; writing is the fign of words. The figns both of writing and of words are different in different nations, but the operations of mind fignified by them are the fame. There are fome operations of thought which are neither true nor falfe. Thefe are expreffed by nouns or verbs fingly, and without compofition.

A

A noun is a found which by compact fignifies fomething without refpect to time, and of which no part has fignification by itfelf. The cries of beafts may have a natural fignification, but they are not nouns: we give that name only to founds which have their fignification by compact. The cafes of a noun, as the genitive, dative, are not nouns. *Non homo* is not a noun, but, for diftinction's fake, may be called a *nomen infinitum.*

A verb fignifies fomething by compact with relation to time. Thus *valet* is a verb; but *valetudo* is a noun, becaufe its fignification has no relation to time. It is only the prefent tenfe of the indicative that is properly called a verb; the other tenfes and moods are variations of the verb. *Non valet* may be called a *verbum infinitum.*

Speech is found fignificant by compact, of which fome part is alfo fignificant. And it is either enunciative, or not enunciative. Enunciative fpeech is that which affirms or denies. As to fpeech which is not enunciative, fuch as a prayer or wifh, the confideration of it belongs to oratory, or poetry. Every enunciative fpeech muft have

a

a verb, or fome variation of a verb. Affirmation is the enunciation of one thing
concerning another. Negation is the e-
nunciation of one thing from another.
Contradiction is an affirmation and negation that are oppofite. This is a fummary of the firft fix chapters.

The feventh and eighth treat of the various kinds of enunciations or propofitions,
univerfal, particular, indefinite, and fingular; and of the various kinds of oppofition in propofitions, and the axioms concerning them. Thefe things are repeated
in every fyftem of logic. In the ninth
chapter he endeavours to prove by a long
metaphyfical reafoning, that propofitions
refpecting future contingencies are not,
determinately, either true or falfe; and
that if they were, it would follow, that all
things happen neceffarily, and could not
have been otherwife than as they are.
The remaining chapters contain many minute obfervations concerning the equipol-
lency of propofitions both pure and modal.

C H A P.

CHAP II.

Remarks.

SECT. 1. *On the Five Predicables.*

THE writers on logic have borrowed
their materials almoſt entirely from
Ariſtotle's Organon, and Porphyry's Introduction. The Organon however was
not written by Ariſtotle as one work. It
comprehends various tracts, written without the view of making them parts of one
whole, and afterwards thrown together
by his editors under one name on account
of their affinity. Many of his books that
are loſt, would have made a part of the
Organon if they had been ſaved. .

The three treatiſes of which we have
given a brief account, are unconnected
with each other, and with thoſe that follow. And although the firſt was undoubtedly compiled by Porphyry and the two
laſt probably by Ariſtotle, yet I conſider
them

them as the venerable remains of a philofophy more ancient than Ariftotle. Ar-
chytas of Tarentum, an eminent mathe-
matician and philofopher of the Pythagorean fchool, is faid to have wrote upon
the ten categories ; and the five predicables probably had their origin in the
fame fchool. Ariftotle, tho' abundantly
careful to do juftice to himfelf, does not
claim the invention of either. And Porphyry, without afcribing the latter to A-
riftotle, profeffes only to deliver the doctrine of the ancients and chiefly of the Peripatetics, concerning them.

The writers on logic have divided that
fcience into three parts ; the firft treating
of fimple apprehenfion and of terms ; the
fecond, of judgement and of propofitions ;
and the third, of reafoning and of fyllogifms. The materials of the firft part are
taken from Porphyry's Introduction and
the Categories ; and thofe of the fecond
from the book of Interpretation.

A predicable, according to the gram-
matical form of the word, might feem to
fignify, whatever may be predicated, that
is, affirmed or denied, of a fubject : and
in that fenfe every predicate would be a
predicable.

predicable. But logicians give a different meaning to the word. They divide propofitions into certain claffes, according to the relation which the predicate of the propofition bears to the fubject. The firft clafs is that wherein the predicate is the *genus* of the fubject; as when we fay, *This is a triangle, Jupiter is a planet.* In the fecond clafs, the predicate is a *fpecies* of the fubject; as when we fay, *This triangle is right-angled.* A third clafs is when the predicate is the fpecific difference of the fubject; as when we fay, *Every triangle has three fides and three angles.* A fourth when the predicate is a property of the fubject; as when we fay, *The angles of every triangle are equal to two right angles.* And a fifth clafs is when the predicate is fomething accidental to the fubject; as when we fay, *This triangle is neatly drawn.*

Each of thefe claffes comprehends a great variety of propofitions, having different fubjects, and different predicates; but in each clafs the relation between the predicate and the fubject is the fame. Now it is to this relation that logicians have given the name of *a predicable.* Hence it is, that
altho'

altho' the number of predicates be infinite, yet the number of predicables can be no greater than that of the different relations which may be in propofitions between the predicate and the fubject. And if all propofitions belong to one or other of the five claffes above mentioned, there can be but five predicables, to wit, *genus, fpecies, differentia, proprium,* and *accidens.* Thefe might, with more propriety perhaps, have been called *the five claffes of predicates;* but ufe has determined them to be called *the five predicables.*

It may alfo be obferved, that as fome objects of thought are individuals, fuch as, *Julius Cæfar, the city Rome;* fo others are common to many individuals, as *good, great, virtuous, vicious.* Of this laft kind are all the things that are expreffed by adjectives. Things common to many individuals, were by the ancients called *univerfals.* All predicates are univerfals, for they have the nature of adjectives; and, on the other hand, all univerfals may be predicates. On this account, univerfals may be divided into the fame claffes as predicates; and as the five claffes of predicates

       above

above mentioned have been called the five predicables, fo by the fame kind of phrafeology they have been called *the five univerfals ;* altho' they may more properly be called *the five claffes of univerfals.*

The doctrine of the five univerfals or predicables makes an effential part of every fyftem of logic, and has been handed down without any change to this day. The very name of *predicables* fhews, that the author of this divifion, whoever he was, intended it as a complete enumeration of all the kinds of things that can be affirmed of any fubject; and fo it has always been underftood. It is accordingly implied in this divifion, that all that can be affirmed of any thing whatever, is either the *genus* of the thing, or its *fpecies*, or its *fpecific difference*, or fome *property* or *accident* belonging to it.

Burgerfdick, a very acute writer in logic, feems to have been aware, that ftrong objections might be made to the five predicables, confidered as a complete enumeration : but, unwilling to allow any imperfection in this ancient divifion, he endeavours to reftrain the meaning of the word *predicable*, fo as to obviate objec-

tions. Thofe things only, fays he, are to
be accounted predicables, which may be
affirmed of *many individuals, truly, properly*, and *immediately*. The confequence of
putting fuch limitations upon the word
predicable is, that in many propofitions,
perhaps in moft, the predicate is not a predicable. But admitting all his limitations,
the enumeration will ftill be very incomplete : for of many things we may affirm
truly, properly, and immediately, their
exiftence, their end, their caufe, their effect, and various relations which they
bear to other things. Thefe, and perhaps
many more, are predicables in the ftrict
fenfe of the word, no lefs than the five
which have been fo long famous.

Altho' Porphyry and all fubfequent writers, make the predicables to be, in number, five; yet Ariftotle himfelf, in the
beginning of the Topics, reduces them to
four ; and demonftrates, that there can be
no more. We fhall give his demonftration when we come to the Topics ; and
fhall only here obferve, that as Burgerfdick juftifies the fivefold divifion, by re-
ftraining the meaning of the word *predicable* ; fo Ariftotle juftifies the fourfold
divifion,

divifion, by enlarging the meaning of the words *property* and *accident.*

After all, I apprehend, that this ancient divifion of predicables with all its imperfections, will bear a comparifon with thofe which have been fubftituted in its ftead by the moft celebrated modern philofophers.

Locke, in his Effay on the Human Underftanding, having laid it down as a principle, That all our knowledge confifts in perceiving certain agreements and difagreements between our ideas, reduces thefe agreements and difagreements to four heads : to wit, 1. Identity and diverfity ; 2. Relation ; 3. Coexiftence ; 4. Real Exiftence (*a*). Here are four predicables given as a complete enumeration, and yet not one of the ancient predicables is included in the number.

The author of the Treatife of Human Nature, proceeding upon the fame principle that all our knowledge is only a perception of the relations of our ideas, obferves, " That it may perhaps be efteemed " an endlefs tafk, to enumerate all thofe

(*a*) Book 4. chap. 1.

S f 2   " qualities

" qualities which admit of comparifon, and
" by which the ideas of philofophical re-
" lation are produced: but if we diligent-
" ly confider them, we fhall find, that
" without difficulty they may be compri-
" fed under feven general heads: 1. Re-
" femblance; 2. Identity; 3. Relations of
" Space and Time; 4. Relations of Quan-
" tity and Number; 5. Degrees of Qua-
" lity; 6. Contrariety; 7. Caufation (*a*)."
Here again are feven predicables given as
a complete enumeration, wherein all the
predicables of the ancients, as well as two
of Locke's, are left out.

The ancients in their divifion attended
only to categorical propofitions which have
one fubject and one predicate; and of
thefe, to fuch only as have a general term
for their fubject. The moderns, by their
definition of knowledge, have been led to
attend only to relative propofitions, which
exprefs a relation between two fubjects,
and thefe fubjects they fuppofe to be always ideas.

(*a*) Vol. 1. p. 33. and 125.

SECT.

SECT. 2. *On the Ten Categories, and on Divisions in general.*

The intention of the categories or predicaments is, to muster every object of human apprehension under ten heads : for the categories are given as a complete e-numeration of every thing which can be expressed without *compofition* and *ftructure*; that is, of every thing that can be either the subject or the predicate of a propofition. So that as every soldier belongs to some company, and every company to some regiment ; in like manner every thing that can be the object of human thought, has its place in one or other of the ten categories ; and by dividing and subdividing properly the several categories, all the notions that enter into the human mind may be muftered in rank and file, like an army in the day of battle.

The perfection of the divifion of categories into ten heads, has been ftrenu-oufly defended by the followers of Ari-flotle, as well as that of the five predica-bles. They are indeed of kin to each o-ther :

ther: they breathe the fame fpirit, and probably had the fame origin. By the one we are taught to marfhal every term that can enter into a propofition, either as fubject or predicate ; and by the other, we are taught all the poffible relations which the fubject can have to the predicate. Thus, the whole furniture of the human mind is prefented to us at one view, and contracted, as it were, into a nut-fhell. To attempt, in fo early a period, a methodical delineation of the vaft region of human knowledge, actual and poffible, and to point out the limits of every diftrict, was indeed magnanimous in a high degree, and deferves our admiration, while we lament that the human powers are un-equal to fo bold a flight.

A regular diftribution of things under proper claffes or heads, is, without doubt, a great help both to memory and judgement. As the philofopher's province includes all things human and divine that can be objects of enquiry, he is naturally led to attempt fome general divifion, like that of the categories. And the invention of a divifion of this kind, which the fpeculative part of mankind acquiefced in

for

for two thoufand years, marks a fuperiority of genius in the inventer, whoever he
was. Nor does it appear, that the general divifions which, fince the decline of
the Peripatetic philofophy, have been fubftituted in place of the ten categories, are
more perfect.

Locke has reduced all things to three
categories ; to wit, fubftances, modes, and
relations. In this divifion, time, fpace,
and number, three great objects of human
thought, are omitted.

The author of the Treatife of Human
Nature has reduced all things to two categories ; to wit, ideas, and impreffions : a
divifion which is very well adapted to his
fyftem ; and which puts me in mind of
another made by an excellent mathemati-
cian in a printed thefis I have feen. In
it the author, after a fevere cenfure of the
ten categories of the Peripatetics, maintains, that there neither are nor can be
more than two categories of things ; to
wit, *data* and *quæfita.*

There are two ends that may be propofed by fuch divifions. The firft is,
to methodize or digeft in order what a
man actually knows. This is neither unimportant

important nor impracticable; and in proportion to the folidity and accuracy of a man's judgement, his divifions of the things he knows, will be elegant and ufeful. The fame fubject may admit, and even require, various divifions, according to the different points of view from which we contemplate it: nor does it follow, that becaufe one divifion is good, therefore another is naught. To be acquainted with the divifions of the logicians and metaphyficians, without a fuperftitious attachment to them, may be of ufe in dividing the fame fubjects, or even thofe of a different nature. Thus, Quintilian borrows from the ten categories his divifion of the topics of rhetorical argumentation. Of all methods of arrangement, the moft antiphilofophical feems to be the invention of this age; I mean, the arranging the arts and fciences by the letters of the alphabet, in dictionaries and encyclopedies. With thefe authors the categories are, A, B, C, &c.

Another end commonly propofed by fuch divifions, but very rarely attained, is to exhauft the fubject divided; fo that nothing that belongs to it fhall be omit-

I   ted.

ted. It is one of the general rules of divifion in all fyftems of logic, That the divifion fhould be adequate to the fubject divided : a good rule, without doubt ; but very often beyond the reach of human power. To make a perfect divifion, a man muft have a perfect comprehenfion of the whole fubject at one view. When our knowledge of the fubject is imperfect, any divifion we can make, muft be like the firft fketch of a painter, to be extended, contracted, or mended, as the fubject fhall be found to require. Yet nothing is more common, not only among the ancient, but even among modern philofophers, than to draw, from their incomplete divifions, conclufions which fuppofe them to be perfect.

A divifion is a repofitory which the philofopher frames for holding his ware in convenient order. The philofopher maintains, that fuch or fuch a thing is not good ware, becaufe there is no place in his ware-room that fits it. We are apt to yield to this argument in philofophy, but it would appear ridiculous in any other traffic.

Peter Ramus, who had the fpirit of a re-

former in philofophy, and who had force
of genius fufficient to fhake the Ariftote-
lian fabric in many parts, but infufficient
to erect any thing more folid in its place,
tried to remedy the imperfection of philofophical divifions, by introducing a new
manner of dividing. His divifions always
confifted of two members, one of which
was contradictory of the other; as if one
fhould divide England into Middlefex and
what is not Middlefex. It is evident that
thefe two members comprehend all England: for the logicians obferve, that a
term along with its contradictory, comprehend all things. In the fame manner,
we may divide what is not Middlefex into
Kent and what is not Kent. Thus one
may go on by divifions and fubdivifions
that are abfolutely complete. This example may ferve to give an idea of the
fpirit of Ramean divifions, which were in
no fmall reputation about two hundred
years ago.

Ariftotle was not ignorant of this kind
of divifion. But he ufed it only as a touch-
ftone to prove by induction the perfection
of fome other divifion, which indeed is
the beft ufe that can be made of it. When
applied

applied to the common purpofe of divifion, it is both inelegant, and burdenfome to the memory; and, after it has put one out of breath by endlefs fubdivifions, there is ftill a negative term left behind, which fhows that you are no nearer the end of your journey than when you began.

Until fome more effectual remedy be found for the imperfection of divifions, I beg leave to propofe one more fimple than that of Ramus. It is this: When you meet with a divifion of any fubject imperfectly comprehended, add to the laft member an *et cætera*. That this *et cætera* makes the divifion complete, is undeniable; and therefore it ought to hold its place as a member, and to be always underftood, whether expreffed or not, until clear and pofitive proof be brought that the divifion is complete without it. And this fame *et cætera* is to be the repofitory of all members that fhall in any future time fhew a good and valid right to a place in the fubject.

SECT. 3. *On Diftinctions.*

Having faid fo much of logical divifions, we fhall next make fome remarks upon diftinctions.

Since the philofophy of Ariftotle fell into difrepute, it has been a common topic of wit and raillery, to enveigh againft metaphyfical diftinctions. Indeed the abufe of them in the fcholaftic ages, feems to juftify a general prejudice againft them: and fhallow thinkers and writers have good reafon to be jealous of diftinctions, becaufe they make fad work when applied to their flimfy compofitions. But every man of true judgement, while he condemns diftinctions that have no foundation in the nature of things, muft perceive, that indifcriminately to decry diftinctions, is to renounce all pretenfions to juft reafoning: for as falfe reafoning commonly proceeds from confounding things that are different; fo without diftinguifhing fuch things, it is impoffible to avoid error, or detect fophiftry. The authority of Aquinas, or Suarez, or even of Ariftotle, can neither ftamp a real value upon diftinctions of bafe metal, nor hinder the currency of thofe of true metal.

Some diftinctions are verbal, others are real. The firft kind diftinguifh the vari-

ous

ous meanings of a word; whether proper, or metaphorical. Diftinctions of this kind make a part of the grammar of a language, and are often abfurd when tranflated into another language. Real diftinctions are equally good in all languages, and fuffer no hurt by tranflation. They diftinguifh the different fpecies contained under fome general notion, or the different parts contained in one whole.

Many of Ariftotle's diftinctions are verbal merely; and therefore, more proper materials for a dictionary of the Greek language, than for a philofophical treatife. At leaft, they ought never to have been tranflated into other languages, when the idiom of the language will not juftify them: for this is to adulterate the language, to introduce foreign idioms into it without neceffity or ufe, and to make it ambiguous where it was not. The diftinctions in the end of the Categories of the four words, *prius, fimul, motus,* and *habere,* are all verbal.

The modes or fpecies of *prius,* according to Ariftotle, are five. One thing may be prior to another; firft, in point of time; fecondly, in point of dignity; thirdly, in point

point of order ; and fo forth. The modes
of *fimul* are only three. It feems this word
was not ufed in the Greek with fo great
latitude as the other, although they are
relative terms.

The modes or fpecies of motion he makes
to be fix, to wit, generation, corruption,
increafe, decreafe, alteration, and change
of place.

The modes or fpecies of *having* are eight.
1. Having a quality or habit, as having
wifdom. 2. Having quantity or magni-
tude. 3. Having things adjacent, as having a fword. 4. Having things as parts,
as having hands or feet. 5. Having in a
part or on a part, as having a ring on
one's finger. 6. Containing, as a cafk is
faid to have wine. 7. Poffeffing, as having lands or houfes. 8. Having a wife.

Another diftinction of this kind is Ariftotle's diftinction of caufes ; of which he
makes four kinds, efficient, material, formal, and final. Thefe diftinctions may
deferve a place in a dictionary of the Greek
language ; but in Englifh or Latin they
adulterate the language. Yet fo fond were
the fchoolmen of diftinctions of this kind,
that they added to Ariftotle's enumeration,

an

an impulfive caufe, an exemplary caufe, and I don't know how many more. We feem to have adopted into Englifh a final caufe; but it is merely a term of art, borrowed from the Peripatetic philofophy, without neceffity or ufe : for the Englifh word *end* is as good as *final caufe*, though not fo long nor fo learned.

SECT. 4. *On Definitions.*

It remains that we make fome remarks on Ariftotle's definitions, which have expofed him to much cenfure and ridicule. Yet I think it muft be allowed, that in things which need definition and admit of it, his definitions are commonly judicious and accurate ; and had he attempted to define fuch things only, his enemies' had wanted great matter of triumph. I believe it may likewife be faid in his favour, that until Locke's effay was wrote, there was nothing of importance delivered by philofophers with regard to definition, beyond what Ariftotle has faid upon that fubject.

He confiders a definition as a fpeech declaring

claring what a thing is. Every thing effential to the thing defined, and nothing
more, muft be contained in the definition.
Now the effence of a thing confifts of thefe
two parts: Firft, What is common to it
with other things of the fame kind; and,
fecondly, What diftinguifhes it from other
things of the fame kind. The firft is called the *genus* of the thing, the fecond its
fpecific difference. The definition therefore
confifts of thefe two parts. And for finding them, we muft have recourfe to the
ten categories; in one or other of which
every thing in nature is to be found. Each
category is a *genus*, and is divided into fo
many fpecies, which are diftinguifhed by
their fpecific differences. Each of thefe
fpecies is again fubdivided into fo many
fpecies, with regard to which it is a genus.
This divifion and fubdivifion continues
until we come to the loweft fpecies, which
can only be divided into individuals, diftinguifhed from one another, not by any
fpecific difference, but by accidental differences of time, place, and other circumftances.

The category itfelf being the higheft
genus, is in no refpect a fpecies, and the
loweft

loweſt *ſpecies* is in no reſpect a *genus;* but
every intermediate order is a genus compared with thoſe that are below it, and a
ſpecies compared with thoſe above it. To
find the definition of any thing, therefore,
you muſt take the genus which is immediately above its place in the category, and
the ſpecific *difference*, by which it is diſtinguiſhed from other ſpecies of the ſame
genus. Theſe two make a perfect definition. This I take to be the ſubſtance of
Ariſtotle's ſyſtem; and probably the ſyſtem of the Pythagorean ſchool before A-
riſtotle, concerning definition.

But notwithſtanding the ſpecious appearance of this ſyſtem, it has its defects.
Not to repeat what was before ſaid of the
imperfection of the diviſion of things into
ten categories, the ſubdiviſions of each category are no leſs imperfect. Ariſtotle has
given ſome ſubdiviſions of a few of them;
and as far as he goes, his followers pretty
unanimouſly take the ſame road. But
when they attempt to go farther, they take
very different roads. It is evident, that
if the ſeries of each category could be
completed, and the diviſion of things into
categories could be made perfect, ſtill the

higheſt genus in each category could not
be defined, becauſe it is not a ſpecies ; nor
could individuals be defined, becauſe they
have no ſpecific difference.   There are alſo
many ſpecies of things, whoſe ſpecific
difference cannot be expreſſed in language,
even when it is evident to ſenſe, or to the
underſtanding.   Thus, green, red, and
blue, are very diſtinct ſpecies of colour ;
but who can expreſs in words wherein
green differs from red or blue ?

Without borrowing light from the ancient ſyſtem, we may perceive, that every
definition muſt conſiſt of words that need
no definition ; and that to define the common words of a language that have no ambiguity, is trifling, if it could be done ;
the only uſe of a definition being to give a
clear and adequate conception of the meaning of a word.

The logicians indeed diſtinguiſh between the definition of a word, and the
definition of a thing ; conſidering the former as the mean office of a lexicographer,
but the laſt as the grand work of a philoſopher.   But what they have ſaid about
the definition of a thing, if it have a meaning, is beyond my comprehenſion.   All
the

the rules of definition agree to the definition of a word: and if they mean by the definition of a thing, the giving an adequate conception of the nature and effence of any thing that exifts; this is impoffible, and is the vain boaft of men unconfcious of the weaknefs of human underftanding.

The works of God are but imperfectly known by us. We fee their outfide; or perhaps we difcover fome of their qualities and relations, by obfervation and experiment affifted by reafoning: but even of the fimpleft of them we can give no definition that comprehends its real effence. It is juftly obferved by Locke, that nominal effences only, which are the creatures of our own minds, are perfectly comprehended by us, or can be properly defined; and even of thefe there are many too fimple in their nature to admit of definition. When we cannot give precifion to our notions by a definition, we muft endeavour to do it by attentive reflection upon them, by obferving minutely their agreements and differences, and efpecially by a right underftanding of the powers of our own minds by which fuch notions are formed.

The principles laid down by Locke with regard to definition and with regard to the abuſe of words, carry conviction along with them. I take them to be one of the moſt important improvements made in logic ſince the days of Ariſtotle : not ſo much becauſe they enlarge our knowledge, as becauſe they make us ſenſible of our ignorance ; and ſhew that a great part of what ſpeculative men have admired as profound philoſophy, is only a darkening of knowledge by words without underſtanding.

If Ariſtotle had underſtood theſe principles, many of his definitions, which furniſh matter of triumph to his enemies, had never ſeen the light : let us impute them to the times rather than to the man. The ſublime Plato, it is ſaid, thought it neceſſary to have the definition of a man, and could find none better than *Animal implume bipes;* upon which Diogenes ſent to his ſchool a cock with his feathers plucked off, deſiring to know whether it was a man or not.

Sect.

SECT. 5. *On the Structure of Speech.*

The few hints contained in the beginning of the book concerning Interpretation relating to the ſtructure of ſpeech, have been left out in treatiſes of logic, as belonging rather to grammar; yet l apprehend this is a rich field of philoſophical ſpeculation. Language being the expreſs image of human thought, the analyſis of the one muſt correſpond to that of the other. Nouns adjective and ſubſtantive, verbs active and paſſive, with their various moods, tenſes, and perſons, muſt be expreſſive of a like variety in the modes of thought. Things that are diſtinguiſhed in all languages, ſuch as ſubſtance and quality, action and paſſion, cauſe and effect, muſt be diſtinguiſhed by the natural powers of the human mind. The philoſophy of grammar, and that of the human underſtanding, are more nearly allied than is commonly imagined.

The ſtructure of language was purſued to a conſiderable extent, by the ancient commentators upon this book of Ariſtotle. Their ſpeculations upon this ſubject, which

which are neither the leaft ingenious nor
the leaft ufeful part of the Peripatetic philofophy, were neglected for many ages,
and lay buried in ancient manufcripts, or
in books little known, till they were lately
brought to light by the learned Mr Harris
in his Hermes.

The definitions given by Ariftotle, of a
noun, of a verb, and of fpeech, will hardly bear examination. It is eafy in practice to diftinguifh the various parts of
fpeech; but very difficult, if at all poffible, to give accurate definitions of them.

He obferves juftly, that befides that
kind of fpeech called a *propofition*, which
is always either true or falfe, there are o-
ther kinds which are neither true nor
falfe; fuch as, a prayer, or wifh; to
which we may add, a queftion, a command, a promife, a contract, and many
others. Thefe Ariftotle pronounces to
have nothing to do with his fubject, and
remits them to oratory, or poetry; and fo
they have remained banifhed from the regions of philofophy to this day: yet I apprehend, that an analyfis of fuch fpeeches,
and of the operations of mind which they
exprefs, would be of real ufe, and perhaps
would

would difcover how imperfect an enumeration the logicians have given of the powers of human underftanding, when they reduce them to fimple apprehenfion, judgement, and reafoning.

S e c t. 6. *On Propofitions.*

Mathematicians ufe the word *propofition* in a larger fenfe than logicians. A problem is called a *propofition* in mathematics, but in logic it is not a propofition : it is one of thofe fpeeches which are not enunciative, and which Ariftotle remits to oratory or poetry.

A propofition, according to Ariftotle, is a fpeech wherein one thing is affirmed or denied of another. Hence it is eafy to diftinguifh the thing affirmed or denied, which is called *the predicate,* from the thing of which it is affirmed or denied, which is called *the fubject ;* and thefe two are called *the terms of the propofition.* Hence likewife it appears, that propofitions are either affirmative or negative ; and this is called *their quality.* All affirmative propofitions have the fame quality, fo likewife have

have all negative ; but an affirmative and a negative are contrary in their quality.

When the fubject of a propofition is a general term, the predicate is affirmed or denied, either of the whole, or of a part. Hence propofitions are diftinguifhed into univerfal and particular. *All men are mortal*, is an univerfal propofition ; *Some men are learned*, is a particular; and this is called *the quantity of the propofition.* All univerfal propofitions agree in quantity, as alfo all particular : but an univerfal and a particular are faid to differ in quantity. A propofition is called *indefinite*, when there is no mark either of univerfality or particularity annexed to the fubject : thus, *Man is of few days*, is an indefinite propofition ; but it muft be underftood either as univerfal or as particular, and therefore is not a third fpecies, but by interpretation is brought under one of the other two.

There are alfo fingular propofitions, which have not a general term but an individual for their fubject ; as, *Alexander was a great conqueror.* Thefe are confidered by logicians as univerfal, becaufe, the fubject being indivifible, the predicate

I   is

is affirmed or denied of the whole, and not of a part only. Thus all propofitions, with regard to quality, are either affirmative or negative; and with regard to quantity, are univerfal or particular; and taking in both quantity and quality, they are univerfal affirmatives, or univerfal negatives, or particular affirmatives, or particular negatives. Thefe four kinds, after the days of Ariftotle, came to be named by the names of the four firft vowels, A, E, I, O, according to the following diftich:

Afferit A, negat E, fed univerfaliter ambæ ;
Afferit I, negat O, fed particulariter ambo.

When the young logician is thus far inftructed in the nature of propofitions, he is apt to think there is no difficulty in analyfing any propofition, and fhewing its fubject and predicate, its quantity and quality; and indeed, unlefs he can do this, he will be unable to apply the rules of logic to ufe. Yet he will find, there are fome difficulties in this analyfis, which are overlooked by Ariftotle altogether; and although they are fometimes touched, they are not removed by his followers. For, 1. There are propofitions in which it is difficult to find a fubject and

a predicate ; as in thefe, *It rains, It fnows.*
2. In fome propofitions either term may
be made the fubject or the predicate as
you like beft ; as in this, *Virtue is the road
to happinefs.*   3. The fame example may
ferve to fhew, that it is fometimes difficult
to fay, whether a propofition be univerfal
or particular.   4. The quality of fome
propofitions is fo dubious, that logicians
have never been able to agree whether
they be affirmative or negative ; as in this
propofition, *Whatever is infentient is not an
animal.*   5. As there is one clafs of propofitions which have only two terms, to wit,
one fubject and one predicate, which are
called *categorical propofitions ;* fo there are
many claffes that have more than two
terms.   What Ariftotle delivers in this
book is applicable only to categorical propofitions ; and to them only the rules
concerning the converfion of propofitions,
and concerning the figures and modes of
fyllogifms, are accommodated.   The fubfequent writers of logic have taken notice
of fome of the many claffes of complex
propofitions, and have given rules adapted
to them ; but finding this work endlefs,
they have left us to manage the reft by the
rules of common fenfe.

CHAP,

C H A P.   III.

Account of the First Analytics.

S e c t. i. *Of the Conversion of Propositions.*

IN attempting to give some account of
the Analytics and of the Topics of A-
riftotle, ingenuity requires me to confefs,
that tho' I have often purpofed to read the
whole with care, and to underftand what
is intelligible, yet my courage and patience
always failed before I had done. Why
fhould I throw away fo much time and
painful attention upon a thing of fo little
real ufe ? If I had lived in thofe ages
when the knowledge of Ariftotle's Organon intitled a man to the higheft rank in
philofophy, ambition might have induced
me to employ upon it fome years of painful ftudy ; and lefs, I conceive, would not
be fufficient. Such reflections as thefe,
always got the better of my refolution,

when the firſt ardor began to cool. All I can ſay is, that I have read ſome parts of the different books with care, ſome ſlightly, and ſome, perhaps not at all. I have glanced over the whole often, and when any thing attracted my attention, have dipped into it till my appetite was ſatisfied. Of all reading it is the moſt dry and the moſt painful, employing an infinite labour of demonſtration, about things of the moſt abſtract nature, delivered in a laconic ſtyle, and often, I think, with affected obſcurity; and all to prove general propoſitions, which when applied to particular inſtances appear ſelf-evident.

There is probably but little in the Categories or in the book of Interpretation, that Ariſtotle could claim as his own invention : but the whole theory of ſyllogiſms he claims as his own, and as the fruit of much time and labour. And indeed it is a ſtately fabric, a monument of a great genius, which we could wiſh to have been more uſefully employed. There muſt be ſomething however adapted to pleaſe the human underſtanding, or to flatter human pride, in a work which occupied men of ſpeculation for more than a thouſand years.

years. Thefe books are called *Analytics;* becaufe the intention of them is to refolve all reafoning into its fimple ingredients.

The firft book of the Firft Analytics, confifting of forty-fix chapters, may be divided into four parts; the firft treating of the converfion of propofitions; the fecond, of the ftructure of fyllogifms in all the different figures and modes; the third, of the invention of a middle term; and the laft, of the refolution of fyllogifms. We fhall give a brief account of each.

To convert a propofition, is to infer from it another propofition, whofe fubject is the predicate of the firft, and whofe predicate is the fubject of the firft. This is reduced by Ariftotle to three rules. 1. An univerfal negative may be converted into an univerfal negative: thus, *No man is a quadruped;* therefore, *No quadruped is a man.* 2. An univerfal affirmative can be converted only into a particular affirmative: thus, *All men are mortal;* therefore, *Some mortal beings are men.* 3. A particular affirmative may be converted into a particular affirmative: as, *Some men are juft;* therefore, *Some juft perfons are men.* When a propofition may be converted

verted without changing its quantity, this
is called *fimple converfion*; but when the
quantity is diminifhed, as in the univerfal affirmative, it is called converfion *per
accidens*.

There is another kind of converfion, o-
mitted in this place by Ariftotle, but fupplied by his followers, called *converfion by
contrapofition*, in which the term that is
contradictory to the predicate is put for
the fubject, and the quality of the propofition is changed; as, *All animals are fen-
tient*; therefore, *What is infentient is not
an animal*. A fourth rule of converfion
therefore is, That an univerfal affirmative,
and a particular negative, may be converted by contrapofition.

SECT. 2. *Of the Figures and Modes of pure
Syllogifms.*

A fyllogifm is an argument, or reafoning, confifting of three propofitions, the
laft of which, called *the conclufion*, is inferred from the two preceding, which are
called *the premifes*. The conclufion having
two terms, a fubject and a predicate, its
predicate

predicate is called the *major* term, and its fubject the *minor* term. In order to prove the conclufion, each of its terms is, in the premifes, compared with a third term, called the *middle* term. By this means one of the premifes will have for its two terms the major term and the middle term; and this premife is called the *major* premife, or the *major* propofition of the fyllogifm. The other premife muft have for its two terms the minor term and the middle term, and it is called the *minor* propofition. Thus the fyllogifm confifts of three propofitions, diftinguifhed by the names of the *major*, the *minor*, and the *conclufion:* and altho' each of thefe has two terms, a fubject and a predicate, yet there are only three different terms in all. The major term is always the predicate of the conclufion, and is alfo either the fubject or predicate of the major propofition. The minor term is always the fubject of the conclufion, and is alfo either the fubject or predicate of the minor propofition. The middle term never enters into the conclufion, but ftands in both premifes, either in the pofition of fubject or of predicate.

According

According to the various pofitions which the middle term may have in the premifes, fyllogifms are faid to be of various figures. Now all thé poffible pofitions of the middle term are only four: for, firft, it may be the fubject of the major propofition, and the predicate of the minor, and then the fyllogifm is of the firft figure ; or it may be the predicate of both premifes, and then the fyllogifm is of the fecond figure ; or it may be the fubject of both, which makes a fyllogifm of the third figure ; or it may be the predicate of the major propofition, and the fubject of the minor, which makes the fourth figure. Ariftotle takes no notice of the fourth figure. It was added by the famous Galen, and is often called *the Galenical figure.*

There is another divifion of fyllogifms according to their modes. The mode of a fyllogifm is determined by the quality and quantity of the propofitions of which it confifts. Each of the three propofitions muft be either an univerfal affirmative, or an univerfal negative, or a particular affirmative, or a particular negative. Thefe four kinds of propofitions, as was before obferved, have been named by the four vowels,

2   A,

A, E, I, O; by which means the mode of a fyllogifm is marked by any three of thofe four vowels. Thus A, A, A, denotes that mode in which the major, minor, and conclufion, are all univerfal affirmatives; E, A, E, denotes that mode in which the major and conclufion are univerfal negatives, and the minor is an univerfal affirmative.

To know all the poffible modes of fyllogifm, we muft find how many different combinations may be made of three out of the four vowels, and from the art of combination the number is found to be fixty-four. So many poffible modes there are in every figure, confequently in the three figures of Ariftotle there are one hundred and ninety-two, and in all the four figures two hundred and fifty-fix.

Now the theory of fyllogifm requires, that we fhew what are the particular modes in each figure, which do, or do not, form a juft and conclufive fyllogifm, that fo the legitimate may be adopted, and the fpurious rejected. This Ariftotle has fhewn in the firft three figures, examining all the modes one by one, and paffing fentence upon each; and from this examination he collects fome rules which may aid the memory in diftinguifhing the falfe from the true, and point out the properties of each figure.

The firft figure has only four legitimate modes. The major propofition in this figure muft be univerfal, and the minor affirmative; and it has this property, that it yields conclufions of all kinds, affirmative and negative, univerfal and particular.

The fecond figure has alfo four legitimate modes. Its major propofition muft be univerfal, and one of the premifes muft be negative. It yields conclufions both univerfal and particular, but all negative.

The third figure has fix legitimate modes. Its minor muft always be affirmative; and it yields conclufions both affirmative and negative, but all particular.

Befides the rules that are proper to each figure, Ariftotle has given fome that are common to all, by which the legitimacy of fyllogifms may be tried. Thefe may, I think, be reduced to five. 1. There muft be only three terms in a fyllogifm. As each term occurs in two of the propofitions, it muft be precifely the fame in both : if it be not, the fyllogifm is faid to have

have four terms, which makes a vitious fyllogifm. 2. The middle term muft be taken univerfally in one of the premifes. 3. Both premifes muft not be particular propofitions, nor both negative. 4. The conclufion muft be particular, if either of the premifes be particular; and negative, if either of the premifes be negative. 5. No term can be taken univerfally in the conclufion, if it be not taken univerfally in the premifes.

For underftanding the fecond and fifth of thefe rules, it is neceffary to obferve, that a term is faid to be taken univerfally, not only when it is the fubject of an univerfal propofition, but when it is the predicate of a negative propofition; on the other hand, a term is faid to be taken particularly, when it is either the fubject of a particular, or the predicate of an affirmative propofition.

SECT. 3. *Of the Invention of a Middle Term.*

The third part of this book contains rules general and fpecial for the invention of a middle term; and this the author

conceives to be of great utility. The general rules amount to this, That you are
to confider well both terms of the propofition to be proved ; their definition, their
properties, the things which may be affirmed or denied of them, and thofe of
which they may be affirmed or denied :
thefe things collected together, are the materials from which your middle term is to
be taken.

The fpecial rules require you to confider
the quantity and quality of the propofition
to be proved, that you may difcover in
what mode and figure of fyllogifm the
proof is to proceed. Then from the materials before collected, you muft feek a
middle term which has that relation to the
fubject and predicate of the propofition to
be proved, which the nature of the fyllogifm requires. Thus, fuppofe the propofition I would prove is an univerfal affirmative, I know by the rules of fyllogifms,
that there is only one legitimate mode in
which an univerfal affirmative propofition
can be proved ; and that is the firft mode
of the firft figure. I know likewife, that
in this mode both the premifes muft be
univerfal affirmatives ; and that the middle

dle term mu{t be the fubject of the major,
and the predicate of the minor. Therefore
óf the terms collected according to the general rule, I feek out one or more which
have thefe two properties ; firft, That the
predicate of the propofition to be proved
can be univerfally affirmed of it ; and fecondly, That it can be univerfally affirmed of the fubject of the propofition to bé
proved. Every term you can find which
has thofe two properties, will ferve you as
a middle term, but no other. In this way,
the author gives fpecial rules for all the
various kinds of propofitions to be proved ; points out the various modes in
which they may be proved, and the properties which the middle term mu{t have
to make it fit for anfwering that end. And
the rules are illuftrated, or rather, in my
opinion, purpofely darkened, by putting
letters of the alphabet for the feveral terms.

SECT. 4.   *Of the remaining part of the Firft*
  Book.

The refolution of fyllogifms requires no
other principles but thefe before laid down
                              for

for conſtructing them. However it is treated of largely, and rules laid down for reducing reaſoning to ſyllogiſms, by ſupplying one of the premiſes when it is underſtood, by rectifying inverſions, and putting the propoſitions in the proper order.

Here he ſpeaks alſo of hypothetical ſyllogiſms; which he acknowledges cannot be reſolved into any of the figures, although there be many kinds of them that ought diligently to be obſerved; and which he promiſes to handle afterwards. But this promiſe is not fulfilled, as far as I know, in any of his works that are extant.

SECT. 5. *Of the Second Book of the Firſt Analytics.*

The ſecond book treats of the powers of ſyllogiſms, and ſhows, in twenty-ſeven chapters, how we may perform many feats by them, and what figures and modes are adapted to each. Thus, in ſome ſyllogiſms ſeveral diſtinct concluſions may be drawn from the ſame premiſes: in ſome, true

true conclufions may be drawn from falfe premifes : in fome, by affuming the con-clufion and one premife, you may prove the other; you may turn a direct fyllogifm into one leading to an abfurdity.

We have likewife precepts given in this book, both to the affailant in a fyllogifti-cal difpute, how to carry on his attack with art, fo as to obtain the victory; and to the defendant, how to keep the enemy at fuch a diftance as that he fhall never be obliged to yield. From which we learn, that Ariftotle introduced in his own fchool, the practice of fyllogiftical difputation, in-ftead of the rhetorical difputations which the fophifts were wont to ufe in more ancient times.

C H A P   IV.

Remarks.

SECT. I.   *Of the Converfion of Propofitions.*

WE have given a fummary view of the theory of pure fyllogifms as deliver-ed by Ariftotle, a theory of which he
claims

claims the fole invention. And I believe it
will be difficult, in any fcience, to find fo
large a fyftem of truths of fo very abftract
and fo general a nature, all fortified by demonftration, and all invented and perfected by one man. It fhows a force of genius
and labour of inveftigation, equal to the
moft arduous attempts. I fhall now make
fome remarks upon it.

As to the converfion of propofitions,
the writers on logic commonly fatisfy
themfelves with illuftrating each of the
rules by an example, conceiving them to
be felf-evident when applied to particular
cafes. But Ariftotle has given demonftrations of the rules he mentions. As a fpecimen, I fhall give his demonftration of
the firft rule. " Let A B be an univerfal
" negative propofition ; I fay, that if A is
" in no B, it will follow that B is in no A.
" If you deny this confequence, let B be
" in fome A, for example, in C; then the
" firft fuppofition will not be true; for
" C is of the B's." In this demonftration, if I underftand it, the third rule of
converfion is affumed, that if B is in fome
A, then A muft be in fome B, which indeed is contrary to the firft fuppofition. If

I   the

the third rule be affumed for proof of the firſt, the proof of all the three goes round in a circle; for the fecond and third rules are proved by the firſt. This is a fault in reaſoning which Ariſtotle condemns, and which I would be very unwilling to charge him with, if I could find any better meaning in his demonſtration. But it is indeed a fault very difficult to be avoided, when men attempt to prove things that are felf-evident.

The rules of converſion cannot be applied to all propoſitions, but only to thofe that are categorical; and we are left to the direction of common fenfe in the converſion of other propoſitions. To give an example: Alexander was the fon of Philip; therefore Philip was the father of Alexander: A is greater than B; therefore B is lefs than A. Thefe are converſions which, as far as I know, do not fall within any rule in logic; nor do we find any lofs for want of a rule in fuch cafes.

Even in the converſion of categorical propoſitions, it is not enough to tranfpofe the fubject and predicate. Both muſt undergo fome change, in order to fit them for their new ſtation: for in every propofition the fubject muft be a fubftantive, or have the force of a fubftantive; and the predicate muft be an adjective, or have the force of an adjective. Hence it follows, that when the fubject is an individual, the propofition admits not of converfion. How, for inftance, fhall we convert this propofition, God is omnifcient?

Thefe obfervations fhow, that the doctrine of the converfion of propofitions is not fo complete as it appears. The rules are laid down without any limitation; yet they are fitted only to one clafs of propofitions, to wit, the categorical; and of thefe only to fuch as have a general term for their fubject.

S e c t. 2. *On Additions made to Ariftotle's Theory.*

Although the logicians have enlarged the firft and fecond parts of logic, by explaining fome technical words and diftinctions which Ariftotle has omitted, and by giving names to fome kinds of propofitions which he overlooks; yet in what concerns the theory of categorical fyllo-gifms,

gifms, he is more full, more minute and particular, than any of them: fo that they feem to have thought this capital part of the Organon rather redundant than deficient.

It is true, that Galen added a fourth figure to the three mentioned by Ariftotle. But there is reafon to think that Ariftotle omitted the fourth figure, not through ignorance or inattention, but of defign, as containing only fome indirect modes, which, when properly expreffed, fall into the firft figure.

It is true alfo, that Peter Ramus, a profeffed enemy of Ariftotle, introduced fome new modes that are adapted to fingular propofitions; and that Ariftotle takes no notice of fingular propofitions, either in his rules of converfion, or in the modes of fyllogifm. But the friends of Ariftotle have fhewn, that this improvement of Ramus is more fpecious than ufeful. Singular propofitions have the force of univerfal propofitions, and are fubject to the fame rules. The definition given by Ariftotle of an univerfal propofition applies to them; and therefore he might think,

that

that there was no occasion to multiply the modes of fyllogifm upon their account.

Thefe attempts, therefore, fhow rather inclination than power, to difcover any material defect in Ariftotle's theory.

The moft valuable addition made to the theory of categorical fyllogifms, feems to be the invention of thofe technical names given to the legitimate modes, by which they may be eafily remembered, and which have been comprifed in thefe barbarous verfes.

> Barbara, Celarent, Darii, Ferio, dato primæ ;
> Cefare, Cameftris, Feftino, Baroco, fecundæ ;
> Tertia grande fonans recitat Darapti, Felapton :
> Adjungens Difamis, Datifi, Bocardo, Eerifon.

In thefe verfes, every legitimate mode belonging to the three figures has a name given to it, by which it may be diftinguifhed and remembered. And this name is fo contrived as to denote its nature : for the name has three vowels, which denote the kind of each of its propofitions.

Thus, a fyllogifm in *Bocardo* muft be made up of the propofitions denoted by the three vowels, O, A, O ; that is, its major and conclufion muft be particular negative propofitions, and its minor an univerfal niverſal affirmative ; and being in the third figure, the middle term muſt be the ſubjeƈt of both premiſes.

This is the myſtery contained in the vowels of thoſe barbarous words. But there are other myſteries contained in their conſonants : for, by their means, a child may be taught to reduce any ſyllogiſm of the ſecond or third figure to one of the firſt. So that the four modes of the firſt figure being direƈtly proved to be concluſive, all the modes of the other two are proved at the ſame time, by means of this operation of reduƈtion. · For the rules and manner of this reduƈtion, and the different ſpecies of it, called *oſtenſive* and *per impoſſibile*, I refer to the logicians, that I may not diſcloſe all their myſteries.

The invention contained in theſe verſes is ſo ingenious, and ſo great an adminicle to the dextrous management of ſyllogiſms, that I think it very probable that Ariſtotle had ſome contrivance of this kind, which was kept as one of the ſecret doctrines of his ſchool, and handed down by tradition, until ſome perſon brought it to light. This is offered only as a conjecture, leaving it to thoſe who are better acquainted

quainted with the moſt ancient commentators on the Analytics, either to refute or
to confirm it.

S E C T. *3. On Examples uſed to illuſtrate
this Theory.*

We may obſerve, that Ariſtotle hardly
ever gives examples of real ſyllogiſms to
illuſtrate his rules.   In demonſtrating the
legitimate modes, he takes A, B, C, for
the terms of the ſyllogiſm.   Thus, the
firſt mode of the firſt figure is demonſtrated by him in this manner.   " For," ſays
he, " if A is attributed to every B, and B
" to every C, it follows neceſſarily, that
" A may be attributed to every C."   For
diſproving the illegitimate modes, he uſes
the ſame manner ; with this difference,
that he commonly for an example gives
three real terms, ſuch as, *bonum, habitus,
prudentiæ ;* of which three terms you are
to make up a ſyllogiſm of the figure and
mode in queſtion, which will appear to be
inconcluſive.
     The commentators and ſyſtematical wri-
ters in logic, have ſupplied this defect ;
                                                and

and given us real examples of every legitimate mode in all the figures. We acknowledge this to be charitably done, in order to affift the conception in matters fo very abftract; but whether it was prudently done for the honour of the art, may be doubted. I am afraid this was to uncover the nakednefs of the theory : it has undoubtedly contributed to bring it into contempt; for when one confiders the filly and uninftructive reafonings that have been brought forth by this grand organ of fcience, he can hardly forbear crying out, *Parturiunt montes, et nafcitur ridiculus mus.* Many of the writers of logic are acute and. ingenious, and much practifed in the fyllogiftical art; and there muft be fome reafon why the examples they have given of fyllogifms are fo lean.

We fhall fpeak of the reafon afterwards; and fhall now give a fyllogifm in each figure as an example.

No work of God is bad ;

The natural paffions and appetites of men are the work of God ;

. Therefore none of them is bad.

In this fyllogifm, the middle term, *work of God*, is the fubject of the major. and

the

the predicate of the minor; fo that the fyllogifm is of the firft figure. The mode is that called *Celarent;* the major and conclufion being both univerfal negatives, and the minor an univerfal affirmative. It agrees to the rules of the figure, as the major is univerfal, and the minor affirmative; it is alfo agreeable to all the general rules; fo that it maintains its character in every trial. And to fhow of what ductile materials fyllogifms are made, we may, by converting fimply the major propofition, reduce it to a good fyllogifm of the fecond figure, and of the mode *Cefare,* thus:

Whatever is bad is not the work of God;

All the natural paffions and appetites of men are the work of God;

Therefore they are not bad.

Another example:

Every thing virtuous is praife-worthy;

Some pleafures are not praife-worthy;

Therefore fome pleafures are not virtuous.

Here the middle term *praife-worthy* being the predicate of both premifes, the fyllogifm is of the fecond figure; and feeing it is made up of the propofitions, A,

2   O,

O, O, the mode is *Baroco*. It will be found to agree both with the general and fpecial rules : and it may be reduced into a good fyllogifm of the firft figure upon converting the major by contrapofition, thus :

> What is not praife-worthy is not vir-
> tuous ;
> Some pleafures are not praife-worthy ;
> Therefore fome pleafures are not virtu-
> ous.

That this fyllogifm is conclufive, common fenfe pronounces, and all logicians muft allow ; but it is fomewhat unpliable to rules, and requires a little ftraining to make it tally with them.

That it is of the firft figure is beyond difpute ; but to what mode of that figure fhall we refer it ? This is a queftion of fome difficulty. For, in the firft place, the premifes feem to be both negative, which contradicts the third general rule ; and moreover, it is contrary to a fpecial rule of the firft figure, That the minor fhould be negative. Thefe are the difficulties to be removed.

Some logicians think, that the two negative particles in the major are equivalent

to an affirmative; and that therefore the
major propofition, *What is not praife-worthy, is not virtuous*, is to be accounted an
affirmative propofition. This, if granted,
folves one difficulty; but the other remains. The moft ingenious folution,
therefore, is this: Let the middle term be
not praife-worthy. Thus, making the negative particle a part of the middle term,
the fyllogifm ftands thus:

  Whatever is *not praife-worthy* is not vir-
    tuous;
  Some pleafures are *not praife-worthy;*
  Therefore fome pleafures are not virtu-
    ous.

By this analyfis, the major becomes an u-
niverfal negative, the minor a particular
affirmative, and the conclufion a particular negative, and fo we have a juft fyllogifm in *Ferio.*

  We fee, by this example, that the quality of propofitions is not fo invariable,
but that, when occafion requires, an affirmative may be degraded into a negative,
or a negative exalted to an affirmative.
Another example:

  All Africans are black;
  All Africans are men;

                    Therefore

Therefore fome men are black.

This is of the third figure, and of the mode *Darapti;* and it may be reduced to *Darii* in the firft figure, by converting the minor.

All Africans are black;

Some men are Africans ;

Therefore fome men are black.

By this time I apprehend the reader has got as many examples of fyllogifms as will ftay his appetite for that kind of entertainment.

SECT. 4.   *On the Demonftration of the Theory.*

Ariftotle and all his followers have thought it neceffary, in order to bring this theory of categorical fyllogifms to a fcience, to demonftrate, both that the fourteen authorifed modes conclude juftly, and that none of the reft do. Let us now fee how this has been executed.

As to the legitimate modes, Ariftotle and thofe who follow him the moft clofely, demonftrate the four modes of the firft figure directly from an axiom called the

Dictum

Dictum de omni et nullo. The amount of
the axiom is, That what is affirmed of a
whole *genus,* may be affirmed of all the
species and individuals belonging to that
genus ; and that what is denied of the
whole genus, may be denied of its species
and individuals. The four modes of the
firſt figure are evidently included in this
axiom. And as to the legitimate modes
of the other figures, they are proved by
reducing them to ſome mode of the firſt.
Nor is there any other principle aſſumed
in theſe reductions but the axioms concerning the converſion of propoſitions, and
in ſome caſes the axioms concerning the
oppoſition of propoſitions.

As to the illegitimate modes, Ariſtotle
has taken the labour to try and condemn
them one by one in all the three figures :
but this is done in ſuch a manner that it
is very painful to follow him. To give a
ſpecimen. In order to prove, that thoſe
modes of the fiı ſt figure in which the major is particular, do not conclude, he proceeds thus : " If A is or is not in ſome B,
" and B in every C, no concluſion follows.
" Take for the terms in the affirmative
" caſe, *good, habit, prudence,* in the nega-
" tive,

" tive, *good, habit, ignorance.*" This laconic ſtyle, the uſe of ſymbols not familiar, and, in place of giving an example, his leaving us to form one from three aſſigned terms, give ſuch embarraſſment to a reader, that he is like one reading a book of riddles.

Having thus aſcertained the true and falſe modes of a figure, he ſubjoins the particular rules of that figure, which ſeem to be deduced from the particular caſes before determined. The general rules come laſt of all, as a general corollary from what goes before.

I know not whether it is from a diffidence of Ariſtotle's demonſtrations, or from an apprehenſion of their obſcurity, or from a deſire of improving upon his method, that almoſt all the writers in logic I have met with, have inverted his order, beginning where he ends, and ending where he begins. They firſt demonſtrate the general rules, which belong to all the figures, from three axioms ; then from the general rules and the nature of each figure, they demonſtrate the ſpecial rules of each figure. When this is done, nothing remains but to apply theſe general and
ſpecial

fpecial rules, and to reject every mode which contradicts them.

This method has a very fcientific appearance ; and when we confider, that by a few rules once demonftrated, an hundred and feventy-eight falfe modes are deftroyed at one blow, which Ariftotle had the trouble to put to death one by one, it feems to be a great improvement. I have only one objection to the three axioms.

The three axioms are thefe : 1. Things which agree with the fame third, agree with one another. 2. When one agrees with the third, and the other does not, they do not agree with one another. 3. When neither agrees with the third, you cannot thence conclude, either that they do, or do not agree with one another. If thefe axioms are applied to mathematical quantities, to which they feem to relate when taken literally, they have all the evidence that an axiom ought to have : but the logicians apply them in an analogical fenfe to things of another nature. In order, therefore, to judge whether they are truly axioms, we ought to ftrip them of their figurative drefs, and to fet them down in plain Englifh, as the logicians

underftand

underſtand them. They amount therefore to this. 1. If two things be affirmed
of a third, or the third be affirmed of
them; or if one be affirmed of the third,
and the third affirmed of the other; then
they may be affirmed one of the other.
2. If one is affirmed of the third, or the
third of it, and the other denied of the
third, or the third of it, they may be denied one of the other. 3. If both are denied of the third, or the third of them;
or if one is denied of the third, and the
third denied of the other; nothing can be
inferred.

When the three axioms are thus put in
plain Engliſh, they ſeem not to have that
degree of evidence which axioms ought to
have; and if there is any defect of evidence in the axioms, this defect will be
communicated to the whole edifice raiſed
upon them.

It may even be ſuſpected, that an attempt by any method to demonſtrate that
a ſyllogiſm is concluſive, is an impropri-
ety ſomewhat like that of attempting to
demonſtrate an axiom. In a juſt ſyllogiſm, the connection between the premiſes and the concluſion is not only real, but
immediate;

immediate; fo that no propofition can come between them to make their connection more apparent. The very intention of a fyllogifm is, to leave nothing to be fupplied that is neceffary to a complete demonftration. Therefore a man of common underftanding who has a perfect comprehenfion of the premifes, finds himfelf under a neceffity of admitting the conclufion, fuppofing the premifes to be true; and the conclufion is connected with the premifes with all the force of intuitive evidence. In a word, an immediate conclufion is feen in the premifes, by the light of common fenfe; and where that is wanting, no kind of reafoning will fupply its place.

Sect. 5. *On this Theory, confidered as an Engine of Science.*

The flow progrefs of ufeful knowledge, during the many ages in which the fyllogiftic art was moft highly cultivated as the only guide to fcience, and its quick progrefs fince that art was difufed, fuggeft a prefumption againft it; and this prefumption

I   tion

tion is ftrengthened by the puerility of the examples which have always been brought to illuftrate its rules.

The ancients feem to have had too high notions, both of the force of the reafoning power in man, and of the art of fyllogifm as its guide. Mere reafoning can carry us but a very little way in moft fubjects. By obfervation, and experiments properly conducted, the ftock of human knowledge may be enlarged without end ; but the power of reafoning alone, applied with vigour through a long life, would only carry a man round, like a horfe in a mill who labours hard but makes no progrefs. There is indeed an exception to this obfervation in the mathematical fciences. The relations of quantity are fo various and fo fufceptible of exact menfuration, that long trains of accurate reafoning on that fubject may be formed, and conclufions drawn very remote from the firft principles. It is in this fcience and thofe which depend upon it, that the power of reafoning triumphs ; in other matters its trophies are inconfiderable. If any man doubt this, let him produce, in any fubject unconnected with mathematics, a train of reafoning of fome length, leading to a conclufion, which without this train of reafoning would never have been brought within human fight. Every man acquainted with mathematics can produce thoufands of fuch trains of reafoning. I do not fay, that none fuch can be produced in other fciences; but I believe they are few, and not eafily found; and that if they are found, it will not be in fubjects that can be expreffed by categorical propofitions, to which alone the theory of figure and mode extends.

In matters to which that theory extends, a man of good fenfe, who can diftinguifh things that differ, can avoid the fnares of ambiguous words, and is moderately practifed in fuch matters, fees at once all that can be inferred from the premifes; or finds, that there is but a very fhort ftep to the conclufion.

When the power of reafoning is fo feeble by nature, efpecially in fubjects to which this theory can be applied, it would be unreafonable to expect great effects from it. And hence we fee the reafon why the examples brought to illuftrate it by

by the moſt ingenious logicians, have rather tended to bring it into contempt.

If it ſhould be thought, that the ſyllo-
giſtic art may be an uſeful engine in mathematics, in which pure reaſoning has
ample ſcope : Firſt, It may be obſerved,
That facts are unfavourable to this opinion : for it does not appear, that Euclid,
or Apollonius, or Archimedes, or Hugens,
or Newton, ever made the leaſt uſe of this
art ; and I am even of opinion, that no
uſe can be made of it in mathematics. I
would not wiſh to advance this raſhly,
ſince Ariſtotle has ſaid, that mathematicians reaſon for the moſt part in the firſt
figure. What led him to think ſo was,
that the firſt figure only yields conclusions
that are univerſal and affirmative, and the
conclusions of mathematics are commonly
of that kind. But it is to be obſerved,
that the propoſitions of mathematics are
not categorical propoſitions, conſiſting of
one ſubject and one predicate. They expreſs ſome relation which one quantity
bears to another, and on that account
muſt have three terms. The quantities
compared make two, and the relation between them is a third. Now to ſuch pro-

pofitions we can neither apply the rules concerning the converfion of propofitions, nor can they enter into a fyllogifm of any of the figures or modes. We obferved before, that this converfion, *A is greater than B*, therefore *B is lefs than A*, does not fall within the rules of converfion given by Ariftotle or the logicians ; and we now add, that this fimple reafoning, *A is equal to B, and B to C;* therefore *A is equal to C*, cannot be brought into any fyllogifm in figure and mode. There are indeed fyllogifms into which mathematical propofitions may enter, and of fuch we fhall afterwards fpeak : but they have nothing to do with the fyftem of figure and mode.

When we go without the circle of the mathematical fciences, I know nothing in which there feems to be fo much demonftration as in that part of logic which treats of the figures and modes of fyllogifm; but the few remarks we have made, fhew, that it has fome weak places : and befides, this fyftem cannot be ufed as an engine to rear itfelf.

The compafs of the fyllogiftic fyftem as an engine of fcience, may be difcerned by

a

a compendious and general view of the conclusion drawn, and the argument used to prove it, in each of the three figures.

In the first figure, the conclusion affirms or denies something of a certain species or individual ; and the argument to prove this conclusion is, That the same thing may be affirmed or denied of the whole genus to which that species or individual belongs.

In the second figure, the conclusion is, That some species or individual does not belong to such a genus ; and the argument is, That some attribute common to the whole genus does not belong to that species or individual.

In the third figure, the conclusion is, That such an attribute belongs to part of a genus ; and the argument is, That the attribute in question belongs to a species or individual which is part of that genus.

I apprehend, that, in this short view, every conclusion that falls within the compass of the three figures, as well as the mean of proof, is comprehended. The rules of all the figures might be easily deduced from it ; and it appears, that there is only one principle of reafoning in all the three; fo that it is not ftrange, that a fyllogifm of one figure fhould be redu- ced to one of another figure.

The general principle in which the whole terminates, and of which every ca- tegorical fyllogifm is only a particular ap- plication, is this, That what is affirmed or denied of the whole genus, may be af- firmed or denied of every fpecies and in- dividual belonging to it. This is a prin- ciple of undoubted certainty indeed, but of no great depth. Ariftotle and all the logi- cians affume it as an axiom or firft prin- ciple, from which the fyllogiftic fyftem, as it were, takes its departure: and after a tedious voyage, and great expence of demonftration, it lands at laft in this prin- ciple as its ultimate conclufion. *O curas hominum ! O quantum eft in rebus inane !*

S E C T. 6.   *On Modal Syllogifms.*

Categorical propofitions, befides their quantity and quality, have another affec- tion, by which they are divided into pure and modal. In a pure propofition, the predicate

predicate is barely affirmed or denied of the fubject; but in a modal propofition, the affirmation or negation is modified, by being declared to be neceffary, or contingent, or poffible, or impoffible. Thefe are the four modes obferved by Ariftotle, from which he denominates a propofition modal. His genuine difciples maintain, that thefe are all the modes that can affect an affirmation or negation, and that the enumeration is complete. Others maintain, that this enumeration is incomplete; and that when an affirmation or negation is faid to be certain or uncertain, probable or improbable, this makes a modal propofition, no lefs than the four modes of Ariftotle. We fhall not enter into this difpute; but proceed to obferve, that the epithets of *pure* and *modal* are applied to fyllogifms as well as to propofitions. A pure fyllogifm is that in which both premifes are pure propofitions. A modal fyllogifm is that in which either of the premifes is a modal propofition.

The fyllogifms of which we have already faid fo much, are thofe only which are pure as well as categorical. But when we confider, that through all the figures and

and modes, a fyllogifm may have one premife modal of any of the four modes,
while the other is pure, or it may have
both premifes modal, and that they may
be either of the fame mode or of different
modes; what prodigious variety arifes
from all thefe combinations? Now it is
the bufinefs of a logician, to fhew how
the conclufion is affected in all this variety of cafes. Ariftotle has done this in
his Firft Analytics, with immenfe labour;
and it will not be thought ftrange, that
when he had employed only four chapters
in difcuffing one hundred and ninety-two
modes, true and falfe, of pure fyllogifms,
he fhould employ fifteen upon modal fyllogifms.

I am very willing to excufe myfelf from
entering upon this great branch of logic,
by the judgement and example of thofe
who cannot be charged either with want
of refpect to Ariftotle, or with a low efteem
of the fyllogiftic art.

Keckerman, a famous Dantzican pro-
feffor, who fpent his life in teaching and
writing logic, in his huge folio fyftem of
that fcience, publifhed *ann.* 1600, calls
the doctrine of the modals the *crux logi-*

2   *corum.*

corium. With regard to the fcholaftic doc-
tors, among whom this was a proverb,
De modalibus non guftabit afinus, he thinks
it very dubious, whether they tortured
moft the modal fyllogifms, or were moft
tortured by them. But thofe crabbed ge-
niufes, fays he, made this doctrine fo very
thorny, that it is fitter to tear a man's wits
in pieces than to give them folidity.
He defires it to be obferved, that the doctrine of the modals is adapted to the Greek
language. The modal terms were frequently ufed by the Greeks in their difputations; and, on that account, are fo
fully handled by Ariftotle : but in the Latin tongue you fhall hardly ever meet with
them. Nor do I remember, in all my experience, fays he, to have obferved any
man in danger of being foiled in a difpute,
through his ignorance of the modals.

This author, however, out of refpect to .
Ariftotle, treats pretty fully of modal propofitions, fhewing how to diftinguifh their
fubject and predicate, their quantity and
quality. But the modal fyllogifms he
paffes over altogether.

Ludovicus Vives, whom I mention,
not as a devotee of Ariftotle, but on ac-

count of his own judgement and learning, thinks that the doctrine of modals ought to be banifhed out of logic, and remitted to grammar; and that if the grammar of the Greek tongue had been brought to a fyftem in the time of Ariftotle, that moft acute philofopher would have faved the great labour he has beftowed on this fub-ject.

Burgerfdick, after enumerating five claffes of modal fyllogifms, obferves, that they require many rules and cautions, which Ariftotle hath handled diligently; but that as the ufe of them is not great and their rules difficult, he thinks it not worth while to enter into the difcuffion of them; recommending to thofe who would underftand them, the moft learned para-phrafe of Joannes Monlorius upon the firft book of the Firft Analytics.

All the writers of logic for two hundred years back that have fallen into my hands, have paffed over the rules of modal fyllo-gifms with as little ceremony. So that this great branch of the doctrine of fyl-logifm, fo diligently handled by Ariftotle, fell into neglect, if not contempt, even while the doctrine of pure fyllogifms con-

tinued

tinued in the higheft efteem. Moved by thefe authorities, I fhall let this doctrine reft in peace, without giving the leaft difturbance to its afhes.

Sect. 7. *On Syllogifms that do not belong to Figure and Mode.*

Ariftotle gives fome obfervations upon imperfect fyllogifms : fuch as, the Enthimema, in which one of the premifes is not expreffed but underftood : Induction, wherein we collect an univerfal from a full enumeration of particulars : and Examples, which are an imperfect induction. The logicians have copied Ariftotle upon thefe kinds of reafoning, without any confiderable improvement. But to compenfate the modal fyllogifms, which they have laid afide, they have given rules for feveral kinds of fyllogifin, of which Ariftotle takes no notice. Thefe may be reduced to two claffes.

The firft clafs comprehends the fyllogifms into which any exclufive, reftrictive, exceptive, or reduplicative propofition enters. Such propofitions are by fome called

3 C 2   *exponible,*

exponible, by others *imperfectly modal*. The rules given with regard to thefe are obvious, from a juft interpretation of the propofitions.

The fecond clafs is that of hypothetical fyllogifms, which take that denomination from having a hypothetical propofition for one or both premifes. Moft logicians give the name of *hypothetical* to all complex propofitions which have more terms than one fubject and one predicate. I ufe the word in this large fenfe; and mean by hypothetical fyllogifms, all thofe in which either of the premifes confifts of more terms than two. How many various kinds there may be of fuch fyllogifms, has never been afcertained. The logicians have given names to fome; fuch as, the copulative, the conditional by fome called hypothetical, and the disjunctive.

Such fyllogifms cannot be tried by the rules of figure and mode. Every kind would require rules peculiar to itfelf. Logicians have given rules for fome kinds; but there are many that have not fo much as a name.

The Dilemma is confidered by moft logicians as a fpecies of the disjunctive fyllogifm.

logifm. A remarkable property of this kind is, that it may fometimes be happily retorted : it is, it feems, like a hand-grenade, which by dextrous management may be thrown back, fo as to fpend its force upon the affailant. We fhall conclude this tedious account of fyllogifms, with a dilemma mentioned by *A. Gellius*, and from him by many logicians, as infoluble in any other way.

" Euathlus, a rich young man, defirous " of learning the art of pleading, applied " to Protagoras, a celebrated fophift, to " inftruct him, promifing a great fum of " money as his reward; one half of which " was paid down; the other half he " bound himfelf to pay as foon as he " fhould plead a caufe before the judges, " and gain it. Protagoras found him a " very apt fcholar; but, after he had " made good progrefs, he was in no hafte " to plead caufes. The mafter, concei- " ving that he intended by this means to " fhift off his fecond payment, took, as " he thought, a fure method to get the " better of his delay. He fued Euathlus " before the judges ; and, having opened " his caufe at the bar, he pleaded to this " purpofe.

" purpofe. O moft foolifh young man,
" do you not fee, that, in any event, I
" muft gain my point? for if the judges
" give fentence for me, you muft pay
" by their fentence; if againft me, the
" condition of our bargain is fulfilled,
" and you have no plea left for your de-
" lay, after having pleaded and gained a
" caufe. To which Euathlus anfwered,
" O moft wife mafter, I might have a-
" voided the force of your argument, by
" not pleading my own caufe. But, gi-
" ving up this advantage, do you not fee,
" that whatever fentence the judges pafs,
" I am fafe? If they give fentence for
" me, I am acquitted by their fentence;
" if againft me, the condition of our bar-
" gain is not fulfilled, by my pleading a
" caufe, and lofing it. The judges, think-
" ing the arguments unanfwerable on
" both fides, put off the caufe to a long
" day."

C H A P.

C H A P   V.

Account of the remaining books of the Organon.

SECT. I.   *Of the Laſt Analytics.*

IN the firſt Analytics, ſyllogiſms are con-ſidered in reſpect of their form ; they are now to be conſidered in reſpect of their matter.   The form lies in the neceſſary connection between the premiſes and the concluſion ; and where ſuch a connection is wanting, they are ſaid to be informal, or vicious in point of form.

But where there is no fault in the form, there may be in the matter ; that is, in the propoſitions of which they are compoſed, which may be true or falſe, probable or improbable.

When the premiſes are certain, and the concluſion drawn from them in due form, this is demonſtration, and produces ſci-ence.   Such ſyllogiſms are called *apodic-tical;*

tical; and are handled in the two books of
the Laſt Analytics. When the premiſes
are not certain, but probable only, ſuch
ſyllogiſms are called *dialectical;* and of
them he treats in the eight books of the
Topicks. But there are ſome ſyllogiſms
which ſeem to be perfect both in matter
and form, when they are not really ſo:
as, a face may ſeem beautiful which is but
painted. Theſe being apt to deceive, and
produce a falſe opinion, are called *ſophiſti-
cal;* and they are the ſubject of the book
concerning Sophiſms.

To return to the Laſt Analytics, which
treat of demonſtration and of ſcience: We
ſhall not pretend to abridge theſe books;
for Ariſtotle's writings do not admit of a-
bridgement: no man in fewer words can
ſay what he ſays; and he is not often
guilty of repetition. We ſhall only give
ſome of his capital concluſions, omitting
his long reaſonings and nice diſtinctions,
of which his genius was wonderfully productive.

All demonſtration muſt be built upon
principles already known; and theſe upon
others of the ſame kind; until we come
at laſt to firſt principles, which neither

can be demonftrated, nor need to be, being evident of themfelves.

We cannot demonftrate things in a circle, fupporting the conclufion by the premifes, and the premifes by the conclufion. Nor can there be an infinite number of middle terms between the firft principle and the conclufion.

In all demonftration, the firft principles, the conclufion, and all the intermediate propofitions, muft be neceffary, general, and eternal truths : for of things fortuitous, contingent, or mutable, or of individual things, there is no demonftration.

Some demonftrations prove only, that the thing is thus affected ; others prove, why it is thus affected. The former may be drawn from a remote caufe, or from an effect : but the latter muft be drawn from an immediate caufe; and are the moft perfect.

The firft figure is beft adapted to demonftration, becaufe it affords conclufions univerfally affirmative ; and this figure is commonly ufed by the mathematicians.

The demonftration of an affirmative propofition is preferable to that of a negative; the demonſtration of an univerſal to that of a particular; and direct demonſtration to that *ad abſurdum.*

The principles are more certain than the concluſion.

There cannot be opinion and ſcience of the ſame thing at the ſame time.

In the ſecond book we are taught, that the queſtions that may be put with regard to any thing, are four: 1. Whether the thing be thus affected. 2. Why it is thus affected. 3. Whether it exiſts. 4. What it is.

The laſt of theſe queſtions Ariſtotle, in good Greek, calls the *What is it* of a thing. The ſchoolmen, in very barbarous Latin, called this, the *quiddity* of a thing. This quiddity, he proves by many arguments, cannot be demonſtrated, but muſt be fixed by a definition. This gives occaſion to treat of definition, and how a right definition ſhould be formed. As an example, he gives a definition of the number *three,* and defines it to be the firſt odd number.

In this book he treats alſo of the four kinds of cauſes; efficient, material, formal, and final.

Another thing treated of in this book is,
the

the manner in which we acquire firſt principles, which are the foundation of all demonſtration. Theſe are not innate, becauſe we may be for a great part of life
ignorant of them : nor can they be deduced demonſtratively from any antecedent
knowledge, otherwiſe they would not be firſt
principles. Therefore he concludes, that
firſt principles are got by induction, from
the informations of ſenſe. The ſenſes give
us informations of individual things, and
from theſe by induction we draw general
concluſions : for it is a maxim with Ariſtotle, That there is nothing in the underſtanding which was not before in ſome
ſenſe.

The knowledge of firſt principles, as it
is not acquired by demonſtration, ought
not to be called ſcience ; and therefore he
calls it *intelligence.*

Sect. 2. *Of the Topics.*

The profeſſed deſign of the Topics is, to
ſhew a method by which a man may be
able to reaſon with probability and con-
ſiſtency

fiftency upon every queftion that can occur.

Every queftion is either about the genus of the fubject, or its fpecific difference,
or fome thing proper to it, or fomething
accidental.

To prove that this divifion is complete,
Ariftotle reafons thus : Whatever is attributed to a fubject, it muft either be, that
the fubject can be reciprocally attributed
to it, or that it cannot. If the fubject and
attribute can be reciprocated, the attribute
either declares what the fubject is, and
then it is a definition ; or it does not declare what the fubject is, and then it is a
property. If the attribute cannot be reciprocated, it muft be fomething contained
in the definition, or not. If it be contained in the definition of the fubject, it muft
be the genus of the fubject, or its fpecific
difference ; for the definition confifts of
thefe two. If it be not contained in the
definition of the fubject, it muft be an
accident.

The furniture proper to fit a man for ar-
guing dialectically may be reduced to thefe
four heads : 1. Probable propofitions of all
forts, which may on occafion be affumed

in

in an argument.   2. Diftinctions of words which are nearly of the fame fignification. 3. Diftinctions of things which are not fo far afunder but that they may be taken for one and the fame.   4. Similitudes.

The fecond and the five following books are taken up in enumerating the topics or heads of argument that may be ufed in queftions about the genus, the definition, the properties, and the accidents of a thing; and occafionally he introduces the topics for proving things to be the fame, or different; and the topics for proving one thing to be better or worfe than another.

In this enumeration of topics, Ariftotle has fhewn more the fertility of his genius, than the accuracy of method.   The writers of logic feem to be of this opinion : for I know none of them that has followed him clofely upon this fubject.   They have confidered the topics of argumentation as reducible to certain axioms.   For inftance, when the queftion is about the genus of a thing, it muft be determined by fome axiom about genus and fpecies ; when it is about a definition, it muft be determined by fome axiom relating to definition, and things defined : and fo of other queftions.

They

They have therefore reduced the doctrine
of the topics to certain axioms or canons,
and difpofed thefe axioms in order under
certain heads.

This method feems to be more com-
modious and elegant than that of Ariftotle. Yet it muft be acknowledged, that
Ariftotle has furnifhed the materials from
which all the logicians have borrowed
their doctrine of topics : and even Cicero,
Quintilian, and other rhetorical writers,
have been much indebted to the topics of
Ariftotle.

He was the firft, as far as I know, who
made an attempt of this kind : and in this
he acted up to the magnanimity of his
own genius, and that of ancient philofophy. Every fubject of human thought
had been reduced to ten categories; every
thing that can be attributed to any fubject, to five predicables : he attempted to
reduce all the forms of reafoning to fixed
rules of figure and mode, and to reduce
all the topics of argumentation under certain heads ; and by that means to collect
as it were into one ftore all that can be
faid on one fide or the other of every queftion, and to provide a grand arfenal, from
                                    which

which all future combatants might be furnifhed with arms offenfive and defenfive
in every caufe, fo as to leave no room to
future generations to invent any thing
new.

The laft book of the Topics is a code of
the laws according to which a fyllogiftical
difputation ought to be managed, both on
the part of the affailant and defendant.
From which it is evident, that this philofopher trained his difciples to contend, not
for truth merely, but for victory.

SECT. 3.   *Of the book concerning Sophifms.*

A fyllogifm which leads to a falfe conclufion, muft be vicious, either in matter
or form : for from true principles nothing
but truth can be juftly deduced.   If the
matter be faulty, that is, if either of the
premifes be falfe, that premife muft be
denied by the defendant.   If the form be
faulty, fome rule of fyllogifm is tranfgreffed ; and it is the part of the defendant to
fhew, what general or fpecial rule it is that
is tranfgreffed.   So that, if he be an able
logician, he will be impregnable in the
defence

defence of truth, and may refift all the at-
tacks of the fophift.　But as there are fyllogifms which may feem to be perfect
both in matter and form, when they are
not really fo, as a piece of money may
feem to be good coin when it is adulterate ; fuch fallacious fyllogifms are confidered in this treatife, in order to make a
defendant more expert in the ufe of his defenfive weapons.

And here the author, with his ufual
magnanimity, attempts to bring all the
fallacies that can enter into a fyllogifm
under thirteen heads ; of which fix lie in
the diction or language, and feven not in
the diction.

The fallacies in diction are, 1. When
an ambiguous word is taken at one
time in one fenfe, and at another time in
another.　2. When an ambiguous phrafe
is taken in the fame manner.　3. and 4.
are ambiguities in fyntax ; when words
are conjoined in fyntax that ought to be
disjoined ; or disjoined when they ought
to be conjoined.　5. is an ambiguity in
profody, accent, or pronunciation.　6.
An ambiguity arifing from fome figure of
fpeech.

　　2　　　　　　　　　　When

When a fophifm of any of thefe kinds is tranflated into another language, or even rendered into unambiguous expreffions in the fame language, the fallacy is evident, and the fyllogifm appears to have four terms.

The feven fallacies which are faid not to be in the diction, but in the thing, have their proper names in Greek and in Latin, by which they are diftinguifhed. Without minding their names, we fhall give a brief account of their nature.

1. The firft is, Taking an accidental conjunction of things for a natural or neceffary connection: as, when from an accident we infer a property; when from an example we infer a rule; when from a fingle act we infer a habit.

2. Taking that abfolutely which ought to be taken comparatively, or with a certain limitation. The conftruction of language often leads into this fallacy: for in all languages, it is common to ufe abfolute terms to fignify things that carry in them fome fecret comparifon; or to ufe unlimited terms, to fignify what from its nature muft be limited.

3. Taking that for the caufe of a thing

which is only an occafion, or concomitant.

4. Begging the queftion. This is done, when the thing to be proved, or fome thing equivalent, is affumed in the premifes.

5. Miftaking the queftion. When the conclufion of the fyllogifm is not the thing that ought to be proved, but fomething elfe that is miflaken for it.

6. When that which is not a confequence is miftaken for a confequence; as if, becaufe all Africans are black, it were taken for granted that all blacks are Africans.

7. The laft fallacy lies in propofitions that are complex, and imply two affirmations, whereof one may be true, and the other falfe; fo that whether you grant the propofition, or deny it, you are intangled: as when it is affirmed, that fuch a man has left off playing the fool. If it be granted, it implies, that he did play the fool formerly. If it be denied, it implies, or feems to imply, that he plays the fool ftill.

In this enumeration, we ought, in juftice to Ariftotle, to expect only the fallacies incident to categorical fyllogifms.

And

And I do not find, that the logicians have made any additions to it when taken in this view ; although they have given fome other fallacies that are incident to fyllo-gifms of the hypothetical kind, particu-larly the fallacy of an incomplete enume-ration in disjunctive fyllogifms and di-lemmas.

The different fpecies of fophifms above mentioned are not fo precifely defined by Ariftotle, or by fubfequent logicians, but that they allow of great latitude in the ap-plication ; and it is often dubious under what particular fpecies a fophiftical fyllo-gifm ought to be claffed. We even find the fame example brought under one fpe-cies by one author, and under another fpecies by another. Nay, what is more ftrange, Ariftotle himfelf employs a long chapter in proving by a particular induc-tion, that all the feven may be brought under that which we have called *miftaking the queftion,* and which is commonly call-ed *ignoratio elenchi.* And indeed the proof of this is eafy, without that laborious de-tail which Ariftotle ufes for the purpofe : for if you lop off from the conclufion of a fophiftical fyllogifm all that is not fup-

ported

ported by the premifes, the conclufion, in
that cafe, will always be found different
from that which ought to have been proved ; and fo it falls under the *ignoratio e-
lenchi.*

It was probably Ariftotle's aim, to reduce all the poffible variety of fophifms,
as he had attempted to do of juft fyllogifms, to certain definite fpecies : but he
feems to be fenfible that he had fallen
fhort in this laft attempt. When a genus
is properly divided into its fpecies, the
fpecies fhould not only, when taken together, exhauft the whole genus ; but e-
very fpecies fhould have its own precinct
fo accurately defined, that one fhall not
encroach upon another. And when an
individual can be faid to belong to two or
three different fpecies, the divifion is imperfect ; yet this is the cafe of Ariftotle's
divifion of the fophifms, by his own ac-
knowledgement. It ought not therefore
to be taken for a divifion ftrictly logical.
It may rather be compared to the feveral
fpecies or forms of action invented in law
for the redrefs of wrongs. For every
wrong there is a remedy in law by one
action or another : but fometimes a man
may

may take his choice among feveral different actions. So every fophiftical fyllogifm may, by a little art, be brought under one or other of the fpecies mentioned by Ariftotle, and very often you may take your choice of two or three.

Befides the enumeration of the various kinds of fophifms, there are many other things in this treatife concerning the art of managing a fyllogiftical difpute with an antagonift. And indeed, if the paffion for this kind of litigation, which reigned for fo many ages, fhould ever again lift up its head, we may predict, that the Organon of Ariftotle will then become a fafhionable ftudy: for it contains fuch admirable materials and documents for this art, that it may be faid to have brought it to a fcience.

The conclufion of this treatife ought not to be overlooked: it manifeftly relates, not to the prefent treatife only, but alfo to the whole analytics and topics of the author. I fhall therefore give the fubftance of it.

" Of thofe who may be called inventers,
" fome have made important additions to
" things long before begun, and carried
" on

" on through a courſe of ages ; others
" have given a ſmall beginning to things
" which, in ſucceeding times, will be
" brought to greater perfection. The be-
" ginning of a thing, though ſmall, is the
" chief part of it, and requires the great-
" eſt degree of invention ; for it is eaſy
" to make additions to inventions once
" begun. Now with regard to the dia-
" lectical art, there was not ſomething
" done, and ſomething remaining to be
" done.   There was abſolutely nothing
" done : for thoſe who profeſſed the art
" of diſputation, had only a ſet of ora-
" tions compoſed, and of arguments, and
" of captious queſtions, which might ſuit
" many occaſions. Theſe their ſcholars
" ſoon learned, and fitted to the occaſion.
" This was not to teach you the art, but
" to furniſh you with the materials pro-
" duced by the art : as if a man profeſ-
" ſing to teach you the art of making
" ſhoes, ſhould bring you a parcel of
" ſhoes of various ſizes and ſhapes, from
" which you may provide thoſe who want.
" This may have its uſe ; but it is not to
" teach the art of making ſhoes. And
" indeed, with regard to rhetorical de-
             " clamation,

" clamation, there are many precepts
" handed down from ancient times; but
" with regard to the conftruction of fyl-
" logifms, not one.

" We have therefore employed much
" time and labour upon this fubjeft; and
" if our fyftem appear to you not to be
" in the number of thofe things, which,
" being before carried a certain length,
" were left to be perfected; we hope for
" your favourable acceptance of what is
" done, and your indulgence in what is
" left imperfect."

C H A P. VI.

Reflections on the Utility of Logic, and
the Means of its improvement.

SECT. 1. *Of the Utility of Logic.*

MEN rarely leave one extreme without
running into the contrary. It is no
wonder, therefore, that the exceffive admiration of Ariftotle, which continued for

fo

fo many ages, fhould end in an undue contempt; and that the high efteem of logic as the grand engine of fcience, fhould at laft make way for too unfavourable an opinion, which feems now prevalent, of its being unworthy of a place in a liberal education. Thofe who think according to the fafhion, as the greateft part of men do, will be as prone to go into this extreme, as their grandfathers were to go into the contrary.

Laying afide prejudice, whether fafhionable or unfafhionable, let us confider whether logic is, or may be made, fubfervient to any good purpofe. Its profeffed end is, to teach men to think, to judge, and to reafon, with precifion and accuracy. No man will fay that this is a matter of no importance; the only thing therefore that admits of doubt, is, whether it can be taught.

To refolve this doubt, it may be obferved, that our rational faculty is the gift of God, given to men in very different meafure. Some have a large portion, fome a lefs; and where there is a remarkable defect of the natural power, it cannot be fupplied by any culture. But this natural

I

power,

power, even where it is the ftrongeft, may
lie dead for want of the means of improvement : a favage may have been born with
as good faculties as a Bacon or a Newton :
but his talent was buried, being never put
to ufe; while theirs was cultivated to the
beft advantage.

It may likewife be obferved, that the
chief mean of improving our rational
power, is the vigorous exercife of it, in
various ways and in different fubjects, by
which the habit is acquired of exercifing
it properly. Without fuch exercife, and
good fenfe over and above, a man who
has ftudied logic all his life, may after all
be only a petulant wrangler, without true
judgement or fkill of reafoning in any fcience.

I take this to be Locke's meaning, when
in his Thoughts on Education he fays,
" If you would have your fon to reafon
" well, let him read Chillingworth." The
ftate of things is much altered fince Locke
wrote. Logic has been much improved,
chiefly by his writings; and yet much
lefs ftrefs is laid upon it, and lefs time
confumed in it. His counfel, therefore,
was judicious and feafonable; to wit,

That the improvement of our reafoning
power is to be expected much more from
an intimate acquaintance with the authors
who reafon the beft, than from ftudying
voluminous fyftems of logic. But if
he had meant, that the ftudy of logic was
of no ufe nor deferved any attention, he
furely would not have taken the pains to
have made fo confiderable an addition to
it, by his *Effay on the Human Underftanding*,
and by his *Thoughts on the Conduct of the
Underftanding*. Nor would he have remitted his pupil to Chillingworth, the acuteft
logician as well as the beft reafoner of his
age; and one who, in innumerable places
of his excellent book, without pedantry e-
ven in that pedantic age, makes the hap-
pieft application of the rules of logic, for
unraveling the fophiftical reafoning of his
antagonift.

Our reafoning power makes no appearance in infancy; but as we grow up, it
unfolds itfelf by degrees, like the bud of
a tree. When a child firft draws an inference, or perceives the force of an inference drawn by another, we may call this
the birth of his reafon: but it is yet like a
new-born babe, weak and tender; it muft
be

be cherished, carried in arms, and have food of easy digestion, till it gather strength.

I believe no man remembers the birth of his reason : but it is probable that his decisions are at first weak and wavering ; and, compared with that steady conviction which he acquires in ripe years, are like the dawn of the morning compared with noon-day. We see that the reason of children yields to authority, as a reed to the wind ; nay, that it clings to it, and leans upon it, as if conscious of its own weaknefs.

When reason acquires such strength as to stand on its own bottom, without the aid of authority or even in oppofition to authority, this may be called its *manly age*. But in most men, it hardly ever arrives at this period. Many, by their fituation in life, have not the opportunity of cultivating their rational powers. Many, from the habit they have acquired of submitting their opinions to the authority of others, or from fome other principle which operates more powerfully than the love of truth, fuffer their judgement to be carried along to the end of their days, either by the authority of a leader, or of a party, or of the multitude, or by their own paffions. Such perfons, however learned, however acute, may be faid to be all their days children in underftanding. They reafon, they difpute, and perhaps write ; but it is not that they may find the truth ; but that they may defend opinions which have defcended to them by inheritance, or into which they have fallen by accident, or been led by affection.

I agree with Mr Locke, that there is no ftudy better fitted to exercife and ftrengthen the reafoning powers, than that of the mathematical fciences ; for two reafons ; firft, Becaufe there is no other branch of fcience which gives fuch fcope to long and accurate trains of reafoning ; and, fecondly, Becaufe in mathematics there is no room for authority, nor for prejudice of any kind, which may give a falfe bias to the judgement.

When a youth of moderate parts begins to ftudy Euclid, every thing at firft is new to him. His apprehenfion is unfteady : his judgement is feeble ; and refts partly upon the evidence of the thing, and partly upon the authority of his teacher. But

every

every time he goes over the definitions, the axioms, the elementary propofitions, more light breaks in upon him : the language becomes familiar, and conveys clear and fteady conceptions : the judgement is confirmed : he begins to fee what demonftration is ; and it is impoffible to fee it without being charmed with it. He perceives it to be a kind of evidence that has no need of authority to ftrengthen it. He finds himfelf emancipated from that bondage; and exults fo much in this new ftate of independence, that he fpurns at authority, and would have demonftration for every thing ; until experience teaches him, that this is a kind of evidence that cannot be had in moft things ; and that in his moft important concerns, he muft reft contented with probability.

As he goes on in mathematics, the road of demonftration becomes fmooth and eafy : he can walk in it firmly, and take wider fteps : and at laft he acquires the habit, not only of underftanding a demonftration, but of difcovering and demonftrating mathematical truths.

Thus, a man, without rules of logic, may acquire a habit of reafoning juftly in
mathematics ;

mathematics; and, I believe, he may, by like means, acquire a habit of reasoning justly in mechanics, in jurisprudence, in politics, or in any other science. Good sense, good examples, and assiduous exercise, may bring a man to reason justly and acutely in his own profession, without rules.

But if any man think, that from this concession he may infer the inutility of logic, he betrays a great want of that art by this inference: for it is no better reasoning than this, That because a man may go from Edinburgh to London by the way of Paris, therefore any other road is useless.

There is perhaps no practical art which may not be acquired, in a very considerable degree, by example and practice, without reducing it to rules. But practice, joined with rules, may carry a man on in his art farther and more quickly, than practice without rules. Every ingenious artist knows the utility of having his art reduced to rules, and by that means made a science. He is thereby enlightened in his practice, and works with more assurance. By rules, he sometimes corrects his

his own errors, and often detects the errors of others : he finds them of great ufe to confirm his judgement, to juftify what is right, and to condemn what is wrong.

Is it of no ufe in reafoning, to be well acquainted with the various powers of the human underftanding, by which we reafon ? Is it of no ufe, to refolve the various kinds of reafoning into their fimple elements ; and to difcover, as far as we are able, the rules by which thefe elements are combined in judging and in reafoning ? Is it of no ufe, to mark the various fallacies in reafoning, by which even the moft ingenious men have been led into error ? It muft furely betray great want of underftanding, to think thefe things ufelefs or unimportant. Thefe are the things which logicians have attempted ; and which they have executed ; not indeed fo completely as to leave no room for improvement, but in fuch a manner as to give very confiderable aid to our reafoning powers. That the principles laid down with regard to definition and divifion, with regard to the converfion and oppofition of propofitions and the general rules of reafoning, are not without ufe, is fufficiently

ciently apparent from the blunders committed by thofe who difdain any acquaint-, ance with them.

Although the art of categorical fyllogifm is better fitted for fcholaftic litigation, than for real improvement in knowledge, it is a venerable piece of antiquity, and a great effort of human genius. We admire the pyramids of Egypt, and the wall of China, tho' ufelefs burdens upon the earth. We can bear the moft minute defcription of them, and travel hundreds of leagues to fee them. If any perfon fhould with facrilegious hands deftroy or deface them, his memory would be had in abhorrence. The predicaments and predicables, the rules of fyllogifm, and the topics, have a like title to our veneration as antiquities : they are uncommon efforts, not of human power, but of human genius ; and they make a remarkable period in the progrefs of human reafon.

The prejudice againft logic has probably been ftrengthened by its being taught too early in life. Boys are often taught logic as they are taught their creed, when it is an exercife of memory only, without underftanding. One may as well expect

to underſtand grammar before he can
ſpeak, as to underſtand logic before he can
reaſon. It muſt even be acknowledged,
that commonly we are capable of reaſoning in mathematics more early than in lo-
·gic. The objeċts preſented to the mind in
this ſcience, are of a very abſtract nature,
and can be diſtinctly conceived only when
we are capable of attentive reflection upon
the operations of our own underſtanding,
and after we have been accuſtomed to reaſon. There may be an elementary logic,
level to the capacity of thoſe who have
been but little exerciſed in reaſoning ; but
the moſt important parts of this ſcience
require a ripe underſtanding, capable of
reflecting upon its own operations. Therefore to make logic the firſt branch of ſcience that is to be taught, is an old error
that ought to be corrected.

SECT. 2.   *Of the Improvement of Logic.*

In compoſitions of human thought expreſſed by ſpeech or by writing, whatever
is excellent and whatever is faulty, fall
within the province, either of grammar,

or of rhetoric, or of logic. Propriety of expreſſion is the province of grammar; grace, elegance, and force, in thought and in expreſſion, are the province of rhetoric; juſtneſs and accuracy of thought are the province of logic.

The faults in compoſition, therefore, which fall under the cenſure of logic, are obſcure and indiſtinct conceptions, falſe judgement, inconcluſive reaſoning, and all improprieties in diſtinctions, definitions, diviſion, or method. To aid our rational powers, in avoiding theſe faults and in attaining the oppoſite excellencies, is the end of logic; and whatever there is in it that has no tendency to promote this end, ought to be thrown out.

The rules of logic being of a very abſtract nature, ought to be illuſtrated by a variety of real and ſtriking examples taken from the writings of good authors. It is both inſtructive and entertaining, to obſerve the virtues of accurate compoſition in writers of fame. We cannot ſee them, without being drawn to the imitation of them, in a more powerful manner than we can be by dry rules. Nor are the faults of ſuch writers, leſs inſtructive or

leſs

lefs powerful monitors. A wreck, left upon a fhoal or upon a rock, is not more ufeful to the failor, than the faults of good writers, when fet up to view, are to thofe who come after them. It was a happy thought in a late ingenious writer of Englifh grammar, to collect under the feveral rules, examples of bad Englifh found in the moft approved authors. It were to be wifhed that the rules of logic were illuftrated in the fame manner. By thefe means, a fyftem of logic would become a repofitory; wherein whatever is moft acute in judging and in reafoning, whatever is moft accurate in dividing, diftinguifhing, and defining, fhould be laid up and difpofed in order for our imitation; and wherein the falfe fteps of eminent authors fhould be recorded for our admonition.

After men had laboured in the fearch of truth near two thoufand years by the help of fyllogifms, Lord Bacon propofed the method of induction, as a more effectual engine for that purpofe. His *Novum Organum* gave a new turn to the thoughts and labours of the inquifitive, more remarkable and more ufeful than that which

the *Organum* of Ariſtotle had given before ; and may be conſidered as a ſecond
grand æra in the progreſs of human reaſon.

The art of ſyllogiſm produced numberleſs diſputes ; and numberleſs ſects who
fought againſt each other with much ani-
moſity, without gaining or loſing ground,
but did nothing conſiderable for the benefit of human life. The art of induction,
firſt delineated by Lord Bacon, produced
numberleſs laboratories and obſervatories ;
in which Nature has been put to the queſtion by thouſands of experiments, and
forced to confeſs many of her ſecrets, that
before were hid from mortals. And by
theſe, arts have been improved, and human knowledge wonderfully increaſed.

In reaſoning by ſyllogiſm, from general
principles we deſcend to a concluſion vir-
tually contained in them. The proceſs of
induction is more arduous ; being an a-
ſcent from particular premiſes to a general
concluſion. The evidence of ſuch general
concluſions is probable only, not demon-
ſtrative : but when the induction is ſufficiently copious, and carried on according
to

to the rules of art, it forces conviction no lefs than demonftration itfelf does.

The greateft part of human knowledge refts upon evidence of this kind. Indeed we can have no other for general truths which are contingent in their nature, and depend upon the will and ordination of the maker of the world. He governs the world he has made, by general laws, The effects of thefe laws in particular phenomena, are open to our obfervation ; and by obferving a train of uniform effects with due caution, we may at laft decypher the law of nature by which they are regulated.

Lord Bacon has difplayed no lefs force of genius in reducing to rules this method of reafoning, than Ariftotle did in the method of fyllogifm. His *Novum Organum* ought therefore to be held as a moft important addition to the ancient logic. Thofe who underftand it, and enter into its fpirit, will be able to diftinguifh the chaff from the wheat in philofophical difquifitions into the works of God. They will learn to hold in due contempt all hypothefes and theories, the creatures of human imagination ; and to refpect nothing but

but facts fufficiently vouched, or conclufions drawn from them by a fair and chafte
interpretation of nature.

Moft arts have been reduced to rules,
after they had been brought to a confiderable degree of perfection by the natural
fagacity of artifts ;   and the rules have
been drawn from the beft examples of the
art, that had been before exhibited : but
the art of philofophical induction was delineated by Lord Bacon in a very ample
manner, before the world had feen any
tolerable example of it.   This, altho' it
adds greatly to the merit of the author,
muft have produced fome obfcurity in the
work, and a defect of proper examples for
illuftration.   This defect may now be eafily fupplied, from thofe authors who, in
their philofophical difquifitions, have the
moft ftrictly purfued the path pointed out
in the *Novum Organum*.   Among thefe Sir
Ifaac Newton appears to hold the firft
rank ; having, in the third book of his
Principia and in his Optics, had the rules of
the *Novum Organum* conftantly in his eye.

I think Lord Bacon was alfo the firft
who endeavoured to reduce to a fyftem
the prejudices or biaffes of the mind,
which

which are the caufes of falfe judgement, and which he calls *the idols of the human underftanding.* Some late writers of logic have very properly introduced this into their fyftem ; but it deferves to be more copioufly handled, and to be illuftrated by real examples.

It is of great confequence to accurate reafoning, to diftinguifh firft principles which are to be taken for granted, from propofitions which require proof. All the real knowledge of mankind may be divided into two parts : the firft confifting of felf-evident propofitions ; the fecond, of thofe which are deduced by juft reafoning from felf-evident propofitions. The line that divides thefe two parts ought to be marked as diftinctly as poffible ; and the principles that are felf-evident reduced, as far as can be done, to general axioms. This has been done in mathematics from the beginning, and has tended greatly to the advancement of that fcience. It has lately been done in natural philofophy : and by this means that fcience has advanced more in an hundred and fifty years, than it had done before in two thoufand. Every fcience is in an unformed ftate until

its

its firſt principles are aſcertained : after which, it advances regularly, and ſecures the ground it has gained.

Altho' firſt principles do not admit of direct proof, yet there muſt be certain marks and characters, by which thoſe that are truly ſuch may be diſtinguiſhed from counterfeits. Theſe marks ought to be deſcribed, and applied, to diſtinguiſh the genuine from the ſpurious.

In the ancient philoſophy, there is a redundance, rather than a defect, of firſt principles. Many things were aſſumed under that character without a juſt title : That nature abhors a *vacuum* ; That bodies do not gravitate in their proper place ; That the heavenly bodies undergo no change ; That they move in perfect circles, and with an equable motion. Such principles as theſe were aſſumed in the Peripatetic philoſophy, without proof, as if they were ſelf-evident.

Des Cartes, ſenſible of this weakneſs in the ancient philoſophy, and deſirous to guard againſt it in his own ſyſtem, reſolved to admit nothing until his aſſent was forced by irreſiſtible evidence. The firſt thing that he found to be certain and e-vident

vident was, that he thought, and reafon-
ed, and doubted. He found himfelf under a neceffity of believing the exiftence of
thofe mental operations of which he was
confcious : and having thus found fure
footing in this one principle of confcioufnefs, he refted fatisfied with it, hoping to
be able to build the whole fabric of his
knowledge upon it; like Archimedes, who
wanted but one fixed point to move the
whole earth. But the foundation was too
narrow; and in his progrefs he unawares
affumes many things lefs evident than
thofe which he attempts to prove. Altho'
he was not able to fufpect the teftimony of
confcioufnefs; yet he thought the teftimony of fenfe, of memory, and of every
other faculty, might be fufpected, and
ought not to be received until proof was
brought that they are not fallacious.
Therefore he applies thefe faculties, whofe
character is yet in queftion, to prove, That
there is an infinitely perfect Being, who
made him, and who made his fenfes, his
memory, his reafon, and all his faculties;
That this Being is no deceiver, and therefore could not give him faculties that are

VOL. III. 3 H fallacious;

fallacious ; and that on this account they deferve credit.

It is ftrange, that this philofopher, who found himfelf under a neceffity of yield-ding to the teftimony of confcioufnefs, did not find the fame neceffity of yielding to the teftimony of his fenfes, his memory, and his underftanding : and that while he was certain that he doubted, and reafon-ed, he was uncertain whether two and three made five, and whether he was dreaming or awake. It is more ftrange, that fo acute a reafoner fhould not per-ceive, that his whole train of reafoning to prove that his faculties were not falla-cious, was mere fophiftry ; for if his fa-culties were fallacious, they might deceive him in this train of reafoning ; and fo the conclufion, That they were not falla-cious, was only the teftimony of his fa-culties in their own favour, and might be a fallacy.

It is difficult to give any reafon for diftrufting our other faculties, that will not reach confcioufnefs itfelf. And he who diftrufts the faculties of judging and reafoning which God hath given him, muft even reft in his fcepticifm, till he

come

come to a found mind, or until God give him new faculties to fit in judgement upon the old. If it be not a firft principle, That our faculties are not fallacious, we muft be abfolute fceptics : for this principle is incapable of proof; and if it is not certain, nothing elfe can be certain.

Since the time of Des Cartes, it has been fafhionable with thofe who dealt in abftract philofophy, to employ their invention in finding philofophical arguments, either to prove thofe truths which ought to be received as firft principles, or to overturn them : and it is not eafy to fay, whether the authority of firft principles is more hurt by the firft of thefe attempts, or by the laft : for fuch principles can ftand fecure only upon their own bottom ; and to place them upon any other foundation than that of their intrinfic evidence, is in effect to overturn them.

I have lately met with a very fenfible and judicious treatife, wrote by Father Buffier about fifty years ago, concerning firft principles and the fource of human judgements, which, with great propriety, he prefixed to his treatife of logic. And

2   indeed

indeed I apprehend it is a fubject of fuch confequence, that if inquifitive men can be brought to the fame unanimity in the firft principles of the other fciences, as in thofe of mathematics and natural philofophy, (and why fhould we defpair of a general agreement in things that are felf-evident ?), this might be confidered as a third grand æra in the progrefs of human reafon.

END of the THIRD VOLUME.

www.ingramcontent.com/pod-product-compliance
Lightning Source LLC
Chambersburg PA
CBHW021324110726
47900CB00005B/1344